Lecture Notes in Artificial Intelligence   7764

Subseries of Lecture Notes in Computer Science

Frank Dignum   Cyril Brom   Koen Hindriks
Martin Beer   Deborah Richards (Eds.)

Cognitive Agents for Virtual Environments

First International Workshop, CAVE 2012
Held at AAMAS 2012
Valencia, Spain, June 4, 2012
Revised Selected Papers

 Springer

Series Editors

Randy Goebel, University of Alberta, Edmonton, Canada
Jörg Siekmann, University of Saarland, Saarbrücken, Germany
Wolfgang Wahlster, DFKI and University of Saarland, Saarbrücken, Germany

Volume Editors

Frank Dignum
Utrecht University, The Netherlands
E-mail: f.p.m.dignum@uu.nl

Cyril Brom
Charles University, Prague, Czech Republic
E-mail: brom@ksvi.mff.cuni.cz

Koen Hindriks
Delft University of Technology, The Netherlands
E-mail: k.v.hindriks@tudelft.nl

Martin Beer
Sheffield Hallam University, UK
E-mail: m.beer@shu.ac.uk

Deborah Richards
Macquarie University, Sydney, Australia
E-mail: deborah.richards@mq.edu.au

ISSN 0302-9743   e-ISSN 1611-3349
ISBN 978-3-642-36443-3   e-ISBN 978-3-642-36444-0
DOI 10.1007/978-3-642-36444-0
Springer Heidelberg Dordrecht London New York

Library of Congress Control Number: 2013930424

CR Subject Classification (1998): I.2.11, K.8.0, K.3.1, I.2.0-1

LNCS Sublibrary: SL 7 – Artificial Intelligence

Typesetting: Camera-ready by author, data conversion by Scientific Publishing Services, Chennai, India

Printed on acid-free paper

Springer is part of Springer Science+Business Media (www.springer.com)

Preface

There is a wide range of activity within the agent community considering various aspects of multi-agent systems, both theoretical as well as practical. This includes communication, team work, coordination, and cooperation of agents. In the First International Workshop on Cognitive Agents for Virtual Environments (CAVE-2012) we explored how these results might be used in the context of games and other virtual applications that require interaction with real users and perhaps identify any additional requirements that should be imposed for these contexts. We also explored similarities between solutions developed within the agent community with those used by people studying cognitive architectures.

The workshop brought individuals working on virtual characters together with those working on agent platforms and languages and cognitive architectures. All three communities have important parts of solutions for creating agents for games and similar applications, but very little is currently being done to combine these solutions. Thus the workshop hoped to connect the different communities and show the benefits from this combination. Although some cross-fertilization took place there is still room for improvement. However, the proceedings give a good indication of the state of the art in this area.

The workshop builds upon the AAMAS AGS 2009/10, EduMAS 2009, and AEGS 2011 workshops where the main issue has been to incorporate elements of agent technology in games and similar virtual environments such as 3D training and educational applications to create more flexible and realistic game play. Although some of the technical issues have been overcome and middleware (such as Pogamut, EIS, and CIGA) has been developed to connect agent platforms to games like Unreal Tournament, there are a number of fundamental challenges both on the technical as well as on the conceptual and design level.

In these proceedings we include papers that address several of these challenges and were presented at CAVE 2012 held on June 4 in Valencia, Spain, in colocation with AAMAS 2012. We received 14 submissions of high quality covering many of the aspects mentioned above. Each submission was reviewed by at least three Program Committee members. We accepted 10 papers for presentation, which can be found in this proceedings. Afterwards we invited several persons to submit additional contributions for this volume in order to make the overview complete. However, we only selected one high-quality contribution of these submissions (reflecting that quality is more important than completeness).

We have grouped the papers into four sections. The first section contains papers that are related to architectures combining agents and game engines.

The paper of Tomas Plch, Tomas Jedlicka, and Cyril Brom discusses the use of HLA, a standard for coupling simulations, for coupling agents to game engines. HLA seems to provide a useful language to define (part of) such a coupling. The second paper by Jeehang Lee, Vincent Baines, and Julian Padget also looks at the more practical side of the coupling and discusses, for instance, performance issues related to tight and loose coupling. The last paper in this section from Joost van Oijen and Frank Dignum discusses the information flow between agents and game engines that is necessary to generate realistic communication between virtual characters. In the second section we included papers that focus on using agents and virtual environments for training team work. It is an excellent area where the use of cognitive agents is imperative for good results, but also where many issues are still open. The paper of Martin Beer, Emma Norling, Peter Wallis and Lyuba Alboul discuss how agents and controllers can work together in order to get (unmanned) aircrafts to discover lost persons in mountainous areas as quickly and efficiently as possible. The second paper in this section is from Nader Hanna and Deborah Richards and looks at the very essential issue of two-way human–agent communication within the context of an educational game. One of the prime challenges is the combination of verbal and non-verbal communication in this context. The paper from Marie Manner and Maria Gini relates how agents can assist people to improve team performance. The third section contains papers that describe how cognitive agents can be used for simulation environments. Both visualization issues as well as issues of efficiency and scale play an important role in this area. The visualization issue is the focus of the first paper in this section, which is from Athanasia Louloudi and Franziska Klügl. The second paper, from Quentin Reynaud, Etienne de Sevin, Jean-Yves Donnart, and Vincent Corruble, breaches the topic of combining cognitive and reactive architectures for urban simulations. The last section groups some papers around performance issues of cognitive agents for virtual environments. The paper from Surangika Ranathunga and Stephen Cranefield discusses the problem of interpreting useful events from the low-level data that an agent receives from the game engine. Having an efficient translation of this low-level information is important for the cognitive agents being able to react to it on time. The second paper in this section is from Rudolf Kadlec, Michal Cermak, Zdenek Behan, and Cyril Brom and discusses issues in generating corpora of daily living memories for cognitive agents. These agents should have some history to be believable, but this history should of course also be manageable! The last paper in this section discusses the tools that should be used to define agents for games. This paper from Jakub Gemrot, Zdenek Hlavka, and Cyril Brom describes an experiment in which different agent behavior specification tools are compared and the authors check whether high-level specification of behavior leads to higher productivity. Read the paper to check the results!

All in all we are very happy with the papers contained in this volume. We are sure they form a valuable overview of the current state of the art of cognitive, intelligent characters in virtual environments. Finally, we would like to thank the Program Committee members and external reviewers without whom the reviewing would not have been possible and who gave valuable comments on all papers.

December 2012

Frank Dignum
Deborah Richards
Koen Hindriks
Martin Beer
Cyril Brom

Organization

Program Committee

Ruth Aylett	Heriot-Watt University, UK
Martin Beer	Sheffield Hallam University, UK
Cyril Brom	Charles University, Czech Republic
André Campos	UFRN, Brazil
Vincent Corruble	LIP6, Universite Pierre et Marie Curie (Paris 6), France
Yves Demazeau	CNRS - Laboratoire LIG, UK
Frank Dignum	Utrecht University, The Netherlands
Virginia Dignum	TU Delft, The Netherlands
Hiromitsu Hattori	Kyoto University, Japan
Koen Hindriks	Delft University of Technology, The Netherlands
Stefan Kopp	University of Bielefeld, Germany
Mei Yii Lim	Heriot-Watt University, UK
Simon Lynch	University of Teesside, UK
Hector Munoz-Avila	Lehigh University, USA
Jeff Orkin	MIT, USA
David Pynadath	University of Southern California, USA
Deborah Richards	Macquarie University, Australia
Avi Rosenfeld	Jerusalem College of Technology (JCT), Israel
Ilias Sakellariou	University of Macedonia, Greece
David Sarne	Bar-Ilan University, Israel
Barry Silverman	University of Pennsylvania, USA
Pieter Spronck	Tilburg University, The Netherlands
Demosthenes Stamatis	Alexander TEI of Thessaloniki, Greece
Ioanna Stamatopoulou	CITY College, International Faculty of the University of Sheffield, Greece
Katia Sycara	Carnegie Mellon University, USA
Duane Szafron	University of Alberta, USA
Joost Van Oijen	University of Utrecht, The Netherlands

Additional Reviewers

Buschmeier, Hendrik
Shamoun, Simon
Van Der Zwaan, Janneke

Table of Contents

HLA Proxy: Towards Connecting Agents to Virtual Environments by Means of High Level Architecture (HLA)

Tomas Plch, Tomas Jedlička, and Cyril Brom

Faculty of Mathematics and Physics, Charles University in Prague
{tomas.plch,jedlickat}@gmail.com, brom@ksvi.mff.cuni.cz

Abstract. Coupling virtual environments (e.g. game engines like Source Engine or Unreal Engine 3) with agent reasoning systems (ARS) is often used in the multi-agent systems (MAS) research field. However, externally connecting ARS or MAS to environments almost always requires individual approach for every coupling. Therefore, we recognize the need for a common method of access, without the need to implement a network stack, network protocol or data management. In this paper, we present our new project *HLA Proxy* utilizing the High Level Architecture (HLA) standard (IEEE 1516-2010) for interconnecting simulations and simulators. We created a C++ prototype middleware providing universal and transparent access to the HLA infrastructure for not HLA-capable applications (i.e. ARS, MAS, visualization tools etc.), thus allowing cross-platform, distributed connection to environments and between environments. Our work is aimed at being directly integrated into the environment (i.e. engine) and application via dynamic linkage. Here, we present our architecture and our proof-of-concept integration into CryENGINE 3 (used for the Crysis game) and Source Engine (used for the HalfLife 2 game) running on Windows XP 32bit and Windows 7 64bit platforms. We also implemented a 64bit Linux console application utilizing HLA Proxy to connect to both engines capable to send console commands and receive environment updates.

Keywords: HLA, High Level Architecture, middleware, Agent Reasoning System, Computer Games, Distributed simulation, Dynamic-Link Library.

1   Introduction

The realism of virtual environments (e.g. computer games) increases with every iteration of their respective engines (e.g. Source engine [1], CryENGINE 3 [2], Unreal engine [3]). These worlds being extensively realistic are excellent candidates for conducting research and experiments in various fields of Artificial Intelligence (AI) [18], ranging from crowd simulations to single agent reasoning systems (ARS) and multi agent systems (MAS). However, it is fairly complicated to access these virtual worlds, possibly by simple, universal and versatile means.

F. Dignum et al. (Eds.): CAVE 2012, LNAI 7764, pp. 1–16, 2013.
© Springer-Verlag Berlin Heidelberg 2013

The CIGA middleware [24] represents an attempt to conceptualize a general architecture needed for coupling computer games with ARS and MAS. CIGA presents a layered fairly complex architecture for accessing game engines, comprised of a physical, semantic and cognitive layer. It is build around the notion of *ontology domain*, which is used to unify the environment's and the agent's view of semantic representations. However, CIGA's physical layer only encapsulates the problem of coupling to an environment. Our opinion is that CIGA creates conceptual and run-time overhead over the coupling, which should be focused on universal data exchange. Actual data interpretation, abstraction and management should be located within the interconnected entities (i.e. MAS, ARS, game engines etc.).

We distinguish the following methods for accessing virtual environment's data (e.g. objects, events etc.) and functionality (e.g. actions of agents): 1) direct access and 2) via external interfaces. Direct access is facilitated via including compiled or scripted code into the engine's runtime, either by dynamic linkage (e.g. Gary's Mod [8]) or loading and executing scripts (e.g. utilizing LUA scripting language [5]). Access based on reverse engineering is rare (e.g. StarCraft Brood War API [7]).

Access over an external interface is commonly realized via network sockets utilizing a text-based or binary protocol. External coupling to an engine requires a bidirectional (network) interface. Often, a custom interface is designed (i.e. network stack, network protocol, data update management, etc.) based on the respective environment's architecture [4] (e.g. event/object based architectures, single/multithread internals etc.). Based on our experience with Source Engine, Cry Engine, Unreal Engine, and Defcon game [13], we consider this task a significant time-consuming effort.

However, need to utilize a 3D virtual environment lead developers and researchers to create an external network interface for Unreal Engine. The resulting text-based GameBots [9] protocol is used to export data and events utilizing the UnrealScript scripting language. The protocol is utilized by many researchers due to the fact it provides an existing network interface for coupling to a capable virtual world.

The Pogamut project [10] capitalizes and extends the idea of GameBots and incorporates the protocol via the GaviaLib library into a NetBeans based platform (Figure 1) for prototyping IVAs utilizing the Java programming language [11]. Presently, Pogamut is limited to few environments – a) Unreal Tournament 2004, b) Unreal Development Kit based projects – e.g. the Emohawk project [12], and c) Defcon game [13].

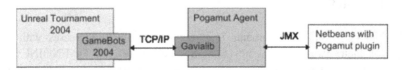

Fig. 1. Pogamut project architecture – connecting a Pogamut Agent via GaviaLib and GameBots 2004 to the Unreal Tournament 2004 computer game. The agent is controlled by a decision making mechanism running in the Netbeans development environment and is written using the Java programming language.

Due to the fact, that coupling methods between applications, ARS, MAS and virtual environments are limited to used protocols (e.g. GameBots) and architectures (e.g. CIGA), we recognize the need for a more universal, platform independent (i.e. Linux/Windows 32/64bit), direct (i.e. without various layers like presented [24]), adaptable and fast solution, which can be easily integrated into most environments or projects with less work on the network and data management overhead currently involved.

This paper presents our C++ based platform *HLA Proxy* for universal, direct, adaptable, cross-platform interconnecting of applications – e.g. simulations, decision making mechanisms, data collecting applications, ARS, MAS etc. HLA Proxy exploits the High Level Architecture (HLA) standard [6] for interconnecting simulations and simulators. Our middleware is aimed at providing the HLA capability to most applications build upon the object oriented programming paradigm, by integrating our middleware via dynamic or static linkage. The target application can utilize a subset of the HLA standard's capabilities and can exchange data in an object or event driven way without the need to implement a network interface or a translation mechanism between the inner representation and a network protocol stack. Our architecture, in contrast with CIGA [24] is aimed at mitigating data between the virtual environment and the ARS or MAS via HLA.

High Level Architecture has already been used for virtual agent's research by (Lees et al.) [25]. HLA compliant agents created with the *SIM_AGENT* high level design toolkit [26] were introduced to a tile world scenario and compared with native SIM_AGENT's agents and their performance was inspected. HLA compliant agents performed worse than native SIM_AGENTs in the presented scenario. However we think this is mostly due to the tendency of the scenario and the HLA agent's design. The low performance of the agent's is mostly due to the overuse of the HLA's synchronization mechanisms. Also the integration with SIM_AGENT toolkit might represent a bottleneck responsible for the degraded HLA compliant agent's performance. However, a degraded performance of HLA in respect to an optimized engine-ARS coupling is expected, because HLA and HLA Proxy are aimed at providing *universal* access to environments and simulations/simulators within large simulation aggregations which requires various non trivial time consuming mechanisms to be present (e.g. time management, data delivery systems etc.).

Note that, the LVC Game proprietal solution by Calitrix [15] provides a similar solution as the HLA Proxy. It provides a network layer for various applications (e.g. Virtual Battle Space 2 (VBS2) [14]) implementing a subset of the DIS/HLA standard. However, LVC Game supports only a limited subset of the military RPR Federation Object Model 2.0 [17]. Therefore, it is not feasible for AI research, because the needs of decision making mechanisms for IVA's are broader then the representation used.

The paper is structured as follows – the following section is focused on presenting basic High Level Architecture concepts. Section 3 is aimed at presenting our middleware. Section 4 and 5 is focused on our proof-of-concept implementation and performance tests of HLA Proxy's internal database. Section 6 concludes and presents future work.

2   High Level Architecture

The purpose of this section is to provide insight into basic High Level Architecture (HLA) concepts and ideas. The standard [6], [16], [21] itself was created for the purpose of interconnecting a multitude of various simulations and simulators in use by the United States Department of Defense [18] without expensive new development or redesign of current simulations and simulators (e.g. life-size tank simulator). HLA recognizes the term *federation*, which represents the aggregation of participants – *federates* (Figure. 2). A federate can be perceived as any application, simulation or any other entity, passively or actively participating in the federation. In our case, federates are either virtual environments or decision making mechanisms.

A federation setup example could be as follows – a virtual fighter jet simulator (e.g. Lock On: Modern Air Combat [19]) being one federate having an AI controlled fighter jet in the simulation, a soldier simulator (e.g. Virtual Battle Space 2 [14]) being operated by a human and a human crew operated tank simulator being the third federate. All these participate and coexist in one simulation environment, where they have different internal data representations and implementations, and care about various degrees of data abstraction – e.g. the fighter jet simulator does not need to know how much health the soldier has, or how the physical model of the tank works. Furthermore, if a virtual soldier mounts a tank as a driver, the soldier simulator is responsible for the abstraction and virtual presentation of the real tank simulator. The data exchanges and communication between federates is done in the HLA environment, where the HLA's mechanisms are responsible for correct exchange and delivery of data to all participants.

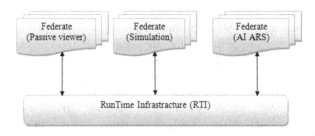

Fig. 2. High Level Architecture – a passive federate (e.g. mission logger), an active federates (e.g. tank simulator and virtual entity managed by an AI)

2.1   Data Representation and Exchange

Interconnecting various federates requires the federation to share a common view of the simulated world, at least conceptually. HLA specifies this common view as the *Federation Object Model* (FOM) [16], which is similar to the domain ontology [24]. The FOM is a tree-like structure based on the object oriented representation of the world (Figure 3) and is represented by a XML document. Nodes within the structure are called *Object Classes*, where the descendant inherits the parent's attributes. The concept allows for backward compatibility, where when adding a new federate with a more detailed notion of the world (i.e. more deep FOM structure) can work with older federates who recognize only a portion of the updated FOM. The HLA standard also allows for complex type creation by type aggregation.

The proper exchange of data within a federation is facilitated via the Run-Time Interface (RTI). The RTI represents the actual implementation of the data exchange protocols. The data exchange between federates is based on ownership, update status and time management. The RTI also provides a multitude of services [21] – e.g. ownership acquisition, object discovery etc.

The data exchanged can be of two major types a) *Object Instances* and b) *Interactions*. The Object Instances represent the object of a certain Object Class and their attributes within a simulation world (e.g. a virtual soldier) specified in the FOM. The attributes and Object Instances can be owned by a particular federate which is responsible for their update and other federates can subscribe to these updates. Parameterized Interactions can be seen as events that occur in the simulated world (e.g. a grenade explosion). The data exchange model is a *publisher/subscriber model*, where federates publish and subscribe to Object Instances and attributes. The data update model is a *one writer, many readers model*, where ownership is acquired or relinquished over RTI.

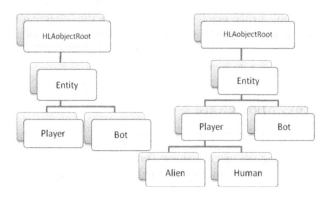

Fig. 3. Federation Object Model representation of two ontological domains. Both domains represent an example of how entities like Players and Bots [4] can be represented. The domain on the right is an extension of the left domain, where the Player objects class is a parent of the Alien and Human object classes.

2.2   Example

To better illustrate HLA's workings, we provide a simple example of a federation's data flow where a computer game engine is coupled with an ARS. Let us assume a virtual world where secret agent bots live and are capable of shooting at each other. The virtual world is run by a computer game engine (e.g. Source Engine) and the ARS is a simple C++ application with simple reactive reasoning. The engine is a federate and every secret agent bot has one dedicated ARS federate. The FOM of this federation specifies only the *Agent* Object Class with a *Health* attribute and one *Attack* Interaction with two parameters – "who attacks who".

The instance of the *Agent* Object Class called *Agent007* is owned by its creator, the Source Engine. The ARS being situated as different federate, can subscribe to some attributes of *Agent007* – e.g. his health, position and enemy agents it can see. Let us assume that, *Agent007* meets an enemy agent called *Agent001* (also an *Agent* Object Class).

The notion of *meeting of two agents* can either reasoned by the agents themselves, based on percepts from the environment (e.g. actual percepts in the agent's field of view, or computations based on the knowledge of all agent's positions). However, this inference can be done by another federate responsible for determining visibility between agents and propagated as an HLA Interaction to the federation. A similar HLA Interaction could also originate from the engine. All variants are equivalent, the difference is only where the information about visibility is processed.

Let us assume that Agent007's ARS reasons the need to shoot Agent001 and it triggers the *Attack*(Agent007, Agent001) HLA Interaction. The Interaction is delivered to the engine (if it has subscribed to receive it) over RTI. Agent007 shoots and may trigger or update various attributes within the engine (e.g. health count of Agent001, ammo count in Agent007's pistol etc.).

It is noteworthy that both Agent001's and Agent007's ARS can have various internal representation's of the ontology domain, even various degrees of perception. Agent007 might not know about having a pistol, only knowing the interaction of *Attack* which is handled engine specific – by pistol, (in a different game) by bow or not at all (i.e. Agent007 has no weapon or no ammo).

3   HLA Proxy Middleware

This section is focused on explaining the basic features of our HLA Proxy middleware, our design goals and decisions. The main idea behind our middleware is to provide any object-based application or engine with the capability to access the HLA and to allow data exchange without being limited to one protocol or architectural design. The HLA Proxy's philosophy is to only load the library into the host's run-time, couple the internal objects to objects represented in the FOM and perform write and read operations on those Object Instances. HLA Proxy should handle all the synchronizing of data between federates, to keep everybody up to date.

3.1   Design

The main design issues we addressed with our HLA Proxy were a) *generality* – virtual environment or application capable of dynamic/static linkage should be capable to use our middleware, b) *adaptability* – if the view of the world or requirements on functionality change, we have to be able to reflect it, c) *transparency & simplicity* - we cannot bother applications or engines with handling network traffic or data management, d) *responsiveness* – the middleware has to be fast to be able to cope with engines.

Our approach is based on the notion of hiding the network management, object management, semantic transformations etc. from the user (Figure 4) thus achieving *simplicity*. We consider the best option to directly couple engine's objects, semantic transformations, and inferences etc., to Object Classes and Interactions specified in the FOM.

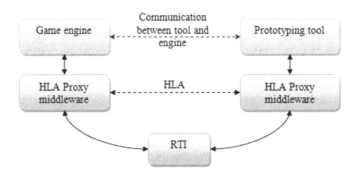

Fig. 4. Coupling of a Prototyping tool (e.g. Pogamut) to a Game Engine over the HLA Proxy middleware over the RTI using HLA. The Game Engine/Prototyping tool integrates the HLA Proxy middleware via DLL linkage and accesses proxy classes generated based on the FOM by get/set methods. The updates are propagated over the RTI between the HLA Proxy nodes and deliver the information to either the Game Engine or Prototyping tool.

The federation's ontology (represented within the FOM specification) can be either taken from already existing FOMs (e.g. RPR FOM 2.0) or developed on a per-case basis as a common derivate of the ontology and abstractions of the participating federates. To our experience, the best practice is to take the existing exported object declarations (e.g. C++ headers of the engine's SDK) and build the FOM based on them. This allows for fast and simple integration of the resulting HLA Proxy's mechanisms into the present engine's or application's code (e.g. the *Player* object instance within the engine calls update functions on the FOM's *Player* class that reflect the actual *Player* Object Instance in the federation and map to a *HumanPlayer* object in another federate that is coupled with the FOM's *Player* Object Class).

The HLA Proxy provides the means to mitigate the ontology over the HLA environment by invoking Interactions or updating and requesting the data on Object Instances from our middleware (Code 1). The update methods of HLA Proxy can be either called directly from an engine code segment (e.g. *Player::setHealth()* method), engine callbacks, engine update loop, or within a code segment present in an additional layer developed for the coupling. This allows for more complex, better tailored integration into an engine or application. Conceptually, this approach allows for a cleaner and less bounding integration in respect to the engine – i.e. the updates can be per objects, or at specific code locations etc (e.g. more important objects are updated every frame, less important objects are updated during update loops).

```
class CPlayer{/* class declaration within CryENGINE 3 */
        /* usual members for engine purposes start here */
        unsigned int m_health;
          . . .
        /* HLA Proxy code starts here */
        HLAProxy::Data::Player *pHLAPlayer;
};

CPlayer::setHealth (unsigned int hp) {
    /* engine specific code goes here */
    m_health = hp;
  /* HLA specific code for propagating updates outwards */
  if (pHLAPlayer != NULL) {
    pHLAPlayer->setHealth(m_health);
    pHLA->updateInstance(pHLAPlayer);
  }
}
```

Code 1. Example of a C++ code from the Cry ENGINE 3 SDK, where the CPlayer is an object within the Cry ENGINE 3 environment representing the player's embodiment. When the engine updates the *health* of the player, the HLA Proxy middleware is called to propagate the update to other federates.

3.2   Internal Architecture

To satisfy *generality*, we designed HLA Proxy as a dynamically linkable library (DLL in Windows based systems, *so* in Linux based systems), which can be introduced into the environment's or application's runtime.

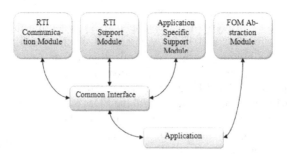

Fig. 5. Barebone HLA Proxy two tier architecture – components are presented in boxes, lines represent communication interfaces between components. The Application box represents the run-time dynamically loading HLA Proxy.

It can be seen in Figure 5, HLA Proxy's architecture is a simple two tier architecture. Application or engine can access the HLA Proxy by two means – the

Common Interface and the *FOM Abstraction Module.* Common Interface provides basic functionalities, like startup, shutdown, registering handlers for HLA Interactions. The other modules, like *RTI Support Module* and *RTI Communication Module* provide support for RTI related network transfer and can be specific or optimized per RTI to gain a performance boost.

The FOM Abstraction Module represents the means for the application to access the federation's ontology domain specified within the FOM XML document. To satisfy the goals *transparency, simplicity* and *adaptability* we needed to address the following issues: 1) extract the ontology domain from the FOM module (satisfies adaptability), 2) provide means for access to the data via simple means (satisfies simplicity), 3) mitigate data exchange from and to HLA in respect to correct data updates (satisfies transparency).

First, we needed to extract the ontology domain specified in the FOM. Due to the fact that multitude FOMs exists for various uses (e.g. RPR FOM 2.0 for military simulations) and the FOM can change, update or be replaced, it is feasible to assume that hard-coding a FOM into HLA Proxy was not a suitable solution. We chose to provide our middleware with the capability to *generate C++ code* based on the FOM XML specification using our XSLT code developed for this purpose. Because the FOM's structure is derived from the object oriented paradigm, the generated code can reflects the ontology by C++ classes in an inheritance schema equivalent to the FOM's specification.

Second, we needed to access the in the FOM specified Object Classes, their attributes as well as Interactions by simple means. Invocation of an Interaction can be done easily by calling the appropriate *global* function from the host (i.e. application, engine) run-time. The host run-time can register callbacks from HLA Proxy to be called when an Interaction occurs within the federation. Objects Instances as being a result of creating an Object Instance (stored in a in-memory database within HLA Proxy) and can be accessed via *Handlers* which are initialized from an internal hash table based on the unique Object Instance names.

To access object attributes, we utilize the *get* and *set* approach, where every attribute has his own *get/set functions* generated (i.e. FOM attribute *Foo* has functions *getFoo()* and *setFoo()*). The *get* and *set* functions are generated based on the access specification of the attribute – i.e. *publish-only attributes* have only *set* functions, *subscribe-only* have only *get* functions and publish/subscribe have both. An example of use can be seen in the code above (Code 1). It is noteworthy, that the attribute *Foo* might represent one attribute within one federate's internal object and a combination of attributes in a different federate's internal representation. Every federate is responsible for its own interpretation of the FOM.

Third, we needed to provide means to synchronize the host run-time with the access to the distributed environment of HLA. On one side, operation requests are inserted by the host run-time, from the other side, updates are received via RTI. We designed our own in-memory internal database of Object Instance Attributes, mostly due to the fact, that available database solutions (i.e. databases like MySQL, PosgreSQL etc.) are either standalone or not suitable for our specific requirements. We need to keep transactions *isolated*, but cannot perform a *rollback* or transaction *aborts*, because virtual worlds tend not to be able to rollback. We also have to keep the data *consistent* and *ordered by timestamps*. We use a combination of locking, assigning unique timestamps to requests and multiversion approach [22]. The internals of our database design are beyond the scope of this paper. As for *responsiveness*, we designed the HLA Proxy's database internals to be *fully multi-threaded*. Internally we use one *dispatching* thread and an army of *worker threads* which execute the request on top of the database.

The resulting FOM Abstraction Module encapsulates all the functionality for the host run-time to access FOM specified federation's ontology domain over RTI in *adaptive*, *simple* and *transparent* way. Our in-memory database provides the host environment with accurate data in respect to the host's run-time HLA time management specification (i.e. update orderings depend on this). The multi-thread design allows for parallel operations on attributes, thus providing more efficient use of today's multicore hardware.

4   Proof-of-Concept Implementation

The aim of our proof-of-concept is see if our approach is feasible and working by exchange information (e.g. health status and command scripts) back and forth between federates (i.e. computer game and application). We also aim at integrating HLA Proxy into two major computer game engines with different internal architecture – Source Engine (Half Life 2 game) and Cry ENGINE 3 (Crysis game). The integration via dynamically loading our DLL was performed without creating additional layers of architecture to the engine (i.e. network layer, abstraction transformation etc.).

We created a federation between our console application and each of the game engines (separately) – i.e. the federation had only 2 federates (due to our license for the MÄK RTI [17]). Both engines were running on a Windows XP 32bit and Windows 7 64bit platform and our console application was developed for a Linux 64bit platform (Figure 6).

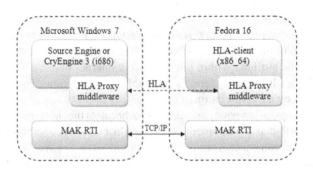

Fig. 6. HLA Proxy proof-of-concept setup where Source Engine/CryENGINE 3 is talking over HLA Proxy with a client application over the MÄK RTI working over TCP/IP network

We considered a simple scenario where our console application receives updates on health status of a Non Player Character (NPC) and sends script commands to the environment (which would appear in the respective engine's console) via HLA Proxy. In our scenario, we forced the NPC via script command to throw a grenade and kill himself, thus receiving health updates before and after the explosion and receiving Interaction notification of the explosion.

The integration into Source engine took us about 9 months of work, due to the fact that the integration was actual HLA Proxy's design and development. We used the Source Engine as a design reference due to its complex internal mechanisms. Our additional findings in respect to integration issues (e.g. memory management issues in Half Life 2 etc.) can be found in [23]. The integration into CryENGINE 3 was rather quicker, due to our experience with Source Engine – it took about 3-4 days.

5   Performance

This section is focused on providing results of our performance benchmarking of the HLA Proxy middleware. We conducted a series of synthetic tests on our in-memory database to inspect the scaling properties of our scheduling algorithm and data storage mechanism. We decided to only benchmark the in-memory database for two reasons – 1) we had no complex enough federation at disposal and 2) a federation wide testing would be about benchmarking the used RTI (i.e. it would depend on the federation properties and network topology).

We base our hypothesis on the observation that frame-rates of game engines is presently around 50–60 frames per second at most. Our expectation would be the database's capability to handle 100 operations (i.e. read/write operations) per frame to satisfy a reasonable assumption on how many objects interact or change during a single frame. It is noteworthy that our expectations are not based on actual measurements, because the amount of interacting objects can vary based on engine and in-game situation.

5.1   Benchmarking Method

Our benchmarking is focused on the duration of read and write operations in a barebone setup of HLA Proxy to avoid resource consumption by other modules (e.g. logging etc.). The HLA Proxy was integrated into an application accessing Object Instances and their attributes. We accessed *one* instance of a HLA Object Instance, because internally we either use direct access over directly linked *handlers*, or a hash table. In most use cases, the handler would be linked once during in-engine object creation and then reused when accessed or updated. We also did not want to benchmark our hash table implementation, but our scheduling mechanism. It is noteworthy, that our database works with Object Instance Attributes, rather than whole Objects Instances, therefore needed only one instance of an Object Instance due to the fact that only concurrent access to Object Instance Attributes are of interest to us – they cause the actual slowdown when scheduling operations. Access to multiple different Object Instances is handled in parallel. It is noteworthy that the in-memory database runs in parallel with the application's code, where one dispatcher thread is responsible for 10 worker threads that perform the requested operations.

We established four use cases for read/write operation ordering:

- series of reads,
- series of writes,
- series of writes followed by a reads,
- random ordering of reads and writes.

For every use-case we perform a series of tests, where we access the attributes in every iteration in the following setups:

1. single attribute from one single thread,
2. multiple (4) attributes accessed from one single thread at once (all in one iteration),
3. multiple (4) attributes access from 4 threads (one attribute per thread).

The iteration count for a batch of tests is increased from 100 to 20000 iterations per run. We conducted 5 runs for every combination of setups and the resulting value is a mean of the measured runs.

Resulting time of executions are normalized to operations processed per second. This representation can easily show whether such performance meets expectations for real-time usage or not. Measurements contain not only time consumed by processing of requests but also time spent in scheduling of request in application code.

We performed our evaluation on a Windows 7 64bit operating system running on a Core 2 Quad 2.4GHz (E6600) processor. Our build target was a 32bit platform. The actual testing application was running on a Virtual Box hosted Fedora 16 platform with one dedicated CPU for the virtualization.

5.2   Results

In Figure 7 we show the read throughput of the database. Because read operations are blocking operations (i.e. have to finish before returning to the caller), we do not need to perform Setup 2, because it behaves like Setup 1. The scheduling mechanism scales properly in both the single and multithreaded setup.

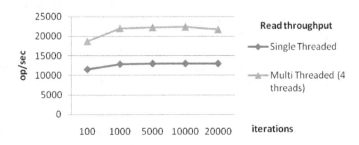

Fig. 7. Read throughput – attributes accessed by long series of reads

In Figure 8 we show the write throughput of the database. The performance for Setup 1 and 2 perform as expected. In Setup 2, write operations are asynchronous and can be performed in parallel - the database works with Object Instance attributes, rather than whole objects. Therefore the increase in Setup 2 in respect to Setup 1 is almost four times. The Setup 3 behaves slightly better, because the inserting into dispatcher's request queues is done on behalf of the requesting thread's runtime and therefore can insert more requests to be processed by the dispatcher thread.

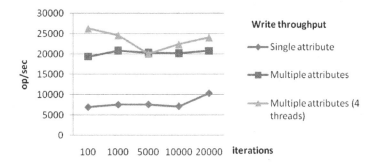

Fig. 8. Write throughput – attributes are access in a long series of writes

In Figure 9 we show a series of writes followed by a read. This ordering of operations is interesting due to the fact that the read has to wait until all the writes are processed to acquire the current data. All setups can be seen to scale well. Setup 1 and 2 behave as expected – write operations are processed asynchronously and only final read operations do block. Parallel processing of asynchronous writes in Setup 2 might provide the observed speedup. The Setup 3 also behaves as expected and scales well. The doubling in speed is due to the same effect described earlier.

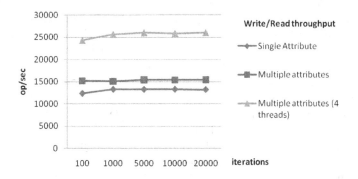

Fig. 9. A series of writes followed by a read operation

In Figure 10 we can see a completely randomized ordering of requests for single thread and multiple thread setups. Both setups behave as expected – they come close to each other because of the necessary synchronization on attribute asynchronous writes and blocking reads which have to wait for each other. The multi-thread setup is still better then the single thread setup, but both are usable, thus HLA Proxy does not favor a single or multi thread design approach.

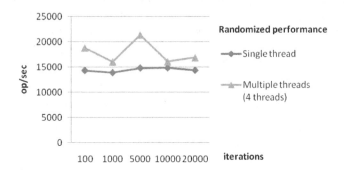

Fig. 10. Randomized ordering of requests on read and write operations

5.3   Discussion

Performance results collected by our benchmark look promising. The middle value of performance equals to 16860.6 (multithreaded) and 14285.7 (single-threaded) random operations per second. Most engines are limiting its frame rate to 50-60 frames per second. Therefore the database can perform around 250 operations per single frame. This result is beyond our initial expectation of 100 operations per single frame. Engines could adapt to the current load of updates by scheduling less operations thus providing a less accurate virtual world's representation. To conclude, the performance meets expectations for usage of the middleware for interconnection between computer game engines and ARS or MAS.

One limitation is that maximum possible performance is limited. Measured limits can be seen in Figure 7 and Figure 8 and are close to 25000 operations per second. The performance bottleneck is the thread scheduling mechanism and it does not matter how many cores the machine has, because we use only one dispatcher thread.

Due to the fact, that most operations on an object's attributes within the engine are performed within one thread's runtime – the most important information is how fast HLA Proxy is processing operation requests from a single thread. A performance improvement might be achieved by using multiple scheduling modules, thus introducing more dispatcher threads for single non-concurrent thread access on different attributes. Unfortunately such modification would introduce a more complex scheduling algorithm and thread synchronization issues.

Due to the fact that the HLA Proxy middleware would run within an engine's runtime it is expected that performance of the internal database will degrade, because game engines tend to consume enormous resources – i.e. memory and processor time. Engine's resource consumption is beyond our reach and this issue has to be addressed on a per integration basis.

6   Conclusion and Future Work

In this paper, we presented the C++ based HLA Proxy middleware prototype for interconnecting applications and engines, as well as various engines with each other in a general, simple, transparent and accessible way. We developed an architecture with good results in synthetic benchmarking in respect to internal operation.

Our proof-of-concept integration with CryENGINE 3 and Source Engine proved to be successful, despite the fact that the SDKs provided are undocumented. Our middleware is aimed at shortening the time for creating an application↔game engine coupling – HLA proxy hides network management and data management layers from the developer and provides simplistic update mechanisms (e.g. simple function calls on *get*, *set* update functions, Interaction notification callbacks etc.). We also managed to connect to CryENGINE 3 in less than a week.

The use of HLA Proxy is simplistic and can be integrated into an application via dynamic or static linkage. The capability to generate code (i.e. get and set update function etc.) based on the FOM provides a unique solution not only to connecting to environments, but also when exchanging data in various domains.

For future work, we need to connect a true decision making mechanism and a development platform to at least one environment. We also look forward to enhance the capabilities of HLA Proxy to support more of the current HLA standard – namely various time management mechanisms. We also plan to test our architecture in a more complex environment with multiple simulations – create a federation where two different engines are connected (e.g. Source engine and CryENGINE 3) to an agent decision making mechanism. We also intend to study integration times and capabilities for HLA Proxy and Pogamut/GameBots integration into a computer game engine.

Acknowledgments. This work was partially supported by SVV Project no. 263 314, student grant GA UK No. 0449/2010/A-INF/MFF, by project P103/10/1287 (GA ČR) and GA UK No. 655012/2012/A-INF/MFF.

References

1. Valve: Source SDK (2011),
   http://source.valvesoftware.com/sourcesdk.php (February 20, 2012)
2. Crytek: CryENGINE 3 SDK (2011), http://mycryengine.com/ (February 20, 2012)
3. Epic Games: Unreal Tournament 2004 (2004), http://www.unreal.com/ (February 20, 2012)
4. Gemrot, J., Brom, C., Plch, T.: A Periphery of Pogamut: From Bots to Agents and Back Again. In: Dignum, F. (ed.) Agents for Games and Simulations II. LNCS, vol. 6525, pp. 19–37. Springer, Heidelberg (2011)
5. Ierusalimschy, R., Celes. W., de Figueiredo L.H.: Lua programming language, http://www.lua.org/ (February 20, 2012
6. IEEE1516.1-2010 IEEE Standard for Modeling and Simulation (M&S) High Level Architecture (HLA) - Federate Interface Specification (2010)

7. BWAPI (2004), http://code.google.com/p/bwapi/ (February 20, 2012)
8. Facepunch Studios: Garry's mod (2004), http://garrysmod.com/ (February 20, 2012)
9. Adobbati, R., Marshall, A.N., Scholer, A., Tejada, S., Kaminka, G., Schaffer, S., Sollitto, C.: Gamebots: A 3d virtual world test-bed for multi-agent research. In: Proceedings of the 2nd International Workshop on Infrastructure for Agents MAS and Scalable MAS (2001)
10. Kadlec, R., Gemrot, J., Bída, M., Burkert, O., Havlíček, J., Zemčák, L., Pibil, R., Vansa, R., Brom, C.: Extensions and Applications of Pogamut 3 Platform. In: Ruttkay, Z., Kipp, M., Nijholt, A., Vilhjálmsson, H.H. (eds.) IVA 2009. LNCS, vol. 5773, pp. 506–507. Springer, Heidelberg (2009)
11. Gemrot, J., Brom, C., Bryson, J., Bída, M.: How to compare usability of techniques for the specification of virtual agents' behavior? An experimental pilot study with human subjects. In: Proceedings of Agents for Games and Simulations, AAMAS workshop (2011)
12. Bida, M., Brom, C.: Emohawk: Learning Virtual Characters by Doing. In: Aylett, R., Lim, M.Y., Louchart, S., Petta, P., Riedl, M. (eds.) ICIDS 2010. LNCS, vol. 6432, Springer, Heidelberg (2010)
13. Introversion Software: DEFCON (2006), http://www.introversion.co.uk/defcon/ (February 20, 2012)
14. Bohemia Interactive: Virtual Battle Space 2, http://vbs2.com (February 20, 2012)
15. Calytrix Technologies: LVC Game
16. IEEE 1516.2-2010 Modeling and Simulation (M&S) High Level Architecture (HLA) - Object Model Tempalte (OMT) Specification
17. VT MÄK, http://www.mak.com (February 20, 2012)
18. Department of Defense, http://www.defense.gov/ (February 20, 2012)
19. van Oijen, J., Dignum, F.: Scalable Perception for BDI-Agents Embodied in Virtual Environments. In: Web Intelligence and Intelligent Agent Technology, WI-IAT (2011)
20. Eagle Dynamics: Lock On: Modern Air Combat (2003)
21. IEEE 1516 Standard for Modeling and Simulation (M&S) High Level Architecture (HLA) – Framework and Rules (2010)
22. Garcia-Molina, H., Ullman, J., Widom, J.: Database Systems: The Complete Book. Prentice Hall (2001)
23. Jedlička, T.: Utilizing HLA for agent based development platforms. Master thesis, Charles University (2012)
24. van Oijen, J., Vanhée, L., Dignum, F.: CIGA: A Middleware for Intelligent Agents in Virtual Environments. In: Proceedings of the 3rd International Workshop on Agents for Education, Games and Simulations, AAMAS 2011 (2011)
25. Lees, M., Logan, B., Theodoropoulos, G.: Agents, games and HLA. Simulation Modelling Practice and Theory (2006)
26. Sloman, A., Poli, R.: SIM_AGENT: A Toolkit for Exploring Agent Designs. In: Tambe, M., Müller, J., Wooldridge, M.J. (eds.) IJCAI-WS 1995 and ATAL 1995. LNCS, vol. 1037, Springer, Heidelberg (1996)

Decoupling Cognitive Agents
and Virtual Environments

Jeehang Lee, Vincent Baines, and Julian Padget

Department of Computer Science, University of Bath,
Bath, BA2 7AY, United Kingdom
{j.lee,v.f.baines,j.a.padget}@bath.ac.uk

Abstract. The development of and accessibility to rich virtual environments, both for recreation and training activities leads to the use of intelligent agents to control avatars (and other entities) in these environments. There is a fundamental tension in such systems between tight integration, for performance and low coupling, for generality, flexibility and extensibility. This paper addresses the engineering issues in connecting agent platforms and other software entities with virtual environments, driven by the following informal requirements: (i) accessibility: we would like (easily) to be able to connect any (legacy) software component with the virtual environment (ii) performance: we want the benefits of decoupling, but not at a high price in performance (iii) distribution: we would like to be able to locate functionality where needed, when necessary, but also be location agnostic otherwise (iv) scalability: we would like to support large-scale and geographically dispersed virtual environments. We start from the position that the basic currency unit of such systems can be events. We describe the Bath Sensor Framework, which is a middleware that attempts to satisfy the above goals and to provide a low-latency linking mechanism between event producers and event consumers, while minimising the effect of coupling of components. We illustrate the framework in two complementary case studies using the Jason agent platform, Second Life and AGAVE (a 3D VE for vehicles). Through these examples, we are able to carry out a preliminary evaluation of the approach against the factors above, against alternative systems and demonstrate effective distributed execution.

1 Introduction

Programming the environment in which a multiagent system is situated has been and continues to be an active research issue [36]. From this perspective, many rich open systems, formed from networked 3D virtual environments such as online games, non-gaming applications or some entertainment context are all potential (programmable) environments, since they offer sufficient variety to simulate real and semi-real world situations. Second Life [27] is an obvious representative example of a 3D virtual environment: it provides a sophisticated, dynamic and realistic virtual world as if duplicating the modern human society with avatars and 3D objects [26]. Such a virtual world may encourage advances

F. Dignum et al. (Eds.): CAVE 2012, LNAI 7764, pp. 17–36, 2013.
© Springer-Verlag Berlin Heidelberg 2013

in agent intelligence, through the demands of sensing and interaction, as agents are situated in more and more complex, dynamic or realistic environments.

However, the integration of agent software and rich environments creates a range of challenges, arising not least from the variety of each and that neither is typically designed to interact with the other. For example, the purpose of the Second Life is to provide an avatar in a networked 3D virtual environment, that it is expected a human will control, so it does not explicitly take into account either the use of AI or integration with other applications. The Jason agent platform [10] is similarly placed: its objective is to provide a BDI-based a deliberative reasoning engine for agent research, so it does not consider standard programming interfaces for other environments.

As a result, the research on agent-environment programming has mostly relied on tightly coupled approaches, characterised by using a specific ontology, protocol and interface that are particular to one system [1, 7–9, 22, 31, 41, 42]. Such a lack of interoperability is possibly not beneficial overall for the development of agent intelligence because there is little scope for the agent that is built for one VE to be exercised in another and so the agent is unavoidably mono-cultural. Besides, such tightly connections between agents and particular environments must somehow inhibit further potential applications arising from alternative agent-environment combinations. We believe that a way forward from this situation may be possible through an appropriate form of middleware.

Thus, our objective is to describe and to demonstrate a kind of integration middleware that serves not only to loosen the coupling between agents and environments, but also to make it possible to consider the connection of any kind of agent and any kind of environment. In software engineering pattern terms, we outline a façade for each agent platform and each environment, where each communicates with the other by means of events (in effect, asynchronous message passing), facilitated by the use of a publish-subscribe server. This constitutes the essence of the Bath Sensor Framework (BSF), which provides the means to link software components independently of programming language, platforms or operating systems, so in principle offering good accessibility, distribution and scalability as an agent-environment integration framework. Performance is a more delicate issue that will take time and experience to establish, depending on the communications overhead (the pub/sub server) and – more likely to dominate – on the decision-making cycle of the agent, although this will clearly depend on the sophistication of the agent architecture.

The remainder of this paper is organised as follows. The overall system design is be described in section 2. Section 3 presents the case studies and their results with example applications. We finish with a brief survey of related work (section 4) followed by discussion and future work (section 5).

2   System Design

In this section, we describe the whole system architecture and how it can integrate an agent platform with a virtual environment. In particular, we will

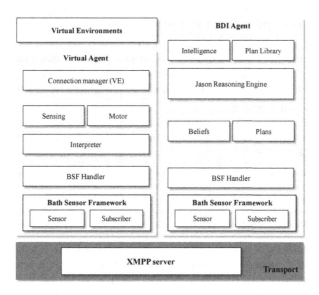

Fig. 1. Overall System Architecture

demonstrate the interaction between the software components and describe the programming model.

For our experimental set-up, the collection, distribution and exchange of data is performed by using publish/subscribe between event producers and consumers via the Extensible Messaging and Presence Protocol (XMPP), an open standard communications protocol [19, 20]. Although XMPP is often cited as a component in real-time (web) systems [40], there is little quantitative evidence to back this up. In consequence, we have carried out some preliminary evaluation (see 3.3) and we return to this issue in related work. For an agent platform, we use the Jason BDI framework and as virtual environments, we use Second Life and the AGents and Autonomous Vehicles Environment (AGAVE).

Any of these components (Jason, SL, AGAVE, XMPP) may be substituted in pursuit of a better fit with the requirements set out earlier, but the primary focus of this paper is our evaluation of the adequacy of the BSF, instantiated as outlined, as a solution to the issues identified above pertaining to agent-environment programming. In doing so, we present case studies that connect Jason agents, Second Life and AGAVE, and discuss how to accommodate differences in platform and programming language.

2.1 Overall System Design

The essence of the design is that the agent platform is decoupled from the virtual environment by means of a publish-subscribe messaging server – in this case, XMPP – as shown in Figure 1.

In the case of Second Life, the virtual agent is created using the openmetaverse library (LIBOMV [30]), which also provides the connection to the Second Life server. The role of the virtual agent is to interpret the actions received from the BDI agent, and then carry out the resulting "physical" actions. In the other direction, the virtual agent perceives the environment and the percepts are delivered to the BDI agent via BSF, where it is becomes a belief that influences the agent's reasoning process.

Clearly the BSF plays a key role in facilitating the interaction between the two components. In particular, through the imposition of a simple communication API, a java-based agent platform and a virtual agent, in this case written in a different language and running on a different platform, can interact with one another. We now explain in more detail about the sensor framework.

2.2   Bath Sensor Framework

The Bath Sensor Framework (BSF) is an abstraction layer for data collection, distribution and exchange built upon XMPP technology. The primary task for which the framework was conceived is the effective collection of data from numerous physical or logical sensors, and its subsequent distribution to the relevant devices or software connected to the XMPP server. The data itself is represented in RDF, although this is not mandatory: the XMPP message structure is just a HTTP body and can be any representation that is suitable.

XMPP is an open standard communication protocol built upon a set of open XML technologies [19, 20]. It is intended to provide not only presence and real-time communication services, but also interoperability by exchanging any type of data in cross domain environments by means of nodes in the XMPP server. To this end, it supports 1-to-1, 1-to-many, and many-to-many data transport mechanisms, so that any data may be be transferred from anywhere to anywhere [6]. Its flexibility, performance and lightweight nature have lead to XMPP being chosen to support research in a diverse range of fields, including Many Task Computing [39], bio-informatics [43] and Cloud Computing [5], as a data distribution service in preference to HTTP or SOAP services.

The above features suggest a number of advantages over pure TCP/IP connections. The latter typically require quite careful set-up and can be fragile where the connection graph is not simple. Moreover, TCP/IP is primarily for 1-to-1 connections, so every additional connection needs an independent additional socket whenever multiple software components are integrated into the main system. In contrast, XMPP provides a star- or bus-like connection model to resolve the m-to-n problem, but through the node abstraction within the server, allows the set-up of multiple virtual circuits. Furthermore, the data producer does not need to know the consumer's identity to set up the connection and through the server's mediation of the connection, the system acquires a degree of fault-tolerance, and permits the observation of system behaviour by third parties, rather than having to replicate such mechanisms in each component. Thus, we conclude that XMPP offers several attractive features, which is why we have chosen to base BSF upon it.

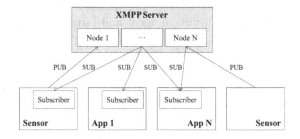

Fig. 2. The System Architecture of Bath Sensor Framework (BSF)

For our purposes, the most notable feature of XMPP and hence the BSF is its provision of a publish/subscribe mechanism. BSF supports these operations by means of *sensor* and *subscriber* classes. When the *sensor* is created in the application which has a role as a data source, a corresponding node is also created in XMPP server. Once created, the application can publish the data sensed from the real or virtual world via the node. If the *subscriber*, which is created in another application, which has a role as a data consumer, sets up a subscription request on that node and registers a corresponding handler in its application, then the data will be transferred from one application to the other. As noted earlier, the data is represented in RDF and published data can be stored in a triple-store (in our case OpenRDF) so that historical data can be retrieved on request from the *subscriber* using the SPARQL query language[1]. In this way, the BSF supports a form of messaging passing with unstructured data between multiple software components.

A particularly valuable aspect of XMPP/BSF is its relative independence from both operating systems and programming languages so that more general programming environments can be provided for users attempting to combine heterogeneous software components. Thus, regardless of language its interfaces reveal the same classes, methods, data structures and interfaces, so that all kinds of applications or libraries can be integrated relatively easily just by adding the classes inside applications.

As can be seen, the features of this framework present a simple and flexible programming environment for heterogeneous software components, with a good level of a accessibility in terms of a simplicity of protocol and ease of connection, performance, and distribution. Consequently, we show how the BSF can facilitate the integration of a cognitive architecture for virtual agents. The next section discusses the programming model of the BSF.

2.3   Programming Model of Bath Sensor Framework

The Bath Sensor Framework can equally be applied to data exchange between distributed software components as to sensor based applications. The perspective

---

[1] Other (structured, relational) databases may equally be connected to the Openfire server and accessed by SQL queries.

of this section is limited to the former. The analogy we draw, in making the connection between BDI agent, virtual agent and virtual environments, is that the virtual agent can be viewed as a sensor for the percepts from the environment. In this context, the *sensor* object is instantiated in a virtual agent in order to collect percepts for the BDI agent. Conversely, the BDI agent needs a *subscriber* object to receive the percepts and subsequent reasoning over acquired beliefs.

In a data consumer such as in the BDI agent, the *subscriber* object has to be instantiated inside the BDI agent. The C# version of this example is identical modulo the grammar of the programming language.

The objective of the design is that it should suffice just to put the *sensor* and *subscriber* object in a wrapper around whichever software component it is desired to integrate into the event processing framework.

3   Case Studies

The aim of the case studies is to demonstrate how the BSF enables the integration of agents and virtual environments; experiments in the actual usage of agents and VEs will be part of future work. In particular, the studies focus on the impact of the use of BSF on the integration of agent platform and virtual environment, in respect of some desiderata for computational models such as generality, modularity and dynamic extensibility [36]. A complementary aspect is the increased capacity for distribution of the components of the software architecture, so that it is not so tightly coupled and that the addition or removal of components is straightforward.

In the preceding section, we outlined how *sensor* and *subscriber* objects are incorporated into a BDI agent and a virtual agent. For the following discussions, the components are (i) Jason, providing a BDI agent, (ii) the openmetaverse library, providing a virtual agent, and (iii) Second Life and AGAVE, providing a virtual environment all linked by the BSF.

3.1   Case Study 1 : Jason Agent and Second Life

The goals of this study are two-fold: (i) to demonstrate the integration of Jason agents with avatars in Second Life via BSF (ii) to identify appropriate mechanism for the control of avatars via BSF, through exploratory scenarios. We also take into account interaction not only between avatars controlled by Jason agents, but also those between humans in real world and avatars in virtual worlds. This latter direction will be explored in more depth as part of future work.

The brief scenario for this section is as follows: one avatar controlled by a human in Second Life server says 'hello' to a Second Life avatar governed by Jason agent. In what follows, we refer to the Jason controlled avatar as the Second Life Bot (SLB). When the SLB receives the greeting message, the SLB sends it to the Jason agent over XMPP via the *sensor*, where it is received via the *subscriber*. The Jason agent then updates the percepts, and performs one cycle of reasoning. As a result, the belief 'hello' triggers the plan 'bow', and appropriate

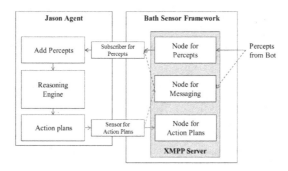

Fig. 3. Basic Operation between Jason agent and Bath Sensor Framework

actions are sent to the SLB. Finally the bot does a 'bow' animation by means of the openmetaverse library after interpreting the action plan 'bow'. Interpretation of the action plans means the conversion of actions from Jason to Second Life animation action(s). For example, if 'bow' is received from Jason, then SLB looks to see whether 'bow' is defined in the action map: if so it perform that animation. More commonly, an action plan is likely to be composed of several atomic actions (or animations) in SLB.

A notable aspect of this scenario is that two heterogeneous software components are able to interact by means of the BSF: because the openmetaverse library is in C#, so too is the SLB, but Jason is Java. Previous work has been able to integrate them by means of the .NET framework [31], but this requires all the components to be in the same location, on a specific platform and also couples them quite tightly. The C# interface to BSF is achieved by an extension of the jabber.net library [25], while the Java interface is built on the Smack library [35], although this is just one of several available Java libraries for XMPP. We are currently using the OpenFire [34] XMPP server, although again there are several other candidates.

Jason Agent and Bath Sensor Framework. There are two ways in which to use Jason agent reasoning engine. The most straightforward is to subclass the environment class, which provides interfaces that are triggered by internal events during the reasoning cycle. This is a quick method of construction, but has limitations: (i) the dynamic update of percepts is impossible because the update interface only can be triggered by the Jason reasoning engine, so external update events from the environment cannot update percepts directly (ii) the other problem is that action execution in the environment class is limited to those actions defined in the base environment class, whle those in the subclass are inaccessible. An alternative approach is to use the Jason agent reasoning engine by subclassing the AgArch class from the Jason class library. The latter is a more general technique for deploying embodied AI into rich environments. Hence we choose this latter approach.

Figure 3 sketches the basic operations between a Jason agent and the BSF. The Jason agent is extended, using the AgArch class, with the *sensor* and

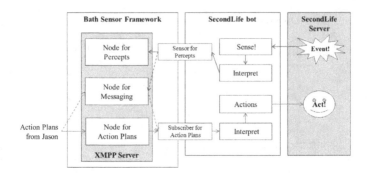

Fig. 4. Basic Operation between Second Life Bot and Bath Sensor Framework

subscriber objects. Percepts from the SLB are received by the *subscriber* object, which results in updates to the beliefs. The next reasoning cycle utilises these beliefs to retrieve an action plan and the *sensor* object publishes the plan to the SLB.

Second Life Bot and Bath Sensor Framework. The open metaverse library provides a set of APIs to program the avatar in terms of creation, appearance, movement, communication – verbal and non-verbal – and interaction with each other, in the same way as the Second Life official viewer application. Thus, with openmetaverse, it is possible to program complex compound actions in the avatar.

Once logged in, the SLB appears as an avatar in Second Life. As such, it has an identity and can move and interact with other participants, as well as perceive events taking place nearby. Consequently, all events occurring in Second Life are detectable in the openmetaverse library and delivered via a callback mechanism to the *sensor* object in the SLB, which collects them and publishes them for the Jason agent to receive. On the other side, the *subscriber* object receives (subscribes to) the action plans from the Jason agent. These are then translated into sequences of atomic actions, which are a combination of defined actions in openmetaverse or user-defined actions. As a result, the SLB carries out these actions in respect of other participants or its environment.

3.2   Case Study 2 : Jason Agents and AGAVE

This case study also has two goals, first to demonstrate the use of Jason agents controlling simulated vehicles within a virtual environment, and second, to replace the simulated vehicle with a physical robot vehicle, but all controlled via the Bath Sensor Framework and XMPP messaging. The AGAVE framework evolved from earlier work based on a Jason-based virtual tank simulation called TankCoders [21]. The solution has now been redesigned, with the Bath Sensor Framework at its core, with integration to the jMonkeyEngine simulation package (to provide a 3D scene), the AllegroGraph data store (for replay and performance analysis), and the Jason BDI framework, to form the AGents and Autonomous Vehicles Environment (AGAVE). Vehicles are controlled via XMPP messages, and report information back via the same mechanism using the BSF. The aim of this work is the construction of scenarios for the exploration of vehicle convoys [4] in the context of automatic driving for their potential benefits in fuel consumption and fatalities, as well as improving traffic efficiency [16].

AGAVE, Jason, and Virtual Vehicles. Unlike the system described in [21], the AGAVE simulation components here are decoupled from Jason for the sake of increased flexibility in where the code is run and the requirements placed on the underlying implementation. As the BSF supports a Resource Description Framework (RDF) data model, the ontology of message exchange is defined, allowing alternative components to be easily integrated. For example, vehicles are expected to publish geo-spatial updates to the BSF, and subscribe to set of defined control messages (e.g. setOrientation, setSpeed). Of course, how those operations are realized depends on the end device, allowing easy substitution for simulated by real vehicles. Similarly, components such as the 3D-view scene subscribe to vehicle updates, and display those positions via the simulated scene.

A vehicle is currently a simple simulated abstraction that publishes its spatial location at a predefined heartbeat, and updates its location based on current orientation and speed. When started, the simulated vehicle is provided with a name, and will publish its spatial position with this name included in the data as well as responding to any control messages that give its name as the subject.

Jason agents are able to interact with a vehicle via the BSF, through the use of customised Jason environment and agent classes. The environment class has been extended, and uses the BSF sensor component with a subscription to spatial data. Received spatial updates are then processed within the environment class, and added as percepts to the relevant coordinator agent for a vehicle. The agent class has been extended with two BSF sensor components, one responsible for sending vehicle commands and one for sending data relating to the state of the Jason agents themselves. The latter is used to display information in the 3D view such as the number of beliefs and agent messages, in order to assist with identifying underlying reasons for observed behaviour of the vehicles. The agent class provides custom actions to the coordinator agent, where the two core actions (`setSpeed` and `setOrientation`) required for vehicle control are implemented. The `setSpeed` action is used by the coordinator agent to request that the vehicle moves at the specified speed, and the class extension passes this to its BSF sensor component, which constructs the appropriate RDF structure for XMPP transmission. The `setOrientation` action follows a similar process, generating a message for the BSF sensor, specifying the desired orientation of the vehicle. The overall process is very similar to that shown in Figure 3, apart from the delivery from the BSF is to vehicles instead of bots.

In this part of the study, the vehicle controlled by the Jason agents is simulated based on the implementation discussed earlier. On receipt of any vehicle control messages via the BSF, the simulated vehicle updates its speed or orientation value, which then takes effect during the next simulation step of the vehicle, as

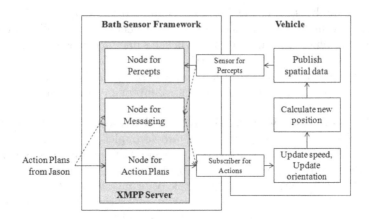

Fig. 5. AGAVE BSF vehicle integration

position changes are determined based on these values. This integration is shown in Figure 5, showing the communication flow between the BSF and the vehicle component.

Each vehicle is controlled by three agents: (i) a coordinator agent that acts as a gateway between other agents responsible for the vehicle and the interface to the vehicle itself – i.e. only this agent directly controls the vehicle), (ii) a driver agent responsible for achieving goals such as moving to a destination, and (iii) a convoy agent responsible for managing vehicle behaviour in convoy formations. Key plans provided by coordinator agent are `+!chosenSpeed(V)` and `+!requestTurnToAngle(A)`. The driver agent provides plans such as `+!emergencyStop`, `+!arrivedAtDestination`, `+!cruise`, `+!speedUp`, `+!slowDown` and `+!moveToKnownPosition` (which is dependent on `desiredXZ(X,Z)`). Finally, the convoy agent provides control largely based on belief updates about the car it is following, which in turn leads to requests for actions by the driver agent such as `desiredXZ(X,Z)` (which X,Z is the location of the vehicle being followed) and `speedUp` or `slowDown` to maintain convoy spacing.

This implementation has been used successfully for a scenario involving a convoy of vehicles navigating in the city centre of Bath (UK). Real world map data in OpenStreetMap format is used for this scenario, with a 3D virtual map created in order to view the simulated vehicles as they traverse the route.

AGAVE, Jason, and Bath Sensor Framework Vehicles. The objective here is to set up a bridge to a simple robot vehicle, such as a Lego Mindstorms, in place of the simulated vehicle used in the previous scenario. At present, both the vehicle control on the Jason side and on the Mindstorms platform are complete, but have not been tested together. In the case of the latter, we utilise an android phone for communications, which runs the BSF component to connect with the XMPP server and bluetooth commincations to send commands to the Mindstorms controller.

As intended, the system structure remains largely the same, due to the decoupled nature of the design as outlined earlier. The robot vehicle interface to the BSF only needs to implement the same functions as the simulated vehicle (i.e. `setSpeed` and `setOrientation`) and by doing so, the simulated vehicle and robot vehicle components become interchangeable, with no changes required to the Jason agents. Consequently, the same process as shown earlier in Figure 5 is used, however the calculation of the new position of the vehicle needs to be based on real world sensors rather than inferred from speed and orientation. This complication however resides with robot vehicle, but brings the benefit of being able to validate Jason agent performance against real sensor data and physical performance issues. As there are no changes required to the BSF design, Jason integration, or the Jason agents themselves, contrasting simulated with real results provides a useful comparison.

3.3   Evaluation

We have prototyped two demonstrators using the BSF: Jason agents controlling Second Life avatars, Jason agents controlling vehicles in a virtual driving environment. A third connecting Jason agents and Lego Mindstorms vehicles is almost completed. At the outset, our informal requirements were stated as (i) accessibility: connection of new software components (ii) performance: decoupling without significant degradation (iii) distribution: connection of components where-ever they might be, and (iv) scalability: in terms of size of environment and number of participants.

Clearly, at this stage, progress on scalability is not feasible, but we can comment on each of the other aspects, although we devote the most space to performance because seems to be the one that raises the most questions.

Accessibility. While each case study started out with the decoupling of the decision-making components (BDI agent) from the virtual environment, each has added other components that demonstrate the practice of our accessibility requirement.

In the context of the first case study, connection with the VE presented a challenge, because the OpenMetaverse library is written in C# and runs in .NET, hence required the construction of a C# client for the BSF, as well as cross-platform communications. Subsequently, we have incorporated a connection with an institutional model (involving Java and Answer Set Programming), following the initial implementation of Balke et al. [3], but decoupled by means of the BSF interface. This has been used to demonstrate norm-mediated behaviour of agents in Second Life (the "hello" example described earlier, and a more complicated one involving making space in a queue for an individual who is given priority).

The development history of the second case study, equally, illustrates how we are starting to meet this requirement. The system started as a decoupled version of the TankCoders [21] system, but the VE has been replaced by the jMonkeyEngine – a 3D game engine written in Java – and subsequently augmented by a 3D viewer that utilises Open Street Map data to produce a more visually credible environment for the convoy than the desert of the original TankCoders. The institutional connection will shortly also be applied here, as we start to treat the management of the convoy as a norm-governed environment problem.

Performance. A qualitative measure of performance might be that the system is performing properly only as long as no events are dropped. That would require even extreme situations to be withing the performance envelope. Quantitative evaluations may not be particularly helpful except perhaps to provide reasssurance that throughput of particular components is probably sufficient not to be the cause of a bottleneck. Even then, it may be hard to say, even if many such components are performing "well", whether their collective performance is adequate. We have, for example, measured round-trip message times between Second Life and the agent controlling an avatar, but this may well say more about the networking infrastructure than about the architecture as whole. As a consequence, it is common to eschew distribution for tight coupling in order to be able to deliver performance guarantees. Thus, performance is less about raw processing power, however that might be measured, but whether the architecture as a whole performs believably. Even then, exhaustive testing all possible states of all possible components is likely to be infeasible, so we are limited, as a poor substitute, to stress-testing individual components as a way of seeking confidence in the overall architecture. In practice, performance is a pervasive issue and tight coupling of components is one way that some control can be exerted over the collective factors that influence it, but in the long term such coupling impacts scalability.

It is too early to have detailed performance profiles of the components in the architecture we have described, but among the primary (new) sources of delay are the network, which is relatively hard to control, and the XMPP server (or servers, since they may be federated). There are several XMPP server implementations, but it is nor surprising, given the application domain, that all aim for high performance within themselves. We have chosen to use Openfire, because of its stated aims of supporting real time communications projects. We have not done a comparative evaluation against other XMPP servers. Openfire claims to be able to support significant numbers of (human) users with relatively few resources (e.g up 500 concurrent users with a minimum of 384Mb RAM on a 1.5GHz processor and up to 100,000 with a minimum of 2.0Gb RAM, 2×3GHz processors and 1–4 connection managers). Further details at [38] measure factors such as the number of concurrent sessions and packet counts.

Since the fundamental mode of communication is publish/subscribe, one approach to evaluating the processing capacity of a component is to quantify the rate at which it can process incoming items, that is the data in the streams to which it is subscribed. Different components will have different subscription capacities, and depending on their role and where they are connected into the subscription network, one of several approaches may be appropriate if this capacity is insufficient, such as: (i) increasing component input capacity (ii) component replication (iii) throttling input volume, and (iv) inserting an aggregator

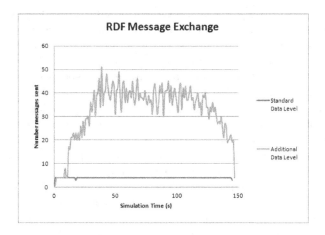

Fig. 6. Effect of additional jason state messaging on RDF quantity

component whose subscription and publication rates match upstream and down-stream components. We have some preliminary data about subscription capacity, such as the frequency at which driver updates (in AGAVE) result in a stable simulation or lead to failure. For example, see Figure 6, where the Standard Data Level is the volume for normal convoy control, resulting in successful arrival at the destination, but the Additional Data Level, which includes full Jason state data, can result in a loss of communication between Jason agents and vehicles, depending on the number of vehicles involved. Openfire developers report of a capacity for ≈250 updates/sec – well in excess of the number observed above – but much more detailed measurements are required to fill out this picture.

There are two forms of mitigation that are possible in the architecture we have outlined: (i) short-circuiting, and (ii) aggregation (as mentioned earlier). Short circuiting is, in effect, taking events from the virtual environment, inter-cepting them before they are forwarded to the controlling agent, and making a decision that is returned to the VE. We do this, for example, in the Mind-storms scenario, where an android handset is physically located on the robot, which may make some (reactive) control decisions and relay them back over the local bluetooth connection to the (lower level) Mindstorms controller. Several such (nested) feedback loops [37] can be inserted into the control chain depend-ing on need. Such a design pattern reflects a hierarchical control framework, where proximity to source implies lower level events and tighter control, as seen in historical multi-layer agent architectures such as InteRRaP [29] and Touring Machines [17]. The technical difference here is that those layers are distributed, reflecting the network-determined (or estimated) capacity for a timely response.

Aggregation is a complementary perspective on the same issue. Our experi-ence and that of others [32] is that the Jason agents cannot handle high percept update frequencies (actual figures are not very useful because they are inevitably application and platform specific useful), which is typically manifested by un-stable and hard to re-produce behaviour. One approach might be to re-engineer

Jason for higher performance, which although possibly desirable, does not consider whether all those events actually need to be processed at the BDI, that is the deliberative, level. In both theory and practice, cognitive architectures use layers to aggregate *small* observations into *bigger* ones. This can be characterised as inference or situational awareness, depending on perspective, but the overall effect is that minor observations are somehow collected, correlated and classified into less minor observations, subject to some degree of probability that reflects the accuracy of the process. In doing so, the volume of data, which possibly at some level may be labelled "information"; is reduced so that frequency of communication is also reduced and the receiving reasoning process is presented with synthesized knowledge reflecting some kind of summary of the situation, rather than having to carry out that process itself. It is a fundamental design challenge, perhaps reflecting the principle of so-called sliding autonomy, to decide which levels should make which decisions, whether those strata are fixed and if not, how those divisions may be determined, or negotiated, in live situations.

We believe that performance is a many-faceted issue in this context and XMPP server throughput, and to a lesser extend network latency, while significant, are not the only factors, and it is as much the other components, but especially the deliberative architectures that we choose to use, the rate at which they can absorb percepts and the rate at which they can make effective decisions. This in turn is significantly affected by the level at which it is demanded they reason: is it sensible to use a BDI agent to monitor and adjust the speed of a vehicle –rather like a cruise control – when the same function can be achieved with a simple numerical procedure? Thus, the second mitigation is the relative ease with which new event processors can be added to this architecture, by subscribing them to existing feeds and publishing their results to existing consumers, through which it becomes possible to balance the factors of event rate, information level and network latency to achieve performance targets.

Distribution. Observations regarding distribution are relatively brief because, like accessibility, it could be viewed as having been demonstrated in principle, but like scalability, more is needed for it to be demonstrated with confidence. Since the XMPP message transport layer is directly built on HTTP, and since XMPP has been used for some years to support Internet Messaging in various guises (Microsoft Messenger, Google Talk, etc.), the mechanism has been demonstrated both to distribute and to scale. We have used the BSF in the context of a distributed sensing project, but the case studies reported here have only been run in the same local area network.

4   Related Work

AI research has paid substantial attention to how agent behaviour should reflect a response to something sensed from the environment in which it is situated. Cognitive architectures analyse this information, make decisions, and carry out planning to determine the next behaviour to execute. In a dynamic environments, SOAR [24] is a well known example of a classical symbolic reasoning architecture. However, it is also known as rather heavy-weight and can hardly be expected to respond in real time. There is also a range of well-known reactive architectures, including subsumption [13], Finite State Machines (FSMs) [12, 14], Basic Reactive Plans (BRP) [14, 18], and POSH plans [11], amongst others. Any of the above, perhaps bar SOAR, are suitable decision-makers for avatars in virtual environments, but our choice from among goal-driven approaches, is the popular the Belief-Desire-Intention (BDI) architecture [33]. Beliefs here refer to knowledge about the world in agents mind, desires are objectives to be achieved, and intentions identify the actions chosen by the agent as part of some plan to help it achieve a particular desire [28].

A distinct line of research has highlighted the notion of the environment programming in multiagent systems [36]. According to [36], agent programming should have balance between the agent itself and its environments in order to achieve a high level of intelligence. This perspective reflects the idea that the environment becomes a meaningful place to support the agent's abilities with many functionalities, rather than the traditional view in which it is simply a place that the agent senses and acts upon.

In this context, there is a fair body of research into the deployment of an embodied artificial intelligence using the above cognitive architectures in rich environments. For example, Bogdanovych et al [7] introduce the 3D Electronic Institution, or Virtual Institution (VI), which is a virtual world with normative regulations governing interactions between participants and environment. They also also propose the introduction of virtual characters capable of learning [8] and the use of VI as environments for imitation learning, providing for the enhancement of virtual agent behaviour by learning from human users or other software agents. Later work from this group puts forward a teaching mechanism, so that the virtual character may become more believable [9]. Although this work is amongst the most developed in the use of Second Life, it offers rather less on the matter of agent-environment programming and the role of cognitive architectures, because of its focus on the regimented normative environment and virtual characters that learn.

Veksler [42] demonstrates integration between ACT-R [2, 23] and Second Life via HTTP web server. In this work, all information are gathered by a 3D object, which is attached to the avatar. It scans the environment around the avatar within a certain radius, and sends what scanner senses to a dedicated web server. The ACT-R module is separate from the Second Life environment, but capable of communicating to the web server. By means of HTTP request to the web server, the decision-making module collects sensing data and executes a 'perceive–think–act' loop. In the end, the decision including motor actions goes back to the intermediate web server, and are then applied to the avatar. Another notable work is [31], in which a Jason agent supplies the reasoning for a virtual agent in an environment provided by Second Life, supported by an external data processing module that handles environment sensing. In the same manner as above, through an attached 3D object, which serves as a virtual sensory system, sets of perceptions generated by the data processing module are delivered to Jason agent, which then deliberates. The results of the reasoning are communicated back to the Second Life avatar, and the action is realised, changing the state of the environment. The scenario in this case is the playing of a football game. This work demonstrates the utilization of an event recognition platform [32] not only to enhance the perception capability, which becomes a source of better reasoning, but also to retrieve more accurate domain-specific information from low level data.

In comparison with the above systems, which are quite tightly coupled, other approaches also exist, that aim for a more general integration between cognitive agents and virtual environments. There are (at least) three representative systems, with similar objectives to ours, against which we contrast what has been presented here: GameBots [1], Pogamut [22], and CIGA [41]. Gamebots [1] has much in common with the virtual agent component in our system, being a kind of programmable agent controller, integrated with the 3D video game Unreal Tournament (UT), in order to create autonomous bots that interact with human players as well as other bot players. The bots are able to sense and act directly from the environment, via TCP/IP socket communication. Gamebot 'agents' appear to be limited to reactive behaviours, while the system as a whole only functions with one game engine, namely Unreal Tournament.

Pogamut [22] incorporates an interface layer between Unreal Tournament and the decision-making agent, by means of TCP/IP sockets. The role of this component is rather like that of the Jason agent in our system, in that it has the task of perceiving the environment, interaction with environment, and decision making, for which it uses the POSH reactive planner [11]. As with Gamebots, Pogamut has seen substantial up-take, from student projects to complex research projects, thanks to their approach that allows greater flexibility in the development of the high level of autonomy in virtual agents. Nevertheless, it still has a high dependency on the particular environment of UT, and on a particular programming language, namely Java.

CIGA [41] also has numerous similarities with our framework in that it aims to resolve the coupling problem between agent and virtual environment. This it does by means of two interface layers and an ontology model: (i) physical interface layer to connect to a environment (game engine), and (ii) cognitive interface layer to connect to a multiagent system, corresponding to the Virtual Agent and the Jason Agent, respectively. The use of ontology model, containing pre-defined ontologies to make a contract between agent and game engine even though they are situated in a specific domain, eases the interpretation of perception and behaviour execution. This architecture offers fair accessibility, and could in principle support distributed execution, thanks to the use of socket-based communications, but this would require careful manual configuration. In this respect, CIGA is the closest to our proposal, but the dependence on a relatively low-level and inflexible network layer seems likely to inhibit distribution and scalability.

To summarise, the short-comings we observe in the above lie in their tight integration of the components, leading to an effectively closed, single platform system. Thus, they do not have the flexibility necessary for distributed software systems. They are tightly coupled by the communication protocol as well as ontology, so that adding/removing a software component is challenging, and deploying such platforms more widely is in general difficult. This is only exacerbated – or probably even rendered impossible – if it is desired to incorporate components in different programming languages or that only run on another operating system.

Earlier, we noted the lack of any comprehensive performance evaluation of XMPP, as far as we can find, in the academic literature. Linden Labs have apparently carried out an evaluation of various message passing protocols[2], noting that the Advanced Message Queueing Protocol [15] implementations demonstrate good single-host performance, but lack figures on maximum capacity when clustered, or the value of clustering. XMPP appears in the list, but was not evaluated for lack of time. Several other protocols are eliminated for not meeting their requirements, but unfortunately there is no definitive conclusion. At best, this indicates that if XMPP proves inadequate, AMPQ may be worth investigation, however it is observed that AMPQ lacks adequate flow control mechanisms, so servers may simply stop when overloaded, unlike XMPP. Also, we note that communication may well finally constitute only a small fraction of the critical costs of round-trip times between agent and VE, compared to the response times of the agent or the VE themselves.

5   Conclusion and Future Work

In this paper, the Bath Sensor Framework has been introduced as a middleware for decoupling cognitive agents and virtual environments. Also, two case studies are presented using the framework for linking heterogeneous software, the Jason BDI reasoning platform, and Second Life and AGAVE which are representative rich 3D virtual environments, respectively. From these studies, it seems clear that the BSF has some useful advantages as an integration middleware. Firstly, it offers good accessibility, because of the simplicity in protocol, and ease of both connection and use. Secondly, in respect of speed and reliability, it inherits from XMPP, so that it is able not only to communicate in real time but also transfer whatever data in the form of open XML, which may become the basis of the interoperability in cross domain applications. Finally, it enables distribution of components, so that it contributes to effective data transport mechanism such as 1-to-1, 1-to-many, or many-to-many, from anywhere to anywhere. As a result, through the use of the BSF, the system as a whole has the potential for flexibility and extensibility.

Furthermore, we have extended the framework to operate in conjunction with an institutional framework based, so that the behaviour of agent in virtual environments can be governed by norms.The notion of institution, as a set of rules for a particular agent society, is appropriate for the regulation of behaviour of

---

[2] http://wiki.secondlife.com/wiki/Message_Queue_Evaluation_Notes, retrieved 20120416, last updated 2010.

virtual agents in a particular situations, by saving the need to incorporate behaviour for all circumstances in the agent themselves.

Plans for future work include a careful evaluation of performance issues, such
as (i) the notion of component subscription profiles, (ii) monitoring of communication in live systems, so that out-of-profile situations can be detected,
(iii) development of mitigations, such as throttling, replication and aggregation,
(iv) experimentation with data handling policies, such as discarding and (finite)
buffering, amongst others and (v) exploring the feasibility of applying corrective
actions during execution, as well, of course, as the application of IVAs to more
demanding scenarios.

Acknowledgements. We would like to thank Surangika Ranathunga, Stephen
Cranefield, and Martin Purvis for useful discussions and observations.

References

1. Adobbati, R., Marshall, A.N., Scholer, A., Tejada, S.: Gamebots: A 3d virtual
   world test-bed for multi-agent research. In: Proceedings of the Second International
   Workshop on Infrastructure for Agents, MAS, and Scalable MAS (2001)
2. Anderson, J.R., Matessa, M., Lebiere, C.: ACT-R: A theory of higher level cognition and its relation to visual attention. Human Computer Interaction 12(4),
   439–462 (1997)
3. Balke, T., De Vos, M., Padget, J., Traskas, D.: On-line reasoning for institutionally-
   situated bdi agents. In: The 10th International Conference on Autonomous Agents
   and Multiagent Systems, AAMAS 2011, Richland, SC, vol. 3, pp. 1109–1110. International Foundation for Autonomous Agents and Multiagent Systems (2011)
4. Bergenhem, C., Huang, Q., Benmimoun, A., Robinson, T.: Challenges of platoon-
   ing on public motorways. In: 17th World Congress on Intelligent Transport Systems
   (2010),   http://www.sartre-project.eu/en/publications/Documents/ITS%20
   WC%20challenges%20of%20platooning%20concept%20and%20modelling%2010%20b
   .pdf (retrieved November 11, 2012)
5. Bernstein, D., Vij, D.: Intercloud directory and exchange protocol detail using
   XMPP and RDF. In: 2010 6th World Congress on Services (SERVICES-1), pp.
   431–438 (July 2010)
6. Bernstein, D., Vij, D.: Using XMPP as a transport in intercloud protocols. In: 2010
   the 2nd International Conference on Cloud Computing, CloudComp (2010)
7. Bogdanovych, A., Esteva, M., Simoff, S., Sierra, C., Berger, H.: A Methodology
   for Developing Multiagent Systems as 3D Electronic Institutions. In: Luck, M.,
   Padgham, L. (eds.) Agent-Oriented Software Engineering VIII. LNCS, vol. 4951,
   pp. 103–117. Springer, Heidelberg (2008)
8. Bogdanovych, A., Simoff, S., Esteva, M.: Virtual Institutions: Normative Environments Facilitating Imitation Learning in Virtual Agents. In: Prendinger, H.,
   Lester, J.C., Ishizuka, M. (eds.) IVA 2008. LNCS (LNAI), vol. 5208, pp. 456–464.
   Springer, Heidelberg (2008)
9. Bogdanovych, A., Simoff, S., Esteva, M., Debenham, J.: Teaching autonomous
   agents to move in a believable manner within virtual institutions. In: Bramer, M.
   (ed.) Artificial Intelligence in Theory and Practice II. IFIP, vol. 276, pp. 55–64.
   Springer, Heidelberg (2008)

10. Bordini, R.H., Wooldridge, M., Hübner, J.F.: Programming Multi-Agent Systems in AgentSpeak using Jason (Wiley Series in Agent Technology). John Wiley & Sons (2007)
11. Brom, C., Bryson, J.J.: Action selection for intelligent systems. In: The European Network for the Advancement of Artificial Cognitive Systems, white paper 044-1 (2006)
12. Brooks, R.A.: Intelligence without representation. Artificial Intelligence 47(1-3), 139–159 (1991)
13. Brooks, R.A.: How to build complete creatures rather than isolated cognitive simulators. In: Architectures for Intelligence. Lawrence Erlbaum Assosiates, Mahwah (2001)
14. Bryson, J.J.: Action selection and individuation in agent based modelling. In: Proceedings of AGENT 2003: Challenges of Social Simulation, pp. 317–330 (2003)
15. OASIS Advanced Message Queueing Protocol (AMQP) Technical Committee. Advanced message queuing protocol 1.0. Technical report, OASIS (2012), https://www.amqp.org/resources/download (retrieved 20120416)
16. Dressler, F., Kargl, F., Ott, J., Tonguz, O., Wischhof, L.: 10402 abstracts collection and executive summary – inter-vehicular communication. In: Inter-Vehicular Communication, Dagstuhl, Germany. Dagstuhl Seminar Proceedings, vol. 10402, Schloss Dagstuhl - Leibniz-Zentrum fuer Informatik, Germany (2011)
17. Ferguson, I.A.: Touring machines: Autonomous agents with attitudes. Computer 25(5), 51–55 (1992)
18. Fikes, R.E., Hart, P.E., Nilsson, N.J.: Learning and executing generalized robot plans. Artificial Intelligence 3, 251–288 (1972)
19. The XMPP Standards Foundation. Extensible messaging and presence protocol(XMPP): Core, and related other RFCs. http://xmpp.org/rfcs/rfc3920.html
20. The XMPP Standards Foundation. The XMPP standard foundation homepage. http://www.xmpp.org
21. Fronza, G.: Simulador de um ambiente virtual distribuido multiusuario para batalhas de tanques 3d com inteligencia baseada em agentes BDI. Final year project report (July 2008),http://campeche.inf.furb.br/tccs/2008-I/2008-1-14-ap-germanofronza.pdf, See also http://sourceforge.net/projects/tankcoders/ (retrieved Novebber 11, 2012)
22. Gemrot, J., Kadlec, R., Bída, M., Burkert, O., Píbil, R., Havlíček, J., Zemčák, L., Šimlovič, J., Vansa, R., Štolba, M., Plch, T., Brom, C.: Pogamut 3 Can Assist Developers in Building AI (Not Only) for Their Videogame Agents. In: Dignum, F., Bradshaw, J., Silverman, B., van Doesburg, W. (eds.) Agents for Games and Simulations. LNCS, vol. 5920, pp. 1–15. Springer, Heidelberg (2009)
23. ACT-R Research Group. ACT-R: Theory and architecture of cognition, http://act-r.psy.cmu.edu/
24. The Soar Group. Soar project homepage, http://sitemaker.umich.edu/soar
25. Jabber-Net. The jabber.net project, http://code.google.com/p/jabber-net
26. Kumar, S., Chhugani, J., Kim, C., Kim, D., Nguyen, A., Dubey, P., Bienia, C., Kim, Y.: Second life and the new generation of virtual worlds. Computer 41(9), 46–53 (2008)
27. Linden Labs. Second life homepage, http://www.secondlife.com
28. Mascardi, V., Demergasso, D., Ancona, D.: Languages for programming bdi-style agents: an overview. In: Corradini, F., De Paoli, F., Merelli, E., Omicini, A. (eds.) WOA, pp. 9–15. Pitagora Editrice Bologna (2005)
29. Müller, J.: The Agent Architecture InteRRaP. In: Müller, J.P. (ed.) The Design of Intelligent Agents. LNCS, vol. 1177, pp. 45–123. Springer, Heidelberg (1996)

30. OpenMetaverse Organization. libopenmetaverse developer wiki,
    http://lib.openmetaverse.org/wiki/

31. Ranathunga, S., Cranefield, S., Purvis, M.: Interfacing a cognitive agent platform
    with a virtual world: a case study using second life. In: The 10th International
    Conference on Autonomous Agents and Multiagent Systems, AAMAS 2011, vol. 3,
    pp. 1181–1182. International Foundation for Autonomous Agents and Multiagent
    Systems, Richland (2011)

32. Ranathunga, S., Cranefield, S., Purvis, M.: Identifying events taking place in second
    life virtual environments. Applied Artificial Intelligence 26(1-2), 137–181 (2012)

33. Rao, A.S., Georgeff, M.P.: BDI agents: from theory to practice. In: Proceedings of
    the First Intl. Conference on Multiagent Systems, San Francisco (1995)

34. Ignite Realtime. The Openfire Project,
    http://www.igniterealtime.org/projects/openfire/

35. Ignite Realtime. The Smack API Project,
    http://www.igniterealtime.org/projects/smack/

36. Ricci, A., Piunti, M., Viroli, M.: Environment programming in MAS: An artifact-
    based perspective. Autonomous Agents and MultiAgent Systems 23(2), 158–192
    (2011)

37. Van Roy, P.: Self management and the future of software design. Electr. Notes
    Theor. Comput. Sci. 182, 201–217 (2007)

38. Jive Software. Openfire scalability,
    http://www.igniterealtime.org/about/OpenfireScalability.pdf   (retrieved
    November 09, 2012)

39. Stout, L., Murphy, M.A., Goasguen, S.: Kestrel: an XMPP-based framework for
    many task computing applications. In: Proceedings of the 2nd Workshop on Many-
    Task Computing on Grids and Supercomputers, MTAGS 2009, pp. 11:1–11:6.
    ACM, New York (2009)

40. In-Band Real Time Text. Xep-301: In-band real time text. Technical report, XMPP
    Standards Foundation (2012) http://xmpp.org/extensions/xep-0301.pdf (re-
    trieved April 16, 2012)

41. van Oijen, J., Vanhée, L., Dignum, F.: CIGA: A Middleware for Intelligent Agents
    in Virtual Environments. In: Proceedings of the 3rd International Workshop on
    the uses of Agents for Education, Games and Simulations (2011)

42. Veksler, V.D.: Second-life as a simulation environment: Rich, high-fidelity world,
    minus the hassles. In: Proceedings of the 9th International Conference of Cognitive
    Modeling (2009)

43. Wagener, J., Spjuth, O., Willighagen, E., Wikberg, J.: XMPP for cloud comput-
    ing in bioinformatics supporting discovery and invocation of asynchronous web
    services. BMC Bioinformatics 10(1), 279 (2009)

Agent Communication
for Believable Human-Like Interactions
between Virtual Characters

Joost van Oijen[1,2] and Frank Dignum[1]

[1] Utrecht University, Utrecht, The Netherlands
{J.vanOijen,F.P.M.Dignum}@uu.nl
[2] VSTEP, Rotterdam, The Netherlands

Abstract. Virtual characters in games or simulations are increasingly
required to perform complex tasks in dynamic virtual environments. This
includes the ability to communicate in a human-like manner with other
characters or a human user. When applying agent technology to create
autonomous, goal-directed characters, interactions have to be generated
at runtime. In this paper we propose a model balancing efficient agent
communication on one hand and believable realizations of human-like
interactions on the other hand.

Keywords: Agent Communication, Intelligent Virtual Agents, Middleware.

1 Introduction

As the technology to create more realistic, complex and dynamic virtual environments advances, there is an increasing interest to create intelligent virtual agents
(IVAs) to populate these environments for the purpose of games, simulations or
training. The use of agent technology in the form of multi-agent systems (MASs)
seems a good fit to realize the cognitive and decision-making aspects of an IVA.
One of the problems one faces when applying a MAS to control the behavior of
virtual characters is how to deal with agent communication in the MAS: agents
now become embodied in a real-time virtual environment and have to communicate through the environment to simulate believable interactions. Additionally,
MASs often do not have to deal with human-like aspects like emotions or empathy and thus standards developed for agent communication (e.g. FIPA) typically
do not support other kinds of communicative intents besides performative acts
(e.g. the ability to communicate an affective state or to associate emotion with
a message).

In current commercial 3D video games or game-based training applications,
human-like interaction between virtual characters has hardly been employed.
When it is, it is often realized during so-called cut scenes or in specific situations
that are known to occur by design (e.g. scripts). Here, the believability of the
graphical and audible realization of an interaction can be of a reasonably good

F. Dignum et al. (Eds.): CAVE 2012, LNAI 7764, pp. 37–54, 2013.

level (e.g. encompassing conversational gestures or emotional expressions). Since the dialog acts and context in which the interaction takes place are fully known beforehand, realization can be crafted in detail at design time.

Now when we turn to agent technology to design autonomous, goal-directed agents, the context in which they might communicate cannot be known beforehand. Hence, communicative behavior has to be generated dynamically at runtime and achieving the same level of believability becomes more difficult to realize. This requires fine-grained multimodal control over an agent's embodiment, believable perception of multimodal behavior in the environment and models for generating outgoing and processing incoming communicative intents.

The use of multi-agent systems to control virtual characters has been considered before [13] and successful attempts have been made to demonstrate its potential. Here, agents are usually integrated in a game engine using a custom developed connection between a specific game engine and MAS [5] or making use of available technologies allowing access to a certain game engine [1,6]. Looking at the facilities for agents to exhibit human-like communicative abilities in these systems, they fall short on delivering the necessary interfaces for agents to express and perceive communicative behaviors, due to the limitations of the underlying intermediate software [1] or game engines they were dependent on.

In this paper we present design issues for realizing believable human-like communication between virtual agents situated cognitively in a MAS and physically in a virtual environment. A model is proposed to tackle these issues allowing agents to effectively communicate any intent at the cognitive level while realizing this in a believable manner at the physical level. By not restricting ourselves to specific intents or intent representations, we leave designers the choice to decide which type of signals agents should be allowed to communicate, whether they are speech acts (e.g. performatives), meta-conversational signals (e.g. turn-taking) or affective signals (e.g. emotional state). This flexibility allows agent designers to employ our model to deal with additional human-like abilities (e.g. flexible interaction management or empathic processing). By discussing a use case scene we aim to show that our model provides an infrastructural basis for realizing the agent communication occurring in such a scene while maintaining a suitable balance between efficiency and believability.

The paper is organized as follows. In section 2 related research areas are discussed. Section 3 addresses issues for realizing human-like interactions using agent communication. A model is proposed in section 4, followed by an implementation and evaluation in sections 5 and 6. Finally, in section 7 and section 8 we conclude.

2   Related Work

As noted above, human-like communication between virtual characters is rarely seen in games or training systems. A more commonly seen type of interaction involves a human player able to have a dialog with a virtual character which often plays a more supportive role during a dialog and does not express much goal-directed communication itself. In current work, we do not consider user-agent interaction but instead focus on communication between virtual characters themselves. Next we provide an overview of related research areas and describe how they relate to our work.

2.1   Agent Communication

In MAS research there is an increasing need for more *open systems* in which agents are situated in more dynamic environments, carrying out complex interactions. In such systems, the situations in which communication can take place is not fully known beforehand and agents require more knowledge about the specific meaning or underlying goal of a message in order to properly deal with it. In [3], research directions in agent communication are presented concerning these issues. For example, the use of *social semantics* is discussed, ascribing meanings to messages based on social concepts such as commitments or conventions. Compared to human-like interactions in virtual worlds, similarities can be drawn: virtual worlds are becoming more complex and dynamic whereas human-like interactions are by definition flexible and full of social semantics. Therefore simulating human-like interactions with agents, the use of standards like FIPA ACL and corresponding fixed protocols is not enough. We really have to make use of rich communication semantics in line of what is discussed in [3].

2.2   Embodied Conversational Agents

Considering the simulation of human-like communication by virtual agents, this is the research focus of the ECA (Embodied Conversational Agent) community. Here, frameworks and computational models are proposed for a wide range of aspects of human-like communication (e.g. multimodal communicative behaviors [9,11], conversation modeling [16] and topics dealing with personality or cultural factors in ECAs [19]. There are several reasons why this research is not always directly applicable for our purposes: the focus is often on interaction with a user situated in the real world where little research is found on human-like interactions between two virtual agents, especially on the perception side. Further, most research focuses on a single aspect and is rarely seen within the scope of a full agent architecture (except for specific instances like [8]). Last, their possible employment for use in real-time games is often not a priority such that important aspects like practicality and efficiency are less focused upon.

2.3   Connecting MASs and Game Engines

Finally we consider the work on the integration of multi-agent platforms or other decision-making systems in virtual environments and look at the communicative abilities of these virtual agents. In [5], the cognitive BDI-architecture of CoJACK was used to control characters in VBS2, a 3D training environment used in military domains. Pogamut [6] is designed as a mediation-layer between a game engine and an agent's decision-making system to bridge the "representational gap". In [18], the agent programming language GOAL was used to integrate BDI agents in the UT game engine using both Pogamut and EIS. The latter is a proposal for an environment interface standard for MAS agents and has been advertised for use in agent platforms including 2APL, Jadex or Jason [2]. In these systems agents have very poor communicative abilities, caused by the employed game engines which offer very limited facilities for expressing and perceiving communicative behaviors. Further, considering multi-agent platforms, this raises the question of how communication should be handled: i.e. when connected to a game engine, communication can be accomplished through the virtual environment. Does this make a platform's communication mechanism obsolete? Or in what situations should agents still use direct communication within the MAS? Such questions have not been addressed in related work.

3   Conceptual Gap

Imagine a scene from a game-based training application for firefighters where each virtual character is controlled by a fully autonomous agent: *"A fire has been reported in a residential home, thought to be uninhabited. A team of fire-fighters arrive at the scene. The team leader assesses the situation and calls for a command huddle. While the leader is giving out orders to each team member to attack the fire, an injured woman stumbles out of the burning house. She is in a panicked state and screams something to the firefighters while pointing to a window on the first floor. Because of an explosion occurring simultaneously, the fire fighters fail to hear the woman but realize something is wrong based on the woman's expressions and gestures. The team leader interrupts the huddle and rushes to the woman who explains that her child is still in the house. A police officer nearby overhears the woman and calls for medical services. Some bystanders get hold of this development and spread the information to others. Meanwhile, the team leader reassesses the new situation, returns to his team and gives out new orders to first save the child and then attack the fire."*

Now when we consider using MAS technology to control human-like characters as illustrated in the example scene, one has to bridge the inherent conceptual gap between typical agent communication in MASs and human-like communication by characters in virtual environments. In the remainder of this section we will discuss concrete issues for realizing human-like interactions using agent communication.

3.1   Issues at the Mind-Body Interface

The first category of issues relate to the technical issues of applying agent communication to simulate character interactions in virtual environments.

Embodiment. Simulating human-like communication, agents should not be allowed to communicate directly with each other within a MAS but resort to expressing communicative behavior through their embodiment, separating *what* is communicated by an agent's mind from *how* this is realized by its embodiment. One aspect involves the use of multiple modalities to express a communicative intent (e.g. speech, gestures, gazing, facial expressions, etc). E.g. referring to our example scene, when the team leader is giving out orders, he may accompany his verbal acts with gestural body movements clarifying the meaning of a task being ordered. Another aspect concerns the *choice* of behavior realization. A similar intent may be communicated many different ways depending on factors like personality, culture, interaction partners or social setting. E.g. in our example, more introvert team members may use less expressive gestures during communication than other members.

The same aspects concern the perception of intents: since intents are communicated using multimodal behavior, they also need to be perceived through the observation of this behavior, requiring an inference step to assign a meaning to the observed behavior. Where the expression of communicative intents has gotten a lot of attention in research on virtual humans (e.g. in [9]), the corresponding perception largely remains untackled for communication between virtual agents.

Environment. Unlike in typical MAS applications, agents required to represent human-like characters have to deal with a different kind of environment, namely a *real-time* and *virtual* environment. This introduces several issues.

First of all, unlike in typical MAS environments, actions now become durative and the successful execution of an act is not immediately known (e.g. speech can last a number of seconds to realize). Now both the environment and the agent's cognitive state may change during the realization of a communicative act and could result in a realization failure or a desire for the agent to interrupt the ongoing realization respectively (e.g. in our example scene, the team leader interrupts his communication when he hears the screaming woman). Further, the perception communicative behavior also becomes a durative process. Even though not fully perceived an intent, one may still require an agent to be aware of ongoing communicative behavior (e.g. for the purpose of situation awareness or providing backchannel feedback).

Second, where MASs usually provide a reliable communication mechanism for inter-agent communication, successful communication realized in a virtual environment depends on the sensory capabilities of the agents and the simulated laws of physics. For example, in our example scene, a bystander walking past the incident may not have perceived the screaming woman simply because she was out of sensory range. And although the team leader perceived the woman's non-verbal behavior, he did not fully understand her because the explosion distorted proper perception of her verbal message. Further, agents within the vicinity are able to overhear communication even if not directed towards them (e.g. the police officer overhearing the screaming woman).

The last issue concerns factors for success. Typically in MASs, semantics for communication success or failure are trivial: either the message was successfully delivered or not. In virtual agent communication, failure can occur at difference conceptual levels: an act was scheduled for realization but there was a problem to physically express it; an act was successfully realized but not perceived; or the act was perceived but not properly interpreted.

3.2 Issues on the Agent-Side

The second category of issues relate to more conceptual issues within the agent itself for simulating human-like interactions. Unlike the technical issues described above, these issues will not be tackled explicitly by our model proposed in the following section. Rather, we aim to summarize the aspects to consider in agent design and the impact it may have on application design.

Communicative Functions. Communication in MASs typically involves the use of performative acts (e.g. FIPA ACL) to effectively allow agents to exchange information or delegate tasks. Signals communicated between virtual agents required to exhibit human-like communicative abilities are much richer. For example, in [14], a taxonomy of communicative functions is given for human communication and amongst others include functions related to conversation management (e.g. turn-taking), meta-cognitive signals, deictic references and emotional expressions. Developing agent frameworks supporting such functions is an active area of research (e.g. [7,10]), though, they often impose strong requirements on the design of the agent. Considering them for use in real-time games, a tradeoff is in place between desired believability and design complexity.

Emotions. Emphasizing a category of communicative functions are affective functions, mandatory for agents required to cope with aspects like emotion or empathy. Computational models and frameworks have been proposed based on theories of appraisal and emotion (e.g. [4,12]). Since emotional factors may impact agent processes like belief formation, deliberation or intent realization, a more complex agent design is required. Employing such affective agents in games, the challenge is deciding why, when and what kind of emotional signals must be communicated between agents and how this can be realized.

Conversation Modeling. In MASs, conversations between two or more agents are often regulated by fixed interaction protocols where each agent takes on a predefined role, either as the initiator or participant (e.g. FIPA *Query* or *Contract Net* protocols). Natural human-like conversations tend to be more flexible and dynamic: participants may take, request or give the turn at any point in time; they can join or leave a conversation any time and may take on different roles (e.g. side participant or overhearer). Human-like conversation modeling has been addressed in previous research on virtual humans (e.g. in [16]). The challenge here is to integrate such models in the deliberation process of a MAS agent coexisting with non-communicative behavioral models (e.g. BDI reasoning on an agent's task model).

Listening Behavior. In MAS communication a message is either delivered as a whole or not at all. In virtual agent communication, performing an intent may take some time and for an addressee, it can look unnatural to restrain from expressing any behavior while the speaker is talking. Here, listening behaviors and backchannel feedback can be used for showing attention or for grounding purposes and are typically expressed as head nods, gaze behavior or short verbal utterances. Research is available proposing models for listening feedback (e.g. [21]). Although increasing believability, such models can add considerably in design complexity: proper listening feedback requires partial understanding of content being communicated.

4   A Middleware Approach

We present a model for virtual agent communication employing a middleware approach to fill the gap between agent communication in a MAS and its realization in a virtual environment. It builds upon our previous effort of designing a middleware bridging the conceptual gap between agent and game engine technology [20].

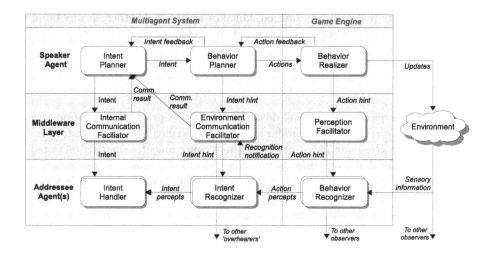

Fig. 1. Communication Model

In figure 1, our model is illustrated and addresses the issues described in section 3.1. More concretely it deals with (1) separating *mind* and *body* allowing agents in a MAS to communicate with each other using multimodal communicative behaviors, (2) separating intent from behavior planning, and behavior from intent recognition respectively, allowing agents to express behaviors and interpret intents depending on contextual factors, (3) durative expression and observation of communicative intents, allowing agents to monitor and interrupt scheduled communication and (4) believable perception based on sensory capabilities and environment physics. It provides an infrastructural basis for dealing with agent-side aspects as presented in section 3.2. Next, we describe the model in more detail.

4.1 Communication Expression

The upper part of the model is responsible for realizing a communicative intent using multimodal behavior expressions. The stages shown are conceptually similar to the behavior generation stages part of the SAIBA framework [9], though, since our goal deviates from the SAIBA initiative, we do not focus on standard data representations used between the stages. First, the *Intent Planner* generates communicative intents a speaker agent wishes to express. Next, the *Behavior Planner* translates an incoming intent to a schedule of communicative actions where each action represents a single modality (e.g. a speech action, gesture or facial expression). Last, the *Behavior Realizer* executes communicative actions for realization in the game engine.

At each stage, feedback information about the progress of a realization is sent to previous stages allowing an agent to monitor the execution of its intent. Feedback about actions is used to determine the feedback to be generated for scheduled intents (e.g. started, finished, failed or aborted). Further, at any point in time, an agent may abort a scheduled intent resulting in the abortion of all scheduled actions.

4.2 Communication Perception

Next, the lower part of the model deals with the perception of communicative intents by an addressee agent. Similar stages are identified as above. First, in reverse order, the *Behavior Recognizer* interprets communicative signals (actions) based on perceived sensory information from the environment. It represents a physical process where the ability to interpret signals is limited by the sensory capabilities of an agent. For example, an agent could recognize a *head nod* performed by a speaker based on head bone positions observed over time. Next, the *Intent Recognizer* assigns a meaning to 'recognized' signals, possibly representing the original intent the speaker agent tried to convey. It represents a cognitive inference process influenced by contextual factors. To give an example, different meanings can be assigned to an observed *head nod*. In some situations it could be interpreted as an *acknowledgement*, in other situations as a form of *greeting*. Last, the *Intent Handler* receives inferred intents for further processing.

4.3 Middleware Facilities

Looking at the software engineering aspects of the perception stages described above, both are computationally heavy processes and contribute to design complexity: the stage of *behavior recognition* requires observations over time to recognize communicative signals like speech (e.g. stream of sound waves) or gestures (e.g. motion of bones). The stage of *intent recognition* can be seen as a pattern matching problem where a set of multimodal communicative signals have to be matched to an intent (taking into account both the type and timing of signals). Although this approach results in a fully autonomous process for the perception of communicative intents, we believe it is not very practical to implement and is overly complex for use in real-time games. As an alternative, we propose a design approach employing a middleware layer to simplify the perception processes, making a tradeoff between efficiency and believability.

Since the data representations for communicative intents and actions that need to be recognized are already available within the speaker agent, we propose to employ this information during the corresponding perception of these actions and intents. First, the *Perception Facilitator* allows agents to perceive communicative actions directly. It simplifies the process of behavior recognition where actions do not have to be interpreted from sensory information. Instead, it is reduced to a query whether an action that was just expressed can be perceived by an observer based on its current sensory capabilities. Here, the middleware provides observing agents with *action hints* which they can use to create percepts (after successfully passing the query). Next, the *Environment Communication Facilitator* facilitates the process of intent recognition within an observing agent by providing a *hint* about the communicative intent currently being expressed by a speaker agent. This hint not only contains the original intent, but also the actions used by the speaker to realize this intent. This reduces the problem of pattern matching to a matter of comparing recognized actions to *expected* actions where the corresponding *expected* intent can be immediately inferred. With this approach, perception can be performed efficiently, though still in a believable manner bounded by environment physics. Also, agents not only perceive the end of an action or intent respectively, but also the beginning, allowing an agent to recognize an intent being communicated *while* the speaker is expressing it (though without full semantics for believability).

To clarify the communication process in our model, figure 2 illustrates the successful communication of a single communicative intent, realized using multimodal behavior consisting of two actions. Note that the focus of the model is on the semantics of the communicated data and not on specific data representations (shown messages have been simplified and *ids* are used to denote a corresponding intent or action). The upper table below the diagram illustrates information being communicated between components *within* the speaker and addressee agent in a time-ordered fashion. The bottom table shows information being send *between* the agents using the middleware's facilities. Referring to the diagram, in phase 1 (P1), the speaker schedules the intent along with the realization actions. In phase 2, the speaker receives feedback stating the realization of the intent has started while the addressee perceives the beginning of the intent (though without actual content). Phase 3 represents the ongoing process of expressing and recognizing actions. In phase 4, the speaker receives feedback about the successful completion of the intent while the addressee perceives the full intent. Finally, phase 5 provides the speaker with feedback about the successful perception of an intent by the addressee. This last phase is optional and is explained next.

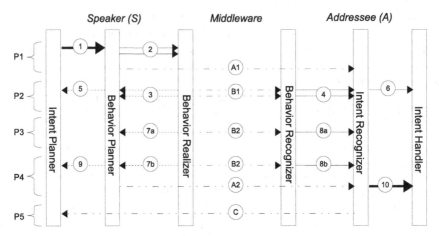

#	Agent	Activity	Message
1	S	schedule intent	*communicate(id=i1,content=inform_child_in_house)*
2	S	schedule action	*speech(id=a1,resource=child_in_house.mp3)*
3	S	receive action feedback	*action_feedback(action=a1,state=started)*
4	A	perceive action	*action_percept(action=a1,state=started)*
5	S	receive intent feedback	*intent_feedback(id=i1,state=started)*
6	A	perceive intent (no content)	*intent_percept(state=started)*
7	S	receive action feedback	*action_feedback(action=a1,state=finsihed)*
8	A	perceive action	*action_percept(action=a1,state=finished)*
9	S	receive intent feedback	*intent_percept(id=i1state=finished)*
10	A	perceive intent	*intent_percept(id=i1,state=ended)*

#	Middleware	Activity	Message
A1	Comm. Facilitator	send intent hint	*intent_hint(intent=i1, actions=a1;a2)(state=started)*
B1	Perception Facilitator	send action hint	*action_percept(action=a1,state=started)*
B2	Perception Facilitator	send action hint	*action_percept(action=a1,state=finished)*
A2	Comm. Facilitator	send intent hint	*intent_hint(intent=i1)(state=finished)*
C	Comm. Facilitator	send communication result	*communication_result(id=i1,observed_by=A)*

Fig. 2. Communication Example

Successful Communication. The success of a non-communicative action can be validated in the physical environment inside the game engine. For example, the success of an action like *open door* can be checked based on the values of certain game state parameters (e.g. status property of the door). But determining whether a communicative intent was successfully communicated cannot easily be done and depends on whether the intent was successfully perceived and interpreted. This would require inspection of agent parameters which are not externally accessible by the speaker agent.

To support an agent in reasoning about the success or failure of communication, in our model we provide feedback about the success or failure of the delivery of an intent to the addressee(s) (i.e. if the corresponding communicative behavior was perceived and interpreted correctly as the original intent). This facility is provided by the *Environment Communication Facilitator*. After successful execution of a communicative intent, this component will inform the speaker agent whether its message has been properly received and recognized and by which addressees. It accomplishes this based on received *recognition notifications* sent by the *Intent Recognizer* from addressee agents.

Direct Communication. One can think of situations where agents may require communication to exchange information or coordinate their actions but where it is not relevant for a human user to notice this during game play. In this situation, instead of realizing this in the environment, direct communication may be more efficient. Our model provides an *Internal Communication Facilitator* allowing agents to send messages directly to any other agent within the MAS. It fulfills the same task as the typical communication mechanism in an agent platform.

4.4 Discussion

Comparing our model to typical agent communication like FIPA ACL, the main difference can be found in the lower-level protocols and medium used to communicate. Where FIPA communication deals with communication over a network medium using a protocol like TCP/IP, communication between virtual agents requires a more complex medium that deals with (1) the cognitive abilities of agents to express and interpret intents, (2) the physical abilities of agents to express and perceive behavior (through actuators and sensors) and (3) a transportation medium represented by a virtual environment. Looking at the protocol from figure 2, FIPA would merely cover line 1 and 10: sending and receiving communicative intents. All the other lines can be seen as a necessary extension to achieve proper realization, efficient interpretation and believable transportation. A concrete application of this protocol is outlined in the following sections.

5   Implementation

In this section we discuss the implementation of a full system design that will be used for further evaluation. It shows a possible interpretation of the communication model from figure 1. The design is illustrated in figure 3 and is

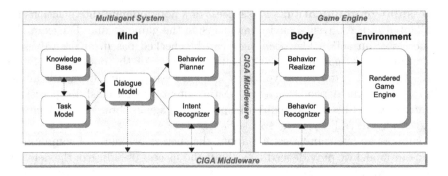

Fig. 3. Agent Architecture in System Design

made up of a MAS and a game engine, coupled by a middleware. It focuses on implemented agent components related to communication (i.e. not a full agent architecture). Current implementation does not support the communication of signals other than performative acts (e.g. no turn-taking, backchanneling or emotions), though this is not a necessity for a proper evaluation. Rather, it should make clear how the proposed communication infrastructure supports the use of additional communicative functions.

As for the MAS and game engine, in-house developed systems have been employed [1]. Further, the system includes a middleware (named *CIGA*) which has been developed as a generic solution to facilitate the coupling between a MAS and game engine. The middleware layer proposed in the communication model has been integrated within this middleware. A more elaborate description of CIGA and its motivation falls outside the scope of this paper and can be found in [20]. Below, the agent's components in its cognitive and physical layer are described shortly.

5.1 Cognitive Layer

Knowledge Base. A storage for propositions that can be accessed during deliberation. Propositions can be created from perceived sensory information (not shown in design) or received information through communication.

Task Model. Deliberation and decision-making rules for non-communicative behavior. Rules according to the BDI-paradigm can be implemented within a task hierarchy representing a certain role for an agent. We have previously experimented with the reasoning engines Jadex and 2APL, though currently a behavior tree implementation is employed which suffices for our evaluation.

Dialogue Model. Deliberation and decision-making rules for communicative behavior. Both the *Intent Planner* and *Intent Handler* from figure 1 are included

---

[1] www.vstep.nl

in this model. To support flexible interactions, the model was implemented as an information state-based dialogue system, inspired by the theory in [17]. To give an example, an incoming dialogue act updates the model's information state (e.g. an obligation to address an act). At the next deliberation cycle the new state is inspected to determine the next dialogue move to perform. This allows flexible interactions not based on specific protocols. Currently dialogue moves are supported for conversation management and for a limited set of core speech acts (inform, enquiry and order).

Behavior Planner. Realizes a communicative intent scheduled by the *Dialogue Model*. An intent is represented by a dialogue act with one or more intended receivers. Custom defined *mapping rules* are used to map an intent to a schedule of actions including instructions for different modalities. For example, a *greeting* could be mapped to an approach behavior, including speech, gaze and an appropriate gesture. Rules can be based on context variables covering aspects like cultural background, relationship with the interlocutor or the current social setting. During realization, feedback information is sent to the *Dialogue Model* whenever an intent was started, finished, aborted or failed its realization (e.g. an intent is started as soon as the first corresponding action is started). A scheduled intent can be aborted at any time and results in the abortion of all corresponding actions that have been scheduled.

Intent Recognizer. Manages intent observations based on *action percepts* received from the *Behavior Recognizer*. From the middleware, this component receives information about the intent being communicated together with the actions used for its realization (the *intent hint*). Based on this information together with the received action percepts, it can determine the progress of an intent observation. *Intent percepts* are then sent to the *Dialogue Model* whenever an intent observation was started or has fully been recognized. In the latter case, the original dialogue act expressed by the actor is included in the percept. In this way an agent could perform a certain listening behavior like gazing knowing its interlocutor has started expressing an intent. Next, after being informed about the intent's full recognition, the agent's *Dialogue Model* can decide on a next course of action.

5.2   Physical Layer

Behavior Realizer. Realizes scheduled communicative actions. Parameterized actions have been defined as control instructions for individual modalities. For concrete action implementations, game engine functionality is used to control and monitor the realization within the virtual character. For example, a gesture expression requires access to the animation engine, gazing requires specific bone control while locomotion requires path finding and collision avoidance. During execution, feedback information about progress is sent to the agent's mind.

Behavior Recognizer. Manages action observations from actions expressed by other agents. This component is dependent on the middleware from whom it receives information about actions expressed by other agents as *action hints*. Upon receival, it checks whether or not the specific action can be perceived. For example, for a speech action this involves querying if the corresponding sound in the environment is observable based on the agent's auditory sensor, loudness and distance towards the source and possible interferences. If observable, an *action percept* containing the action's original representation and its current progress (e.g. started or ended) is generated and sent upstream to the *Intent Recognizer* for further processing.

6   Evaluation

We evaluate the communication model at the functional level by realizing a set of scenarios for different interactional situations. Based on the implemented system described in the previous section, a simple base scenario has been developed in which the required functionality can be demonstrated. The base scenario concerns a two-turn conversation between two IVAs where small variations to this scenario are run for testing different aspects of the model.

Below we list the requirements that will be evaluated for the implemented system and correspond to the issues outlined in section 3.1.

1. Context-dependent multimodal behavior expressions
2. Multimodal behavior perception
3. Monitoring durative intent realizations
4. Monitoring durative observation of communicative intents
5. Interruption of scheduled communication
6. Believable perception based on sensory capabilities and environment physics

An impression of the implemented base scenario and its variations is illustrated in figure 4. The base scenario demonstrates a successful conversation covering requirements 1 through 4; variation (a) demonstrates interruption of communication (requirement 5); remaining variations relate to requirement 6 and demonstrate failed communication because of no perception (out of range) or partial perception (variation b and c respectively) concluding with overhearing of communication by bystanders (variation d). Due to space limitations, below we only describe the base scenario and variation (a).

Base Scenario: An agent starts a conversation with a passerby agent and asks for the current time. The participant answers by giving the time after which they both terminate the conversation and resume their way. This base scenario illustrates a primitive successful conversation. From the communication model, it covers all stages for behavior generation and recognition. Middleware facilitators allow for efficient behavior and intent recognition for the initiator and participant where a speaker is notified about the successful delivery of its intent.

Variation a: The same situation is simulated though here while the initiator is asking for the time, both agents hear an explosion and notice a fire starting. The current speaker interrupts its current communicative intent while the addressee

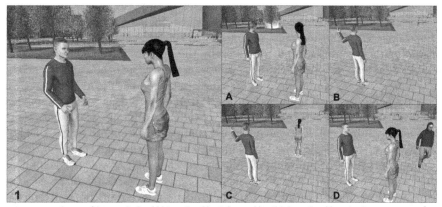

1 successful communication; (a) interruption; (b) out of range; (c) partial observation; (d) overhearing

Fig. 4. Scenario Impressions

interrupts its listening behavior. Both agents end the conversation implicitly and pursue a new goal to deal with the situation. This variation illustrates agents coping with external events in the middle of a dialogue. Referring to the communication model, the speaker aborts its intent realization (and therefore behavior realization) from the *Intent Planner*; correspondingly the addressee's *Intent Handler* is informed that the intent was not fully perceived (i.e. was aborted). In the implemented system, the dialogue model (encompassing both the above components), at both agents, decides to end the conversation caused by a higher priority goal originating from the task model.

The base scenario and its variations have been realized successfully in our system. Although the involved agent components were implemented in an ad-hoc manner based on simple rules and policies, it suffices in demonstrating the basic principles of our model. More complex scenarios can be created based on the same principles but using more complex rules and policies. These may support for example: the use of more complex (multi-party) dialogues; the use of a richer context for expressing an intent; dealing with more believable ways of reacting on partial intent observations; or a more generic and context dependent way of decision-making for overheard communications. Often such aspects relate to different research areas as mentioned in section 3.2.

7 Discussion

In this paper we have focused mainly on directed communication of dialogue acts between two or more agents. However, as we have already shortly mentioned in section 3.2, there are more types of meanings that human-like agents could communicate through signals, concerning information on the speaker's mind like beliefs, goals or emotions [15]. For example, through specific verbal or nonverbal signals information can be conveyed about the speaker's meta-cognitive or affective state. Our communication model does not restrict one to use specific types of meaning involved in communication. As long as they can be expressed and observed through the agents actuators and sensors, they can be represented as a communicative intent and processed by the middleware's facilitators. This allows designers to develop their own intents geared towards their specific needs. For example, for agents required to be emotional or empathic one could design affective signals to be communicated. Such signals could then be accompanied by a directed dialogue act, but also used as undirected intents (i.e. where there is no specific addressee). E.g. one might use undirected intents to support leaked emotions or 'communicate' an agent's mood expressed through certain postures or facial expressions. The ability to observe such signals would be helpful as input for an agent's empathic processing.

Now when we consider using our model to communicate intents not directed towards a specific agent, this raises the question of whether the model could also be used to efficiently 'communicate' non-communicative intents and if this would be desirable from an conceptual point of view. Knowing another's agent's intent could ease the realization of certain social behaviors. To give an example, consider an agent walking towards a door with the intent to open it. Another agent observing this intent could assist the agent by informing it that the door is locked. The possible advantages and disadvantages of using the model for non-communicative intents is currently being investigated.

8   Conclusion

In this paper we proposed a design approach for modeling agent communication in a MAS to be represented in a human-like manner in a game engine. We focused on the benefits of employing a middleware layer to facilitate perception and decision-making aspects involved in communication. The middleware layer allows IVAs to (1) communicate intents efficiently at the cognitive level on the MAS side and (2) realize this at the physical level in the game engine through the expression and perception of multimodal communicative behaviors. This is accomplished by the middleware's communication protocol which couples the cognitive and physical channels of communication between sender and receiver agents. Here, the perception stages of receiver agents do not require fully autonomous processes for recognizing communicative actions and intents (which are computationally expensive). Further, decision-making in dialogues can be handled more efficiently based on the acquired knowledge of the success or failure of communication (provided to sender agents by the middleware layer). Although requiring a more complex protocol for agents to adhere to (compared to FIPA), it does not enforce any specific implementation for any involved agent component. Nor does it enforce any specific data representation for communicative intents and actions used between agent components or channeled between agents themselves.

We believe with this more practical approach, one can achieve a proper balance between believability and efficiency for simulating human-like interactions (e.g. suitable for real-time games). The proposed model provides an infrastructure one can build upon to implement additional aspects of human-like communication like described in section 3.2. It therefore provides a first stepping stone to realize the example scene described in the beginning of this paper.

References

1. Adobbati, R., Marshall, A.N., Scholer, A., Tejada, S.: Gamebots: A 3d virtual world test-bed for multi-agent research. In: Proceedings of the Second International Workshop on Infrastructure for Agents, MAS, and Scalable MAS (2001)
2. Behrens, T., Hindriks, K., Dix, J.: Towards an environment interface standard for agent platforms. Annals of Mathematics and Artificial Intelligence, 1–35 (2010)
3. Chopra, A.K., Artikis, A., Bentahar, J., Colombetti, M., Dignum, F., Fornara, N., Jones, A.J.I., Singh, M.P., Yolum, P.: Research directions in agent communications. ACM Transactions on Intelligent Systems and Technology, 1–26 (2001)
4. Dias, J., Masceranhas, S., Paiva, A.: FAtiMA Modular: Towards an Agent Architecture with a Generic Appraisal Framework. In: Proceedings of the International Workshop on Standards for Emotion Modeling (2011)
5. Evertsz, R., Pedrotti, M., Busetta, P., Acar, H., Ritter, F.: Populating VBS2 with realistic virtual actors. In: Proceedings of the 18th Conference on Behavior Representation in Modeling and Simulation, pp. 1–8 (2009)
6. Gemrot, J., Brom, C., Plch, T.: A Periphery of Pogamut: From Bots to Agents and Back Again. In: Dignum, F. (ed.) Agents for Games and Simulations II. LNCS, vol. 6525, pp. 19–37. Springer, Heidelberg (2011)
7. Heylen, D., Kopp, S., Marsella, S.C., Pelachaud, C., Vilhjálmsson, H.H.: The Next Step towards a Function Markup Language. In: Prendinger, H., Lester, J.C., Ishizuka, M. (eds.) IVA 2008. LNCS (LNAI), vol. 5208, pp. 270–280. Springer, Heidelberg (2008)
8. Kenny, P., Hartholt, A., Gratch, J., Swartout, W., Traum, D., Marsella, S., Piepol, D.: Building interactive virtual humans for training environments. In: The I/ITSEC (2007)
9. Kopp, S., Krenn, B., Marsella, S.C., Marshall, A.N., Pelachaud, C., Pirker, H., Thórisson, K.R., Vilhjálmsson, H.H.: Towards a Common Framework for Multimodal Generation: The Behavior Markup Language. In: Gratch, J., Young, M., Aylett, R.S., Ballin, D., Olivier, P. (eds.) IVA 2006. LNCS (LNAI), vol. 4133, pp. 205–217. Springer, Heidelberg (2006)
10. Lee, J., DeVault, D., Marsella, S., Traum, D.: Thoughts on FML: Behavior generation in the virtual human communication architecture. In: Proceedings of The 1st Functional Markup Language Workshop (2008)
11. Lee, J., Marsella, S.: Nonverbal Behavior Generator for Embodied Conversational Agents. In: Gratch, J., Young, M., Aylett, R.S., Ballin, D., Olivier, P. (eds.) IVA 2006. LNCS (LNAI), vol. 4133, pp. 243–255. Springer, Heidelberg (2006)
12. Marsella, S.C., Gratch, J.: EMA: A process model of appraisal dynamics. Cognitive Systems Research 10(1), 70–90 (2009)
13. Norling, E., Sonenberg, L.: Creating interactive characters with BDI agents. In: IE 2004: Proceedings of the Australian Workshop on Interactive Entertainment, pp. 69–76 (2004)
14. Poggi, I.: Mind markers. In: Trigo, N., Rector, M., Poggi, I. (eds.) Gestures, Meaning and Use. University Fernando Pessoa Press, Oporto (2003)

15. Poggi, I., Pelachaud, C., Rosis, F., Carofiglio, V., Carolis, B.: Greta. a believable embodied conversational agent. In: Stock, O., Zancanaro, M., Ide, N. (eds.) Multimodal Intelligent Information Presentation. Text, Speech and Language Technology, vol. 27, pp. 3–25. Springer, Netherlands (2005)
16. Traum, D., Rickel, J.: Embodied agents for multi-party dialogue in immersive virtual worlds. In: Proceedings of AAMAS 2002, pp. 766–773 (2002)
17. Traum, D., Swartout, W., Gratch, J., Marsella, S.: A virtual human dialogue model for non-team interaction. In: Dybkjær, L., et al. (eds.) Recent Trends in Discourse and Dialogue, vol. 39, pp. 45–67. Springer Netherlands (2008)
18. Hindriks, K.V., van Riemsdijk, B., Behrens, T., Korstanje, R., Kraayenbrink, N., Pasman, W., de Rijk, L.: UNREAL GOAL Bots. In: Dignum, F. (ed.) Agents for Games and Simulations II. LNCS, vol. 6525, pp. 1–18. Springer, Heidelberg (2011)
19. Vala, M., Blanco, G., Paiva, A.: Providing Gender to Embodied Conversational Agents. In: Vilhjálmsson, H.H., Kopp, S., Marsella, S., Thórisson, K.R. (eds.) IVA 2011. LNCS, vol. 6895, pp. 148–154. Springer, Heidelberg (2011)
20. van Oijen, J., Vanhée, L., Dignum, F.: CIGA: A Middleware for Intelligent Agents in Virtual Environments. In: Beer, M., Brom, C., Dignum, F., Soo, V.-W. (eds.) AEGS 2011. LNCS, vol. 7471, pp. 22–37. Springer, Heidelberg (2012)
21. Wang, Z., Lee, J., Marsella, S.: Towards More Comprehensive Listening Behavior: Beyond the Bobble Head. In: Vilhjálmsson, H.H., Kopp, S., Marsella, S., Thórisson, K.R. (eds.) IVA 2011. LNCS, vol. 6895, pp. 216–227. Springer, Heidelberg (2011)

Using Agents in Virtual Environments
to Assist Controllers to Manage Multiple Assets

Martin D. Beer[1], Lyuba Alboul[2], Emma Norling[3], and Peter Wallis[4]

[1] Communication & Computing Research Centre
Faculty of Arts, Computing, Engineering & Sciences
Sheffield Hallam University
Sheffield, United Kingdom
m.beer@shu.ac.uk
[2] Centre for Automation & Robotics Research
Faculty of Arts, Computing, Engineering & Sciences
Sheffield Hallam University
Sheffield, United Kingdom
LAlboul@shu.ac.uk
[3] Centre for Policy Modelling,
Manchester Metropolitan University
Manchester, United Kingdom
norling@acm.org
[4] The NLP Group, Dept. of Computer Science, University of Sheffield
Sheffield, United Kingdom
p.wallis@dcs.shef.ac.uk

Abstract. Search and rescue operations often require complex coordination of a range of resources, including human and robotic resources. This paper discusses a proposed new framework that allows agent technology to be used in conjunction with a virtual environment to provide a human controller with an effective visualisation of the distribution of a collection of autonomous objects, in our case, Unmanned Aerial Vehicles (UAVs) so that they can be managed in a way that allows them to successfully complete the task in the minimum possible time. It is our contention that to do this effectively there needs to be two-way initiation of verbal conversations, but that it is not necessary for the system to completely understand the conversations required. An example scenario is presented that illustrates how such a system would be used in practice, illustrating how a single human can communicate with a swarm of semi-autonomous actors verbally and envisage their activities in a swarm based on the visual cues provided within the virtual environment. An agent-based solution is proposed that meets the requirements and provides a command station that can manage a search using a collection of UAVs effectively.

1 Introduction

Agent technology has been used extensively with virtual environments for a range of educational [1], gaming [2] and training applications [3]. This paper considers another situation where virtual environments could provide a vital link with between humans

F. Dignum et al. (Eds.): CAVE 2012, LNAI 7764, pp. 55–69, 2013.

and real world activities. One area of considerable interest is the use of multiple robots or other autonomous agents to perform some large scale cooperative task, such as search and rescue [4]. Robots are considered to be a valuable asset in search and rescue activities as they can be sent into areas which have not been made safe for human rescuers. Initially single robots were used with a human controller. While it is relatively straightforward for a single human to remotely control a single robot, teams of robots can be used in more complex and efficient searches. It has still proved necessary for individual human operators to provide both the intelligence and coordination [5].

This paper proposes a framework that provides a single operator with the means to control large teams of autonomous agents in complex operations via a virtual environment. The human operator is immersed in a virtual environment where the (semi) autonomous physical agents are represented by virtual agents. The operator coordinates the behaviour of physical agents by interacting with their counterparts in the virtual representation of the physical world. It is an open question as to where the intelligence lies but typically the physical agents will have limited (if any) cognitive abilities, that simply enable the physical agent to operate autonomously for short periods of time. The on-board processing limitations of these platforms precludes much in the way of higher-level reasoning; instead, this would be performed by the physical agent's virtual counterpart, who would receive sensory data from the physical agent and send instructions back to it. In addition, these virtual agents are also "embodied conversational agents," allowing the human operator to coordinate the agents through a natural language interface. The use of a spoken language interface in this scenario has two advantages. The first is that language is our best example of a mixed initiative interaction in which the human can initiate an interaction by issuing a command or requesting information, but the agent can also provide information in a timely manner without being asked. The second advantage is that natural language allows us humans at least to negotiate new information.

The scenario we use to illustrate the problems involved is of a search and rescue operation involving unmanned aerial vehicles (UAVs). A single human controlling (say) twenty surveillance UAVs introduces a range of problems but, for such mixed teams to work at all, a certain level of autonomy for the UAVs is required. The assumption is that each has sufficient intelligence that once it has received specific instructions, it is able to maintain itself on station and to perform its allotted task, which may include relaying messages to peers over the horizon from the base station, and so out of direct contact, acting as a mobile telephone relay station and collecting and relaying sensor data. Sensors may be a standard set that are common to all individuals, or they may be configured specifically for each operation. For the purposes of this analysis it does not matter. It also requires a means of communication – both machine with machine and machine with human. We therefore provide a virtual world for the human operator in which real UAVs are represented by embodied conversational agents (ECA) that can be seen performing their duties, and that can be conversed with in plain English. These agents have limited cognitive abilities and these limitations are, like the plans and goals of each agent, something that the agent can talk about. A spoken language interface is not only intuitive and flexible, being able to "call out" allows agents to initiate a conversation in a graded manner that is difficult with simple alarms. The challenge however is to provide an agent that can hold even simple conversations. From the very early days of AI research it has been possible to hold a conversation with a machine in a limited domain [6, 7]; the problem is that we humans are not very good at sticking to the topic. This issue has been considered [8, 9] together with ways to bring the user back on topic without them noticing.

The approach taken in this paper is to develop a typical scenario based around real situations that rescue services experience, and to construct a suitable system to meet that need. The scenario chosen is close at hand, and therefore rescue personnel with real experience of similar situations are available to advise us. This approach allows the system to be validated with these real users at an early stage, and they can be updated and comment on each development cycle. This leads to a more usable and functional system as all the components are validated at each stage. This is particularly important with the development of the "virtual world" as this needs to be functional enough to represent the actual situation on the ground, but abstract enough to show the essential information without distracting the controller with unnecessary detail.

2   The Scenario

The scenario is based on a search and rescue mission in the Northern Peak District in the United Kingdom, which despite the relative smallness of the area covered, involves most, if not all, of the activities that such operations typically require. This is because of the poor communications across the area, its relative popularity particularly with inexperienced and ill-equipped visitors who have easy access from nearby large cities, and the rapid changes in weather, particularly in winter, when time is often of the essence in successfully evacuating casualties. BBC reports [10–14] illustrate the wide range of incidents that the rescue services have to deal with within this small area.

2.1   A Typical Incident

The scenario starts with a set of UAVs each carrying a mobile phone repeater station "brick" as used to fix dead-spots in the mobile telephone network, for example within steep valleys (locally called cloughs). Each UAV flies at a fixed height and, within limits, can re-position where it "loiters" based on the amount of communication traffic it is relaying and how close it is to other UAVs in the team. The point however is the model for human-machine interaction based on the virtual world and conversational representations of the robots.

Sergeant Jones is three hours into a shift providing radio coverage for a search and rescue mission over the Peak District. A Duke of Edinburgh Award Group set off from Edale to follow the southern part of the Pennine Way across Kinder Scout. They have failed to report in as expected, the weather is closing in and a search and rescue operation has been launched. They are not responding to mobile phone messages, but communication in the area is notoriously difficult.

The Kinder plateau is a large upland area with few markers, and it is easy to become disorientated in poor weather. The fear is that the group may have become lost, possibly separated, and that as the weather deteriorates towards nightfall they will become increasingly at risk both from the terrain, which includes peat bogs and deep ravines, and exposure. A ground search has commenced involving Mountain Rescue, the Fire and Rescue Service, National Trust and National Park Rangers. Figure 1 shows the area of the National Park. The area of the scenario consists of northern upland fells where there are few roads, and plenty of opportunities for hiking and other outdoor pursuits.

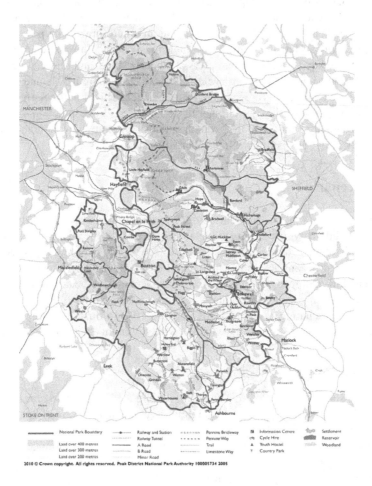

Fig. 1. A Map of the Peak District National Park. The Scenario considers the northern fells north of Edale where roads and habitations are very sparse.

Because of the diversity of groups involved, the primary means of communication is mobile telephones. In view of the poor communications coverage, Sergeant Jones' team has been asked initially to back up and "fill out" the existing mobile telephone infrastructure's coverage. Jones is the controller for twenty semi-autonomous UAVs that can provide temporary mobile telephone base stations. She is standing in a virtual environment provided by a data cave with images of The Peak topology displayed on all four walls, as viewed from the centre of the search area at a height of 2km as shown in Figure 2. The system can modify the lighting to represent day and night, and can provide various shadings to assist Jones in both visualising conditions on the ground and have a clear overview of the topology over which she is working. She can also superimpose simulated weather patterns generated from Meteorological Office data to assist her in her task. She can move to a different location by sitting in a virtual electric wheelchair and motoring in any direction, but usually she stands or walks about. In either case, her effective position as represented in the cave moves to follow her. Looking west she can see, super imposed on a recent photograph of the weather in that direction, the flight paths of airliners heading to and from Manchester Airport (the flight paths cross the search area), and north of that she can see a set of icons representing the electrical storm coming in from the west. Also projected on her view are twenty coloured deltas, each representing the position and travel of one of her UAVs.

Fig. 2. The Control Station

3   Meeting the Requirement

She has just made a cup of tea when a voice off to her right calls out

"Sir"

She turns to it and addresses the blue delta

"Yes Blue?"

"Sir, I am low on fuel and request permission to return to base."

"Granted"

The blue delta turns west and heads off to its temporary landing field for a service and to refuel. Jones knows that it will return in about 90 minutes and need redeploying. Ten minutes later she notices one of the deltas is heading north. She points at it and says

"You. What are you doing?"

A voice from that direction says

"Sir, there has been no radio activity in my area and I am following a lead."

Jones asks to listen in on the call and hears a conversation about a party. That UAV is, it seems, following a car travelling westwards towards the Snake Pass (the A57) and away from the search area. She looks about and sees a fairly vacant area just west of the Howden Reservoir. She calls up the map reference for this area and directs the stray UAV saying:

"Head to 53 degrees 26 north by 01 degrees 42 west and look there."

The UAV's agent confirms by repeating the coordinates it thinks it heard:

"53 26 north by 10 42 west."

which would take it a long way west and far away from the search area. Jones corrects it by saying:

"No no, zero one forty two west."

The agent confirms that it now has the correct coordinates:

"Oh, 53 26 north by 01 42 west. Okay."

and sends them to the UAV which takes up position as requested.

A bit later a new UAV appears from the west. One of the current UAV team – White – interrogates it (it is still outside of direct communication with the base station) and (White's virtual agent) calls out

"Sir."

Sergeant Jones says

"Yes White."

"A Shadow AAI RQ-7 has come to join the search. Can you see it?"

Jones looks in the appropriate direction in the virtual world and sees a new delta that has just appeared. She interrogates it with:

"Yes, thank you" says Jones. She goes on: *"RQ-7, what are your capabilities?"*

The virtual agent for the new UAV pops up a photo of its physical agent with some detailed text and introduces itself by saying:

"I am a Shadow RQ-7 with a gimbal-mounted EO/IR camera, standard communications monitoring a G23 PA system and about 6 hours of fuel."

Jones does not know the capabilities of the PA system so asks the new UAV's agent to explain:

"How do you use the PA system?"

and is given this answer:

"I can fly at 200 feet and play a pre-recorded message. If the message is less than ..."

This gives her enough information for now and she closes the conversation with:

"Okay RQ-7"

Some time later Sergeant Jones decides to use the PA system to try to send a message to the lost hikers and gives the following instruction:

"go to 53 19 north, 10 42 west and then use your PA on a run to 53 23 north, 10 42 west with the following message: ..."

An hour before sunset a mobile phone message is received from the group, who are completely lost. The initial message is only relayed by UAV White, so there is insufficient information to pinpoint their location. Jones instructs the nearest UAVs (Red and Indigo) to form a holding pattern around White and to listen for further messages. She then calls the number from which the original message was sent, and the message is relayed by all the UAVs. When the call is answered, the location of the caller is pinpointed, and Jones hears that the group is together and safe. Jones relays this information to the rescue teams and a search group with all-terrain vehicles is redirected to locate and evacuate them. As soon as it is clear that the entire group have been located, the other search teams are instructed to stand down and return to base. The UAVs are however still required to provide communication and track the search teams until they are all safely off the moor. As the weather closes in the live images are updated and visibility is effectively zero. Met Office data is however imposed on Jones' view allowing her to see the extent of the bad weather. One rescue team will be caught before they can reach safety and a UAV is tasked to stay with them. As the storm approaches, its virtual agent calls out

"Sir."

Jones replies

"Yes Red"

The virtual agent requests, based on the sensor information communicated from the UAV

"The weather is getting rough. Requesting permission to return to base."

Jones replies that she wishes the UAV to stay on station despite the weather

"No Red, stay with that signal."

A little while later UAV Red requests to return to base and is again denied. A while later Red reports that it will need to land in the next 15 minutes and again it is told to say where it is. Finally the fuel runs out and it requests coordinates for a crash landing. Jones instructs it to go down in Ladybower Reservoir. All the people are out and safe two hours after sundown with the loss of one UAV that is later recovered and refurbished ready for the next incident.

While the use of UAVs as described is a future vision, the situation in this scenario is typical of a wide range of deployments that the emergency services have to undertake in often hostile conditions. In this case, we are looking at comparatively large tracts of open country, rather than the more normal firefighting situation of searching in the confined spaces of burning buildings as was the case in GUARDIANS [15]. This in itself provides a different set of challenges. UAVs are seen as a useful tool both to search larger areas very quickly and to provide temporary communication when necessary in what are inevitably poorly covered areas. They are becoming increasingly autonomous, and no longer need individual 'pilots' to control them, but pilots previously were able to communicate naturally with an overall controller, providing an important coordination element. Our hypothesis is that humans are better able to coordinate complex sets of operations involving multiple participants by giving instructions and receiving feedback by voice, rather than text- or image-based interfaces that are more commonly used when coordinating with robots. This scenario describes a mechanism that seamlessly integrates machine decision making and human interaction. Our research aim is therefore to explore its potential and identify its limitations. Within this project, we are developing the virtual world interface and a suitable simulation mechanism for development and evaluation. We see no barriers to success regarding a base-line implementation; the question is primarily how far can we push it?

3.1 Approach to Language

The approach we are taking is to minimise the use of full understanding, and instead pay attention to the social roles and cues, to politeness and capturing the details of how people manage social relations with language [16]. Following Tomasello [17], we view language in use as intentional and cooperative; as long as the system can maintain its status as a social actor, the user will assume a cooperative intent. As an example consider how the dialogue in the scenario is not as smart as it may look. Consider what might happen if a person unfamiliar with the language capabilities of the virtual agent tried to interrogate the RQ-7 with questions such as

"Do you have a camera?"

to which the formal answer might be

"Yes,"

but the response can be, quite appropriately,

"I am a Shadow RQ-7 with a gimbal-mounted EO/IR camera, standard communications monitoring a G23 PA system and about 6 hours of fuel".

With this second response, the user assuming a charitable intent is unlikely to realise that the system cannot answer the question, but rather assume that the system is taking the opportunity to help out with other information that might be relevant. By taking a situated approach to the dialogue, the point is to discuss the behaviours available to the system rather than its equipment. Rather than question answering, our vision for the system looks more like browsing.

The scenario makes extensive use of the autonomous control capabilities of modern UAVs. This allows them to operate within the operational area without continuous human intervention. They are able to fly to a specified location and to remain there by flying a pre-programmed circuit without further interaction. Not only can they act singly, but when a number are deployed they will establish a search pattern that efficiently covers the area in question, and if communication to the base station is impeded – for example by uneven terrain, or inclement weather patterns – they will arrange themselves in such a way that some of the group act as relays to the others so that communication is always maintained as shown in Figure 3.

The key objective therefore is to provide an environment for a single controller to maintain effective control of all aspects of the search so that the UAVs effectively become part of the team, and work in coordination with the other search parties, rather than as an independent resource. The controller is in verbal contact with the Emergency and Search services on the ground, so it is only natural that verbal communication should be used to manage the UAVs as well.

The UAVs are assumed to be standard production models, communicating with the system through special interface agents. The virtual counterpart of each UAV performs higher-level reasoning on its behalf, thus avoiding the need to modify the UAVs. The overall system architecture is shown in Figure 4.

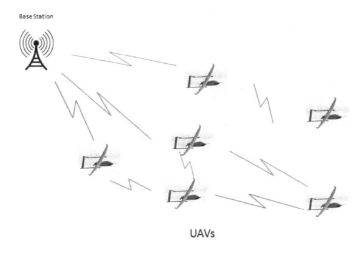

Fig. 3. The Communication Pattern of UAVs with the Ground Station

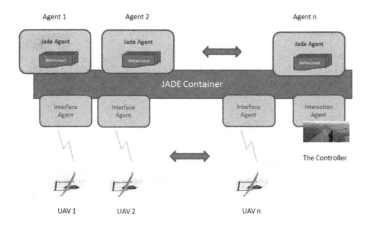

Fig. 4. The Agent Architecture to be used for Controlling a Group of Cooperating UAVs

From a language perspective, perhaps the first challenge is is to decide on the appropriate level of representation to store explanations. At one extreme the person developing plans for UAV behaviour would provide an explanation of the behaviour in text (say) and the text itself would be stored, and somehow stitched together when the agent is asked to explain its behaviour. At the other extreme, the provided explanations would be mapped into some formal representation of the text meaning and, when an explanation is required, the dialogue manager would use a text generation system would produce an appropriately tailored utterance. The second challenge is to have the dialogue manager choose what to say and when to say it in an appropriate manner – for example, which of the two responses to the "Do you have a camera?" question given previously would be appropriate?

3.2   The Agent Perspective

A layered approach has been adopted, as shown in Figure 5. The first layer provides the interface with the UAVs, and the last layer manages the virtual world and voice and video interfaces. It is the middle layer that is most interesting, as it provides the management and control at the core of the system. We propose to use BDI agents at this level, and an approach based on applied cognitiva task analysis (ACTA) [18] to furnish these agents with domain-specific knowledge from experts [19].

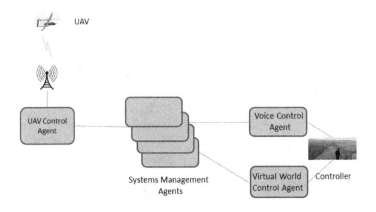

Fig. 5. Layering of Agents

A BDI architecture has been used on numerous occasions to drive simulated agents (both human and other) to drive robots and to drive dialogue. The GUARDIANS project has integrated a BDI language (JADE) with robot middleware (Player) and a simulation environment for search and rescue in a fire environment using the architecture shown in Figure 6[5].

3.3   The Use of BDI Architecture

The Belief, Desire and Intention (BDI) agent architecture was first developed in the 1980's at SRI International and implemented as PRS. [20] BDI is a software model developed for programming intelligent agents. Superficially characterised by the implementation of an agent's beliefs, desires and intentions, it actually uses these concepts to solve a particular problem in agent programming. In essence, it provides a mechanism for separating the activity of selecting a plan (from a plan library or an external planner application) from the execution of currently active plans. Consequently, BDI agents are able to balance the time spent on deliberating about plans (choosing what to do) and executing those plans (doing it). A third activity, creating the plans in the first place

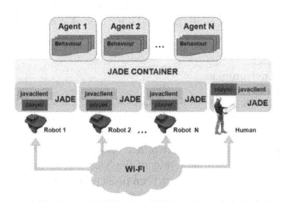

Fig. 6. The GUARDIANS Agent Architecture

(planning), is not within the scope of the model, and is left to the system designer and programmer.

The idea is not to do planning, but to use plans to achieve goals. By separating plans from goals, the system can automatically re-plan on plan failure. Having recognised the problem it is easy enough for a programmer to write a rule that stops a UAV running out of fuel; the problem is there are so many commonsense rules and they are hard to notice until something goes wrong. Separating goals from plans goes some way toward alleviating the need to explicitly identify every rule. Here, the more important feature of a BDI approach is the way reasoning with BDI plans looks very much like the way we humans think other people think [21]. Based on our everyday "folk psychology," a BDI approach provides a clear path to autonomous systems that can explain their behaviour [22].

The basis in folk psychology has another advantage: it can be used to facilitate knowledge acquisition [23, Ch. 6]. Following this approach, we hypothesise that we can develop cognitive agents to populate the virtual environment, using knowledge gathered from subject matter experts, with goals, plans and actions that are easily explicable to a human controller. Each of these cognitive agents will be linked to a single physical agent, performing the high-level reasoning and relaying the low-level commands to its physical counterpart.

First however, in order for a machine to perform any kind of interesting autonomous action, it must have sensor input. The classic is GPS positioning but this does not leave much room for autonomous decision making. Internal sensing (fuel/battery, vibration, system functionality) are all sensor inputs that help, but some means of sensing the environment opens up the possibilities and make the nature of autonomous action more appealing and far more challenging. These sensor readings can be interpreted locally on board the UAV to provide local feedback control, or the information can be transferred back to the virtual agent for further processing. The question of *which* data should be transferred to the virtual agent is an open one: this agent must have sufficient data reason accurately about its physical counterpart, but will not necessarily require all the raw sensor data. There is also the possibility that the virtual agent may have incomplete knowledge about its physical counterpart, and it must be able to reason appropriately in this situation[1].

3.4 The Virtual Environment

Development of the virtual environment starts with the construction of an initial 3D model of the scenario environment by using digital terrain models photographic images, bitmaps etc. A challenge will be to impose (integrate) the data obtained from the sensors (cameras, GPS) into this virtual world in real-time. At SHU some results in this direction have been achieved in the remits of the View-Finder project. The data from LRF (laser range finder) and camera have been fused to obtain a 3D photo-realistic representation of the environment, which then was 'inserted' in a 2D map obtained by a SLAM algorithm [24].

4 Further Work

We propose to take the knowledge acquisition process one step further by tagging plans for explanation. Behaviours can then be explained in terms of the plans driving those behaviours, and the conditions that caused those particular plans to be selected. The naturally hierarchical nature of BDI plans will facilitate the varying levels of detail that can be presented to the controller. It is the development of a suitable tagging mechanism for plans that will enable the generation of natural dialogue that will be the focus of this area of research.

The dialogue manager is an often-ignored part of a conversational system. For instance a classic approach to a natural language interface to a relational database is to treat the SQL query that would answer the query as the meaning of the text. The aim then is to translate the user input into SQL, perform the query, and then use text generation techniques to present the result. This is however not what people do. When we look at what people actually do, we find they put considerable effort into being polite [25], managing social relations [26] and, going out of their way to be helpful [17]. If the SQL query returns no matching records, it is not enough to say "no records match your request." People expect more. What do they expect, and how do our conversational partners go about providing it?

There has been a growing interest in using partially observable Markov decision processes (POMDPs) [27] for spoken dialogue systems. The motivation is that Markov decision processes can model what the human will say next (based on some hidden brain state) and hence provide what the system should say next. Young at Cambridge has championed this approach in the UK and Lemon has been doing interesting work at Heriot-Watt [28]. Such machine learning techniques however are data hungry and simplifying assumptions need to be made. For instance, in the work by Young et al [29] it is assumed that user goals don't change very much, that speech acts can be identified using

---

[1] It should be noted though that a remote human controller of a single UAV may also find him-/her-self in this situation, and as such, our proposed knowledge acquisition approach should handle these cases in as much as they can be handled by a human controller.

intuition, and training data can be produced by "simulated users." Such work certainly results in interesting machine learning challenges, but is only peripherally relevant to better algorithms for human-machine conversation. Rather than modelling language itself as represented by a corpus, our approach models the language production process. This has been criticised by Wilks for only doing "one half of dialogue" (the non user's half) [30] but this is indeed how much of linguistics views the process. Our approach is theoretically well-founded, not in mathematics, but in linguistics. Rather than reasoning with uncertainty – a task for which statistical approaches are eminently suited – we find that humans reason about the uncertainties; rather than betting on the horses, human conversational tactics look more like the bookmaker and play the odds. Human language as used is full of contingency planning and mitigation strategies. The way to better machine dialogue systems is to find and copy those strategies.

The challenge therefore, is to capture understanding from the conversational dialogue, in form and detail suitable for a BDI plan library:

– the way an expert would fly a UAV in the context of the chosen scenario, and
– the way a human would explain the resultant plans-in-use to a human overseer.

With a system in place – either Wizard of Oz [31] or automated – we can record interactions and use those recordings to develop the system. Techniques for doing this have been developed as described, and related techniques have been developed for dialogue over the years including Conversation Analysis [25], Applied Cognitive Task Analysis [18] and, hopefully, our new Narrative approach [32].

5   Conclusions

There are many challenges with the scenario that we have described, but the opportunities offered by successfully deploying such a system are huge. As well as providing more effective search and rescue capabilities, similar systems can be used for exploration in difficult terrain, monitoring such things as traffic and large sporting events and if suitable data is available, large buildings and other structures that have met with some disaster. An example of this would be the rescue mission launched when the cruise ship Costa Concordia capsized. Search parties not only had the problems of exploring an unfamiliar enclosed environment, but it was at an unfamiliar angle and water levels had to be assessed and monitored. This was before the effects of damage had been taken into account. Small flying autonomous robots could rapidly explore the area and monitor human searchers, maintaining contact with the controller and warning them of potential dangers in good time, so that they can take evasive action, and keep themselves safe. If a swarm of swimming robots with similar capabilities could also be deployed, the complete ship could be explored in a coordinated manner.

We believe that a limited conversational interface in conjunction with a Belief Desire and Intention architecture can provide an effective way to provide flexible operations, reduce work load, and minimise bandwidth requirements. Ultimately of course autonomous vehicles could look after themselves, providing only timely and relevant sensor data. With the state of the art, they need supervision and the proposed virtual environment provides a highly flexible human machine interface.

References

1. Mehlmann, G., Häring, M., Bühling, R., Wißner, M., André, E.: Multiple Agent Roles in an Adaptive Virtual Classroom Environment. In: Allbeck, J., Badler, N., Bickmore, T., Pelachaud, C., Safonova, A. (eds.) IVA 2010. LNCS, vol. 6356, pp. 250–256. Springer, Heidelberg (2010)
2. Gemrot, J., Brom, C., Plch, T.: A Periphery of Pogamut: From Bots to Agents and Back Again. In: Dignum, F. (ed.) Agents for Games and Simulations II. LNCS (LNAI), vol. 6525, pp. 19–37. Springer, Heidelberg (2011)
3. Richards, D., Taylor, M., Porte, J.: Allowing trainers to author their own learning content. In: Proceedings of Workshop on Education and MAS (EduMAS 2009) (2009)
4. Saez-Pons, J., Alboul, L., Penders, J.: Experiments in cooperative human multi-robot navigation. In: International Conference on Robotics and Automation (ICRA 2011), Shanghai, China, pp. 6512–6516. The IEEE Robotics and Automation Society (2011)
5. Saez-Pons, J., Alboul, L., Penders, J., Nomdedeu, L.: Multi-robot team formation control in the GUARDIANS project. Industrial Robot: An International Journal 37(4), 372–383 (2010)
6. Schank, R.C., Abelson, R.P.: Scripts, Plans, Goals, and Understanding. Lawrence Erlbaum Press (1977)
7. Allen, J.F., Schubert, L.K., Ferguson, G., Heeman, P., Hwang, C.H., Kato, T., Light, M., Martin, N.G., Miller, B.W., Poesio, M., Traum, D.R.: The TRAINS project: A case study in defining a conversational planning agent. Journal of Experimental and Theoretical AI (1995)
8. Wallis, P.: Robust normative systems: What happens when a normative system fails? In: de Angeli, A., Brahnam, S., Wallis, P. (eds.) Abuse: The Darker Side of Human-Computer Interaction (CHI 2005) (2005)
9. Wallis, P.: Believable conversational agents: Introducing the intention map. In: Pelachaud, C., Andre, E., Kopp, S., Ruttkay, Z. (eds.) Creating Bonds with Humanoids (Proceedings of the Workshop at AAMAS 2005) (2005)
10. http://news.bbc.co.uk/1/hi/england/derbyshire/7765014.stm
11. http://www.bbc.co.uk/news/uk-england-derbyshire-11081145
12. http://www.bbc.co.uk/news/uk-england-derbyshire-12648565
13. http://www.bbc.co.uk/news/uk-england-stoke-staffordshire-13036916
14. http://www.bbc.co.uk/news/uk-england-south-yorkshire-17028351
15. Penders, J., Alboul, L., Witkowski, U., Naghsh, A., Saez-Pons, J., Herbrechtsmeier, S., Habbal, M.E.: A robot swarm assisting a human fire fighter. Journal of Advanced Robotics 25(1-2), 93–117 (2011)
16. Payr, S., Wallis, P.: Socially situated affective systems. In: Petta, P., Pelachaud, C., Cowie, R. (eds.) Emotion-Oriented Systems: The Humaine Handbook, pp. 497–516. Springer (2011)
17. Tomasello, M.: Origins of Human Communication. The MIT Press, Cambridge (2008)
18. Militello, L.G., Hutton, R.J.B.: Applied Cognitive Task Analysis (ACTA): A practitioner's toolkit for understanding cognitive task demands. Ergonomics 41(11), 1618–1641 (1998)
19. Norling, E.: What should the agent know?: The challenge of capturing human knowledge. In: Proceedings of the 7th International Joint Conference on Autonomous Agents and Multiagent Systems, Richland, SC, vol. 3, pp. 1225–1228. International Foundation for Autonomous Agents and Multiagent Systems (2008)
20. Rao, A.S., Georgeff, M.P.: BDI agents: From theory to practice. In: Lesser, V. (ed.) Proceedings of the First International Conference on Multi-Agent Systems (ICMAS 1995), pp. 312–319. MIT Press (1995)
21. Heinze, C., Smith, B., Cross, M.: Thinking quickly: Agents for modeling air warfare. In: Proceedings of the Eighth Australian Joint Conference on Artificical Intelligence, Brisbane, Australia, pp. 47–58 (1998)

22. Heinze, C., Goss, S., Pearce, A.: Plan recognition in military simulation: Incorporating machine learning with intelligent agents. In: Proceedings of the Sixteenth International Joint Conference on Artificial Intelligence, Workshop on Team Behaviour and Plan Recognition, Stockholm, Sweden, pp. 53–63 (1999)
23. Norling, E.: Modelling Human Behaviour with BDI Agents. PhD thesis, University of Melbourne, Australia (June 2009)
24. Alboul, L., Chliveros, J.: A system for reconstruction from point clouds in 3D: simplification and mesh representation. In: 11th International Conference on Control, Automation, Robotics and Vision, ICARCV 2010, Singapore, pp. 2301–2306. IEEE (2010)
25. Wallis, P., Mitchard, H., Das, J., O'Dea, D.: Dialogue Modelling for a Conversational Agent. In: Stumptner, M., Corbett, D.R., Brooks, M. (eds.) Canadian AI 2001. LNCS (LNAI), vol. 2256, pp. 532–544. Springer, Heidelberg (2001)
26. Payr, S., Wallis, P., Cunningham, S., Hawley, M.: Research on social engagement with a rabbitic user interface. In: Tscheligi, M., de Ruyter, B., Soldatos, J., Meschtscherjakov, A., Buiza, C., Streitz, N., Mirlacher, T. (eds.) AmI 2009, ICT&S Center, Salzburg (2009)
27. Williams, J.D., Young, S.: Partially observable Markov decision processes for spoken dialog systems. Computer Speech & Language 21(2) (2007)
28. Lemon, O.: Learning what to say and how to say it: joint optimization of spoken dialogue management and natural language generation. Computer Speech and Language 25(2) (2011)
29. Young, S., Gasic, M., Keizer, S., Mairesse, F., Schatzmann, J., Thomson, B., Yu, K.: The hidden information state model: A practical framework for pomdp-based spoken dialogue management. Computer Speech & Language 24(2), 150–174 (2010)
30. Wilks, Y., Catizone, R., Worgan, S., Dingli, A., Moore, R., Field, D., Cheng, W.: A prototype for a conversational companion for reminiscing about images. Computer Speech & Language 25(2), 140–157 (2011)
31. Janarthanam, S., Lemon, O.: A wizard-of-Oz environment to study referring expression generation in a situated spoken dialogue task. In: Proceedings of the 12th European Workshop on Natural Language Generation, ENLG 2009, Stroudsburg, PA, pp. 94–97. Association for Computational Linguistics (2009)
32. Wallis, P.: From data to design. Applied Artificial Intelligence 25(6), 530–548 (2011)

A Collaborative Agent Architecture
with Human-Agent Communication Model

Nader Hanna and Deborah Richards

Department of Computing
Macquarie University
NSW, 2109, Australia
{nader.hanna,deborah.richards}@mq.edu.au

Abstract. Designing a virtual agent architecture that comprises collaboration between the agents and human users remains a challenging issue due to differences in beliefs, ways of reasoning and the abilities used to achieve the common goal. Allowing the agent and human to communicate verbally and non-verbally while achieving the collaborative task, further increases the difficulty of the challenge. In this paper, we present an overview of existing research involving collaborative agents in virtual environments and extend our Multi-Agent Collaborative VIrtuaL Learning Environment (MACVILLE) agent architecture to handle two-way human-agent collaboration. A scenario is provided.

Keywords: Collaborative Learning, Agent Architecture, Human-Agent Collaboration, BDI Model, Human-Agent Communication Model.

1   Introduction

Computer-Supported Collaborative Learning (CSCL) goes beyond Intelligent Tutoring Systems (ITS) by introducing the concept of collaboration in learning [1]. CSCL is not considered a new branch of knowledge rather it can be viewed as a natural extension of one-to-one learning done in ITS to the group learning environment [2]. Virtual Environment technology offers a potential group learning environment particularly suited to exploration of problems that are hazardous or difficult to deal with in reality. A Collaborative Virtual Environment (CVE) is where multiple individuals interact and co-operate with each other in the virtual world. Collaborative learning in a virtual environment includes collaboration between learners. Benford et al. [3] assert that a CVE may support collaboration in ways which go beyond what is possible using alternative technologies such as video conferencing.

However, collaboration is difficult and humans often need assistance to [learn how to] effectively collaborate. Autonomous agents and Multi-Agent Systems (MAS) can play an important role in providing this assistance. Autonomous agents are able to control the environment they are embedded in as well as their internal state and behavior; perform a specific role or achieve determined goals; and due to their proactive and reactive ability, they are ideally suited to problem-solving situations [4].

F. Dignum et al. (Eds.): CAVE 2012, LNAI 7764, pp. 70–88, 2013.

Agent-based systems are used in different areas, including team analysis [5], workflow systems [6] and affective tutoring systems [7].

The idea of human-machine collaboration for educational purposes is not a new research topic. There is a range of research which presents collaborative agents with properties and behaviors appropriate to a range of roles to support the learner. These roles include agents acting as a simulated student [8, 9], computational learner [10], learning companion [11] and teachable agent [12].

Agents in a collaborative environment may have to play multiple roles. Zhang and Li [13] mention a number of general aims to be achieved by an agent in a collaborative environment including facilitating the team work between humans. A less explored combination involves making the human and agent one team in performing a certain task. This combination adds further system requirements such as monitoring human and agent performance, checking if individual and overall goals are achieved, management of turntaking and replanning.

Among the factors that encourage collaboration, Maddux [14] mentions 3 factors: 1) identification of areas of interdependence; 2) open communication channels; and 3) let the team members know that teamwork will positively influence individual recognition. Larson and LaFasto [15] assert the importance of communication between collaborative teamwork member.

Smith-Jentsch et al.[16] define four factors that are crucial to effective teamwork: Information Exchange, Communication, Supporting Behaviour and Initiative/Leadership. The greatest challenge in designing agents that can act as a teammate with a human lies in communicating their intent and making results intelligible to them [17]. Lenox et al. [18] use agents to support the team as a whole, this support includes facilitating communication, allocation of tasks, coordination among the human agents, and improving attention focus. Sycara and Lenox [19] [18] identify three roles for agents in interacting with human teams: agents support individual team members in completion of their own tasks, agents support the team as a whole and agents assume the role of an equal team member. All three agent roles require communication.

In this paper we first review the literature relevant to collaborative agents, considering alternative agent and human team combinations (Section 2). In Section 3, a collaborative agent architecture is presented that, in addition to having a reasoning core, will enable collaborative behavior when interacting with the learner. In Section 4, a scenario is presented to demonstrate implementation of the collaboration agent architecture in Omosa virtual world. In section 5, future work, challenges and conclusions are given.

2   A Review of Agent Collaboration Approaches

There is a vast range of agent-based research that has some relevance to collaborative agents due to the complexity of collaborative behavior and the modeling of human behavior in general. In designing a collaborative agent we need to consider the cognitive module of the agent and how to execute reasoning tasks. However in this review we want to go beyond that basic functionality. Some recent research pays attention to other aspects of an agent, such as extending the ability of a virtual agent to include personality-like traits. For example, Huang et al. [20] propose a self-awareness agent model that contains two personality traits (super-ego and ego) and includes an external learning mechanism and internal cognitive capacity. The model claims to provide better learning performance over classical agent models and improved agent reasoning capabilities.

Other research concerns the social abilities of an agent. Social ability is the ability of an agent to interact with other agents, and possibly humans, in order to achieve its design objectives [21]. Zhang et al. [22] define a social agent architecture based on roles using Ðcalculus (a process calculus for describing and analyzing properties of concurrent computation). According to the authors, human social ability means that an individual is able to select a role, play the role, and locate their role in some organized society at any time. Agents as simulations of human-beings should have the same social capabilities.

Adaptability to dynamic situations is the focus of some research work. Buford et al. [23] extend the Belief-Desire-Intention (BDI) agent model by enabling the agent's beliefs to be based on real-time situations so the agent can dynamically adapt its representation for situations over time. Decision making is the focus of some research. For example, Luo et al. [24] present a decision process model for modeling the decision making process of virtual agents in time-critical and uncertainty situations and Norling [25] integrates a psychological decision making model into an agent BDI framework.

Although there are many varied attempts to extend agent abilities, as exemplified above, the ability to collaborate remains a challenge due to the nature of collaboration. Collaboration requires the individual to have an insight into the situation as a whole, to the task requested to be done and the performance of the peer with whom they are collaborating. Though many researchers present agents in a CVE with a variety of roles and responsibilities, there have been two main foci. Firstly, agents may take the role of facilitators or trainers/teachers to assist one or more humans achieve a task, or acquire knowledge or a skill, for example, as in the case of pedagogical agents. Secondly, some collaborative systems involve separation of tasks into teams of humans and teams of agents, where each carry out the task most appropriate to them. For example, in first responder/emergency systems the team of agents may go into remote or dangerous locations to gather data before human teams are sent in.

The idea of grouping the agent and the human learner to form a collaborative learning team has not been much discussed. This is the key focus of our work. Before presenting our cognitive and social architecture for an agent who can collaborate with a human, we consider the possible collaboration combinations between humans and agents in virtual environments that are found in the literature. Accordingly; the following three sections categorize the research work into three possible combinations of agent collaboration: 1) agent-to-agent collaboration that makes use of a shared/global model between agents to achieve the determined goal; 2) one-way human-agent collaboration which usually includes actions performed by the human with assistance from the agent; and 3) two-way human agent collaboration where the actions of both the human and agent interleave and depend on each other.

2.1 Agent-Agent Collaboration

Numerous research projects focus on the collaboration of two or more agents in a virtual world while achieving a common objective. The nature of the virtual world should itself be dynamic and allow the agents to impact on and change their surrounding environment.

Hadad et al. [26] present a temporal reasoning mechanism for an individual agent collaborating with other agents in a dynamic environment. The reasoning mechanism consists of two components: Planning subsystem and Real-Time (RT) Scheduling subsystem. The Planning subsystem generates a partial order plan dynamically. During the planning it sends the RT Scheduling subsystem basic actions and time constraints. The RT Scheduling subsystem receives the dynamic basic action set with associated temporal constraints and inserts these actions into the agent's schedule of activities. Shakshuki and Matin [27] present an agent architecture which is able to monitor the user's actions and learn using a reinforcement learning algorithm. The learning agent architecture consists of eight main components: communication component, assignment component, knowledge base, the problem solver component, the filter component, the execution component, knowledge update component, the learning component.

Extending work on situation-aware BDI agents [23] that can respond to an event, Jakobson et al. [28] present a collaboration-enabled BDI agent to respond to multiple events. According to their design when a situation is recognized, an existing plan is invoked or a trigger is automatically generated to create a plan from a specification embedded in the situation. To extend the situation-aware BDI agent with agent collaboration capabilities, the authors added a new layer to their previous design. The new layer is composed of two elements: Collaboration Manager that receives request for collaboration either from other agents or from its inner intention; Inter-Agent Collaboration Models that include scenario or policy-based collaboration.

Liu et al. [29] present a collaborative learning system. The system is composed of three modules. The User module provides the interface between the agent, learners and the teacher. In the Agent module, when a user logs in, an agent for the user is built automatically. This agent can assist the user to interact with the system. Agents can do some tasks themselves and cooperate with other agents. Finally there is a Data module divided into two parts: the database that saves the agents beliefs, and the other part saves information resources.

Agent Collaboration Approaches

There are several approaches related to agent collaboration [30], including Tuple-Spaces, Group Computation, Activity Theory and Roles. A Tuple-space is an unordered container of tuples. A "space" is a shared persistent memory in which clients may read, write, and take objects. A "tuple" can be thought of as a data structure or a set of attributes to be used as a template for matching. Tuple-spaces provide a multi-agent-like architecture, where agents can collaborate through writing, reading or removing tuples in the space [31]. The tuple-space mechanism could be centralized or decentralized. There are various implementations for centralized tuple-spaces; the most well-known are Sun Java Space and IBM TSpaces [32]. LIME as an example of the decentralized tuple-space which was implemented and extended by Murphy and Picco [33]. Group Computation is another approach to address how to program the agent's reasoning for group based activities [34].

Activity Theory is used as a framework to design the mediated interaction that may happen between the user and computer system or between agents. There are a few projects (e.g. [35, 36]) that present frameworks for collaborative activity in a virtual environment. Some frameworks analyze needs, tasks, and outcomes for designing constructivist learning [37], others identify any difficulties that users may have when navigating through Virtual Reality Environments [38] and others design virtual problem-based learning environments [39].

Roles are used to define common interactions between agents in virtual environments. Roles include all information and capabilities needed in a particular execution environment for an agent to communicate and collaborate with other agents. One of the characteristics of a role-based collaborative agent is the separation in implementation between the agent and the roles that are going to be used [30, 40].

While these approaches may be used in contexts involving humans, we see them as agent-agent approaches due to the use of shared spaces/processes which do not seem appropriate for human-agent collaboration. We admit that there may be shared understandings, even a set of common beliefs, desires and intentions, however, it is an oversimplification to bundle them together as one.

2.2   One-Way Human-Agent Collaboration

Other research work considers one-way interaction between the user and agent, such as making the agent a team leader. Aguilar et al. [41] present a system that makes use of an Intelligent Collaborative Virtual Environment (ICVE) that incorporates a Pedagogical Virtual Agent (PVA) to assist the group during the execution stage of a Team Training Strategy (TTS). The system has four stages: the first Integration stage has the purpose of integrating the human team. In the following stage (Execution), the team uses an ICVE for training to execute the planned activities, a PVA plays a team leader role to assist the trainees, and it may offer its help to the team, giving preference to activities that are critical for the task's success. In the third stage (Evaluation), the team members have to evaluate their previous execution and must identify both individual and group errors. Finally, in the last stage (Improvement) the team members in a virtual meeting co-construct a new plan. Another feature of one way interaction is to make the agent answer the user's questions while navigating in a virtual world [42].

There are other approaches that limit the role of the agent to a mediator in the collaboration environment while users interact with one another via the system. Yacine and Tahar [43] present an architecture of a collaborative learning system which is composed of a set of artificial agents. The collaboration occurs between users using technical tools such as chat rooms, electronic mail and forums; the agent's role is to facilitate the collaboration between users and give feedback.

Zhang et al. [13, 44] present an approach to support collaborative design by providing intelligent multi-agent technology. The MAS includes: User Interface Agent,

Assisting Agent, Collaboration Agent, and Mediator Agent. The role of the mediator agent is to facilitate the communication of a user with other users, while the collaborative agent's role is to look after the collaboration process between users starting with the project design but also including associated problems.

2.3   Two-Way Human-Agent Collaboration

Research concerning human-agent collaboration is sparse. Miller et al. [45] present an approach called Collaborative Agent architecture for Simulating Teamwork (CAST). It is an agent-based approach to designing intelligent team training systems. The team is a group of entities (humans or agents) that are working together to achieve a goal. The intelligent agents play two roles in the system: virtual team members and coach.

A COLLaboration manager for software interface AGENts called COLLAGEN presented by Lesh et al. [46] uses a plan recognition algorithm in order to reduce communication during collaboration between a human and an agent. Using attention, partial plans, and clarification enables COLLAGEN-based agents to interact with humans in an intelligent fashion. Miao et al. [47] adopt a multi-agent multi-user system to train learners to handle abnormal situations while driving cars. Multiple users can drive cars in a shared virtual driving place. The authors employ multiple pedagogical agents. The *coach* agent warns, advises, or gives feedback on the user's driving performance. The *situation creator* is a kind of pedagogical agent represented as a car that drives according to traffic rules and can deliberately create normal situations within a collaborative 3D car driving simulation environment. The *problem creator* agent can be represented as a vehicle, a pedestrian, a bicycle, a motorbike, or an animal and is able to create a small number of highly abnormal and dangerous situations. The problem creator agent does not communicate directly with users however; it interacts with learners through the simulation environment. In Miao et al.'s work, both the trainee and the agent do not collaborate to achieve any task, but the user may be affected by the agent's actions/responses.

Another example of limited agent-human collaboration is presented by Hedfi et al. [48] who developed a negotiation architecture for product design. When the user designs the product using a 3D interface, the agent will negotiate over the possible optimal design of the product. The system is an online negotiation framework.

In considering teamwork that may involve a human and agent, Fan and Yen [49] introduce the shared belief map concept and propose the use of Hidden Markov Model (HMM)-based cognitive load models for an agent to estimate its human partner's cognitive load.

3   Proposed Collaborative Agent Architecture

While a number of agent-based architectures for collaborative learning have been proposed e.g. [28, 44], these architectures either focus on the reasoning module (core) of the agent neglecting to address the social and collaborative aspects of the agent's behavior e.g. [44], or the collaboration is directed by goals without consideration of the performance of individual peers in the team (one-way human-agent collaboration, e.g. [28]). In the literature, the previously presented intelligent agent architectures were designed to be used in situations that did not involve two-way agent-human collaboration, and the embedded processes in the reasoning core of their agent architectures were designed to be general purpose.

In this section we extend our initial Multi-Agent Collaborative VIrtuaL Learning Environment (MACVILLE) architecture with communication components. Among the different collaboration features, we target human-agent two-way collaboration, as two-way collaboration gives the learner a more interactive and interesting way to learn. Agents should combine both reasoning and social elements, plus they should be aware of the human learner's activity and adapt its own performance to the changes in the human's actions. Thus, the proposed novel agent architecture includes a social and collaborative core in addition to the reasoning core. Furthermore, the collaborative agent should be aware of the partner's attitude and their objectives to be achieved. Thus, the social and collaborative core enables the collaborative agent to be aware of the human learner's activities while learning, and to give appropriate feedback such as encouraging the user when collaboration is occurring or urging the user to collaborate when insufficient collaborative activity is taking place. The collaborative agent should contain components to handle their cognitive processes including memory and its related processes as well as the social and collaborative processes. Besides the novel collaborative core, the proposed agent architecture will adjust the processes included in the reasoning core of agent to be suitable for collaboration with a partner. Interaction and negotiation will be handled via the communication components. The complete architecture is shown in Fig.1 and discussed further below.

3.1   The Intelligent and Cognitive Processes

This component includes two processes: *Memory* and *Cognitive*. The memory or the knowledge base is where the agents store information, knowledge and experience. There are two processes related to memory: *Knowledge Integration* to add a new experience to the stored knowledge, and *Information Retrieval* to get the appropriate piece of information for the current situation. Retrieving information from memory could be done during any process.

Cognitive Processes include the reasoning model needed by the agent to handle the current situation. Cognitive Processes begin with *Situation Understanding* and determining if this situation has appropriate knowledge in memory or it is a new situation requiring the agent to infer new knowledge. The agent also needs the ability to plan what activity to do, its share in this activity and what is the human learner's role.

After specifying the role the agent is going to play, it needs to plan how its share in the activity should be done. By knowing its share, the agent should have solutions/plans for possible problems it may encounter, and the ability to decide the best solution for the dynamic situation it faces. At the end of the reasoning process, the agent may add a piece of knowledge that is not in its memory for later use; this process is similar to learning. Collaboration between the agent and human requires that there is an activity or a task to be completed by both of them. To support real

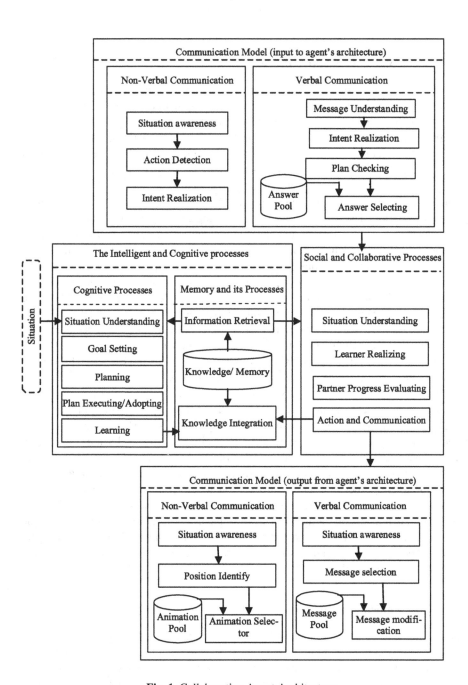

Fig. 1. Collaborative Agent Architecture

time collaboration, the agent should have a set of processes that enable it to estimate the current situation, think about its step, and analyze the situation after the human's step.

3.2   Social and Collaborative Process

One of the most important elements of learning which is absent from a traditional text based learning system is social interaction with other learners. The agent in a collaborative learning environment should have the ability to socially interact with the human learner and encourage collaboration together. The social processes begin with understanding whether the social situation is competitive or collaborative. The agent may have a mechanism to identify the learning and the social properties of the learner.

The *Situation Understanding* process includes identifying the variables in the surrounding environment. Identifying these variables will help in building the agent's general perception. The variables of the surrounding environment will vary depending on the joint task. It may include the agent's position in the virtual world, the agent's orientation and the human's action. Because collaboration between two partners need each one to be aware of the other's action and form a complete understanding of the partner's actions, the *Learner Realizing* process aims at forming an understanding of the actions of the human partner by continuously keeping the agent aware of both the verbal and non-verbal interaction of the human partner.

Collaboration between two or more partners to achieve a shared task needs them to be involved in the collaborative task and at the same time watch the action of the partner to make sure that individual behaviours lead towards the overall achievement of the activity. The *Partner Progress Evaluation* process is a continuous process that the agent should perform during execution of the collaborative activity with the human learner; the agent should make sure that the learner is participating in the activity. The agent is then going to evaluate the progress of the task relying on another three processes: 1) the *Planning* process to determine the workload share of the agent and the learner, 2) the *Plan Executing/Adopting* process to acquire the properties of the learner which may lead the agent to adopt different evaluation criteria and 3) the *Learner Realizing* process to gather information about the human's actions.

At the end of the social and collaborative module the agent will need to take a social action such as encouraging the learner to put in more effort, or congratulate the learner for his/her hard work. In the *Action and Communication* process the agent expresses its internal state and its feedback to the human action via both verbal and non-verbal communication.

3.3   Communication Model

The communication model is included in Fig. 1. and contains two separate modules to handle two-way communication. At the top, we see the input to the agent's architecture, that is, the communication from the human. At the bottom we see the output from the agent's architecture, that is, the communication sent to the human. The communication model includes both verbal communication (i.e. textual communication) and from non-verbal communication (i.e. behavioural communication). Interaction will involve alternating between textual and behavioural communication. That is to say, the human will send a text request to the agent, and the agent will reply with acceptance or rejection depending on its plan to complete the shared task. The agent may also send a text request to the human user asking for his/her help to achieve the task, and the human user may reply with acceptance or rejection. The rejection of the agent's request by the human user will lead the agent to modify its plan to the new state of the task. Behavioural communication is also handled in an alternating fashion and relies on the agent planning process. As part of behavioural communication the agent has to monitor the surrounding environment and observe the actions of the human teammate and continuously adapt the plan in accordance with the behaviour of the human.

The agent will begin either its cognitive and intelligent processes or social and collaborative processes by following the *situation understanding* process. Situation understanding will enable the agent to gather the required information from the surrounding virtual environment in order to provide input to the other processes in the cognitive or collaborative module. The situation understanding process should keep the agent updated with any change made be either the human or the agent itself.

Textual Communication

Textual communication is a structured conversation-like interaction between the agent and the human learner. The basic process allows both parties to select a request, based on their plans/intentions, from a list which is presented to the party and the other party will be able to answer the request either with accept or reject.

The agent-human textual communication model will enable the agent to ask the human learner to take certain steps to help in achieving the targeted task according to the plan of the agent. The request of the agent will rely on the plan created by the agent planner. The agent will get the answer from the human learner either to accept or to reject the request. If the answer of the human user is to accept the agent proposed step, the agent will go on carrying out the plan. If the answer is rejection, the agent should identify the new action of the human via the behavioural component of the communication model (that is, the agent will observe what the human decided to do in place of the request they rejected), then the agent should begin changing its plan in accordance with the new action of the human.

On the other side as part of human-agent textual communication, the human can ask the agent to take a certain step to help in achieving the targeted task according to the point of view of the human. When the human selects a request and directs it to the agent, the agent begins the process of Request Understanding to identify which request was issued by the human. After identification, the agent will understand the intent of the human from their request. In order to give a response to the human request, the agent should check its plan to make sure if the request matches the plan. If the request matches the plan, the agent will accept the human request; otherwise the request will be rejected.

Behavioural Communication

In behavioural communication, both the human and agent will understand what the other did by observing the other's action in achieving the shared task. It may be easy for the human to automatically understand what the agent aims to do from observing its current actions, but in the case of the agent, the agent should follow some process to infer the intent of the human. The first process should be *Situation Awareness* where the agent should have some information about its own location coordinates and orientation, the human's location coordinates and orientation, the task situation, remaining time, how many steps were undertaken and whose turn it is to take the next step. In the *Action Detection* process, the agent should be able to detect any changes in the human's location and orientation and what action the human performed. Based on information collected in the *Action Detection* process, the agent can understand the intention of the human user and determine whether this intent helps in achieving the agent's plan or the agent may have to use textual communication to direct the human to do specific task.

4   A Scenario to Demonstrate the Collaboration Agent Architecture in Omosa Virtual World

In order to test the successfulness of the human-agent interaction in achieving a shared objective in a virtual world, we have extended a virtual learning environment (VLE) that has been created [50] to help students to learn scientific knowledge and science inquiry skills. The VLE represents an ecosystem on an imaginary island called Omosa. The system was designed using the Unity3D game engine, and the animation was programmed using the JavaScript language which is supported by Unity3D along with C# and Boo scripting languages.

Currently, Omosa supports only collaboration in the real world and only between companion learners and not among learning groups; interaction and activities in the virtual world are not collaborative yet. The goal that is set for the learner is to determine why the fictitious animals, known as Yernt, are dying out. In the scenario we present here, the scientist agent named Alan, needs the assistance of a human to capture a Yernt so he can study its anatomy and behavior. Capturing an animal is a task that is much easier with someone else to help trap the animal. We wanted an authentic task that did not just involve dividing up the workload, but one that would be difficult to achieve alone and that needs coordination and dynamic planning.

To achieve the task in this scenario, both the learner and the agent should collaborate together. This specifically means that they should try to help one another, rather than compete. In order to trap the Yernt, after the human or agent draws the first line near the animal, they will continue to take alternating turns to form a geometric shape around the animal by drawing a line beginning from the two ends of the existing drawn shape. This process is shown in Fig. 2. For practicality, the Yernt will first be shot with a tranquilising gun by one of the parties to ensure it remains calm for a specific pre-determined amount of time before it runs away, therefore the task of capturing the animal should be done before the time deadline is reached. Communication that will take place between the human learner and agent will include both textual communication and behavioural communication.

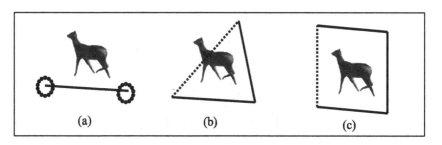

Fig. 2. (a) After the initial step, each following step should begin at any of the two ends; (b) Yernt is outside the scope of the fence and cannot be trapped in one step; (c) Yernt is inside the scope of the fence and can be trapped in one step.
NOTE: other geometric shapes are possible.

The agent will begin its activity by gathering information from the virtual world regarding its position and orientation, the surrounding objects and the target Yernt and its position. The agent will determine the goal of the shared task with the human, which is trapping the animal by creating a fence around it. The agent should persistently make sure that the goal is not yet met in order to continue planning and evaluating human partner progress. In the beginning the agent will select one of the Yernt to be the target to be trapped. Virtual numbered markers will appear around the target Yernt to make it easy for both the human and virtual agent to identify and discuss locations around the animal (see Fig. 3 & 4). The human will take the first step and select one of the 8 regions around the target animal. After selecting one of the regions, Alan will ask the human if s/he would like to give any suggestion for him to go to a particular region. The human will have the option to accept or reject the agent's suggestions. In the case of accepting to given suggestions, a GUI window will appear to enable the human to select possible regions for the agent to go to. When it is the agents' turn, Alan will begin by evaluating the human's request through matching the request with the agent's plan. Either there is a match between the human's request and the agent's plan or not. The agent will reply to the human with its agreement or disagreement along with its reason in either case. After replying to the human's request, the agent will make its selection to one of the two edge points around the virtual animal. This selection would be according to the optimal output from the planning process.

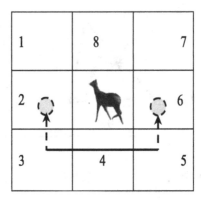

Fig. 3. Region 3, 4 and 5 are selected by both human and agent, the next two optimal regions will be 2 and 6

Fig. 4. Snapshot from the collaborative virtual world, it is initial state where 8 region markers around Yernt and Alan the virtual agent is standing waiting for the first step from the human

After finishing the selection of the optimal region according to its reasoning, the agent will make a request to the human, asking him/her to go to one of two proposed regions. The human will have the option to get an explanation from the agent about the reason behind this request. Then, the human will have their turn to select another region; his/her selection could agree or disagree with the agent's request. Next, when it is the agent's turn, the agent will gather information from the surrounding environment regarding its current position, Yernt's current position, the edge of the two regions used in the last step and the region request given to the human. Then, the agent will observe and realize what was the actual region selected by the human. Through the process *Partner Progress Evaluating*, the agent will evaluate how the human responded to the agent's request for selection, and if the human actually selected the suggested region this will help the agent in achieving its plan. The agent will express his evaluation to the human partner's action via sending a feedback message to the human telling him the result of his selection and whether it assisted the agent to achieve the final goal according to the agent's plan.

As long as the goal is not completed, the agent will resume its reasoning by gathering information from the surrounding virtual environment including its own position and orientation, the Yernt's position and which region was initially selected by the human. During its turn, the agent will reason what next step will be optimal towards achieving the task. The process *Planning* will play a major role in calculating and updating the plan of the agent to complete the task. Continuous re-planning will be crucial in real-time collaborative task due to the changes in the surrounding environment such as changes in the Yernt's position or unexpected selections from the human. Planning/re-planning is not only needed for the intelligent and cognitive module of collaborative agent architecture, but is also vital for the social and collaborative module of the architecture. The process of *Partner Progress Evaluating* in the collaborative module will rely on both realizing the human learner's actions as well as the expected plan from planning process.

5   Future Work, Challenges and Conclusion

To deliver virtual agents that can collaborate with human learners in a virtual environment includes a number of conceptual, design and implementation challenges. Conceptual and design challenges may include:

1. Determining the factors that control human collaboration. To design collaborative agents that mimic human collaborative behavior requires an understanding of the factors that manage human social collaboration. Human collaborative behavior is not fully understood; getting humans to collaborate is itself a challenge.
2. Extending the abilities of virtual agents to be collaborative will involve not only the cognitive capabilities, but also social and affective characteristics [51]. Agent affective behavior has a positive influence on the learner's satisfaction while learning [52]. There is an extensive and growing body of work in the area of empathic and affective agents. To keep the scope of our project manageable, emotion handling is not a major focus in our project. Particularly we note that we will not be exploring the use of facial expressions and body gestures to convey emotion as these are large and difficult topics to address and also the small size of the agent in our implemented virtual system means that facial expressions and body gestures would not be clearly noticed. The social and the affective characteristics of the proposed agent will include adjusting the agent's behavior

(actions and language) in the virtual world to cope up with the changes in learning behavior of the human, and also providing text feedback to urge or encourage learner actions.

3. The difficulties in capturing and measuring the levels and nature of collaboration taking place. Evaluating the effect of collaboration between the human learner and agent is an even greater challenge. There are research approaches that try to assess and evaluate collaboration (e.g [53]). We will be employing some of these methods. For example, in our studies we plan to evaluate the development of social skills among learners as a result of human-human interaction by conducting pre and post assessment of learners' attitude toward collaborative learning and companion learners. Collecting and evaluating data regarding the collaborative learning activity can also be done through analysis of video recordings of the collaborative learning session [54] using analysis methods such as Decision Function Coding Scheme (DFCS) [55, 56]. However, these methods often require transcription of dialogues, manual coding, interpretation and inter-rater agreement and are thus open to error and very costly in time and money. As a less biased and more sustainable and scalable approach, we have designed and developed a technique to automate data collection while the learners use the virtual world [57]. In this technique, learners' activities are traced in log files. The log files record data and notes regarding: the users' navigational paths; the agents met by the learner; the questions asked by the learner; which items were collected; what activities they conducted and the duration of these activities. The log files also include measurements of the level of collaboration between the human learner and agent by measuring the ratio of participation of both the learner and the agent in completing different tasks in the virtual world.

Implementation challenges may include:

1. Creating, selecting or adapting an appropriate implementation framework to extend the [BDI] reasoning model of the agent. Although there are a number of existing frameworks that implement the BDI model of an agent, not all of them allow extension of the abilities of the agent.

2. Integrating the framework of agent reasoning with a 3D game engine, as usually game engines support the programming languages that could be integrated with graphic scripting languages. For example, Omosa Virtual World is implemented using the Unity 3D game engine which supports specific programming languages (C#, JavaScript and Boo script), while the majority of agent reasoning frameworks are implemented in Java e.g. jadex, Jason. To overcome this challenge, we may search for a framework with levels of abstraction e.g. [58].

In this paper we discussed the various approaches to designing an agent-based collaborative virtual environment and proposed an architecture to allow agents to collaborate with humans to achieve a shared objective. Currently, we have implemented the scenario presented and will test the scenario with undergraduate students in a second year animal behavior unit to evaluate how well our agent-human communication model works in practice.

References

1. Lafifi, Y., Bensebaa, T.: Supporting Learner's Activities in a Collaborative Learning System. International Journal of Instructional Technology & Distance Learning 4, 3–12 (2007)
2. Inaba, A., Okamoto, T.: The Intelligent Discussion Coordinating System for Effective Collaborative Learning. In: Proceedings of IV Artificial Intelligence in Education, Workshop in the International Conferene (AI-ED 1997), pp. 26–33 (1997)
3. Benford, S., Bowers, J., Fahlen, L.E., Mariani, J., Rodden, T.: Supporting Co-operative Work in Virtual Environments. The Computer Journal 37, 653–668 (1994)
4. Jennings, N.R.: An Agent-Based Approach for Building Complex Software Systems. Communications of the ACM 44, 35–41 (2001)
5. Raines, T., Tambe, M., Marsella, S.: Automated assistants to aid humans in understanding team behaviors. In: Proceedings of the Fourth International Conference on Autonomous Agents, pp. 419–426. ACM, Barcelona (2000)
6. Tony, B., Savarimuthu, B.T.R., Purvis, M.: A Collaborative Multi-agent Based Workflow System. In: Negoita, M.G., Howlett, R.J., Jain, L.C. (eds.) KES 2004. LNCS (LNAI), vol. 3214, pp. 1187–1193. Springer, Heidelberg (2004)
7. Mao, X., Li, Z.: Agent-based Affective Tutoring Systems: A Pilot Study. Computers & Education 55, 202–208 (2010)
8. Virvou, M., Manos, K.: A Simulated Student-Player in Support of the Authoring Process in a Knowledge-Based Authoring Tool for Educational Games. In: Proceeding of the Third IEEE International Conference on Advanced Learning Technologies (ICALT 2003), pp. 338–339 (2003)
9. Vizcaíno, A.: A Simulated Student Agent for Improving Collaborative Learning. Interactive Technology and Smart Education 1, 119–126 (2004)
10. Dillenbourg, P., Self, J.: People Power: A Human-Computer Collaborative Learning System Intelligent Tutoring Systems. In: Frasson, C., McCalla, G.I., Gauthier, G. (eds.) ITS 1992. LNCS, vol. 608, pp. 651–660. Springer, Heidelberg (1992)
11. Kim, Y., Baylor, A.: Pedagogical Agents as Learning Companions: The Role of Agent Competency and Type of Interaction. Educational Technology Research and Development 54, 223–243 (2006)
12. Blair, K., Schwartz, D.L., Biswas, G., Leelawong, K.: Pedagogical Agents for Learning by Teaching: Teachable Agents. Educational Technology 47, 56–61 (2007)
13. Zhang, P., Li, X.: The Framework of Multi Intelligent Agent Based on Collaborative Design. In: International Conference on Future BioMedical Information Engineering (FBIE 2009), pp. 513–517 (2009)
14. Maddux, R.B., Wingfield, B.: Team Building: An Exercise in Leadership. Crisp Publications (2003)
15. Larson, C.E., LaFasto, F.M.J.: TeamWork: What Must Go Right, what Can Go Wrong. USA Publications. Sage Publications, CA (1989)
16. Smith-Jentsch, K.A., Johnston, J.H., Payne, S.C.: Measuring Team-Related Expertise in Complex Environments. In: Making decisions Under Stress: Implications for Individual and Team Training, pp. 61–87. APA Press, Washington (1998)
17. Lewis, M.: Designing for Human-Agent Interaction. AI Magazine, 19 (1998)
18. Lenox, T., Lewis, M., Roth, E., Shern, R., Roberts, L., Rafalski, T., Jacobson, J.: Support of Teamwork in Human-Agent Teams. In: IEEE International Conference on Systems, Man, and Cybernetics 1998, 1341–1346 (1998)
19. Sycara, K., Lewis, M.: Integrating Agents into Human Teams. In: Proceedings of the Human Factors and Ergonomics Society 46th Annual Meeting, pp. 413–417 (2002)

20. Huang, C.-Y., Wang, S.-W., Sun, C.-T.: Modeling Agent Self-awareness, Individual Performance and Collaborative Behavior. In: 9th World Congress on Intelligent Control and Automation (WCICA 2011), pp. 759–763 (2011)
21. Wooldridge, M.: An Introduction to Multiagent Systems. John Wiley & Sons, Inc. (2002)
22. Zhang, J., Zeng, G.-Z., Li, Z.-F.: The Study of a Sociality Agent Architecture Based on Role. In: Proceedings of the 2010 Second International Conference on Information Technology and Computer Science, pp. 232–235. IEEE Computer Society Press (2010)
23. Buford, J., Jakobson, G., Lewis, L.: Extending BDI Multi-Agent Systems with Situation Management. In: 9th International Conference on Information Fusion, Florence, Italy, pp. 1–7 (2006)
24. Luo, L., Zhou, S., Cai, W., Lees, M., Low, M.Y.H.: Modeling Human-like Decision Making for Virtual Agents. In: Time-Critical Situations 2010 International Conference on Cyberworlds (CW), Singapore, pp. 360–367 (2010)
25. Norling, E.: Folk Psychology for Human Modelling: Extending the BDI Paradigm. In: Proceedings of the Third International Joint Conference on Autonomous Agents and Multiagent Systems, vol. 1, pp. 202–209. IEEE Computer Society, New York (2004)
26. Hadad, M., Kraus, S., Gal, Y., Lin, R.: Temporal Reasoning for a Collaborative Planning Agent in a Dynamic Environment. Annals of Mathematics and Artificial Intelligence 37, 331–379 (2003)
27. Shakshuki, E., Matin, A.W.: RL-Agent That Learns in Collaborative Virtual Environment. In: Third International Conference on Information Technology: New Generations (ITNG 2006), pp. 90–95 (2006)
28. Jakobson, G., Buford, J., Lewis, L.: Collaborative Agents for C2 Of Tactical Urban Combat Operations. In: Defense Transformation and Net-Centric Systems 2008, vol. 6981, p. 69810. SPIE, Orlando (2008)
29. Liu, Z., Jin, H., Fang, Z.: Collaborative Learning in E-Learning based on Multi-Agent Systems. In: 10th International Conference on Computer Supported Cooperative Work in Design (CSCWD 2006), pp. 1–5 (2006)
30. Cabri, G., Ferrari, L., Leonardi, L.: Agent role-based collaboration and coordination: a survey about existing approaches. In: IEEE International Conference on Systems, Man and Cybernetics, vol. 5476, pp. 5473–5478 (2004)
31. Xing, J., Qin, Z., Zhang, J.: A Replication-Based Distribution Approach for Tuple Space-Based Collaboration of Heterogeneous Agents. Research Journal of Information Technology 2, 201–214 (2010)
32. Lehman, T., McLaughry, S., Wyckoff, P.: TSpaces: The Next Wave. In: The 32nd Annual Hawaii International Conference on System Sciences (HICSS-32), pp. 1–9 (1999)
33. Murphy, A.L., Picco, G.P.: Using Coordination Middleware for Location-Aware Computing: A Lime Case Study. In: De Nicola, R., Ferrari, G.-L., Meredith, G. (eds.) COORDINATION 2004. LNCS, vol. 2949, pp. 263–278. Springer, Heidelberg (2004)
34. Hirsch, B., Fisher, M., Ghidini, C.: Programming Group Computations. In: The First European Workshop on Multi-Agent Systems, EUMAS 2003 (2003)
35. Ricci, A., Omicini, A., Denti, E.: Activity Theory as a Framework for MAS Coordination. In: Petta, P., Tolksdorf, R., Zambonelli, F. (eds.) ESAW 2002. LNCS (LNAI), vol. 2577, pp. 96–110. Springer, Heidelberg (2003)
36. Gifford, B.R., Enyedy, N.D.: Activity Centered Design: Towards a Theoretical Framework for CSCL. In: Proceedings of the 1999 Conference on Computer Support for Collaborative Learning, pp. 22–37. International Society of the Learning Sciences, Palo Alto (1999)
37. Lim, C.P., Hang, D.: An Activity Theory Approach to Research of ICT Integration in Singapore Schools. Computers & Education 41, 49–63 (2003)

38. Norris, B.E., Wong, B.L.W.: Activity Breakdowns in QuickTime Virtual Reality Environments. In: Proceedings of the First Australasian User Interface Conference (AUIC 2000), pp. 67–72. IEEE Computer Society, Canberra (2000)
39. Miao, Y.: An Activity Theoretical Approach to A Virtual Problem Based Learning Environment. In: Proceedings of the 2000 International Conference on Information in the 21 Century: Emerging Technologies and New Challenges, pp. 647–654 (2000)
40. Naoyasu, U.: RoleEP: Role Based Evolutionary Programming for Cooperative Mobile Agent Applications. In: International Symposium on Principles of Software Evolution, pp. 232–232 (2000)
41. Aguilar, R.A., de Antonio, A., Imbert, R.: An Intelligent Collaborative Virtual Environment for Team Training – A Preliminary Report. In: 15th International Conference on Computing (CIC 2006), pp. 236–239 (2006)
42. van Luin, J., op den Akker, R., Nijholt, A.: A Dialogue Agent for Navigation Support in Virtual Reality. Extended Abstracts on Conference on Human Factors in Computing Systems (CHI 2001), pp. 117–118. ACM, Seattle (2001)
43. Yacine, L., Tahar, B.: Supporting Collaboration in Agent-Based Collaborative Learning System (SACA). In: Information and Communication Technologies (ICTTA 2006), pp. 2843–2848 (2006)
44. Zhang, C., Xi, J., Yang, X.: An Architecture for Intelligent Collaborative Systems Based on Multi-agent. In: 12th International Conference on Computer Supported Cooperative Work in Design (CSCWD 2008), pp. 367–372 (2008)
45. Miller, M.S., Yin, J., Volz, R.A., Ioerger, T.R., Yen, J.: Training Teams with Collaborative Agents. In: Proceedings of the 5th International Conference on Intelligent Tutoring Systems, pp. 63–72. Springer, Heidelberg (2000)
46. Lesh, N., Rich, C., Sidner, C.L.: Using plan recognition in human-computer collaboration. In: Proceedings of the Seventh International Conference on User Modeling, pp. 23–32. Springer-Verlag New York, Inc., Banff (1999)
47. Miao, Y., Hoppe, U., Pinkwart, N.: Naughty Agents Can Be Helpful: Training Drivers to Handle DangerousSituations in Virtual Reality. In: Sixth International Conference on Advanced Learning Technologies (ICALT 2006), pp. 735–739 (2006)
48. Hedfi, R., Ito, T., Fujita, K.: Towards Collective Collaborative Design: An Implementation of Agent-Mediated Collaborative 3D Products Design System. In: 2010 International Symposium on Collaborative Technologies and Systems (CTS), pp. 314–321 (2010)
49. Fan, X., Yen, J.: Realistic cognitive load modeling for enhancing shared mental models in human-agent collaboration. In: Proceedings of the 6th International Joint Conference on Autonomous Agents and Multiagent Systems, pp. 1–8. ACM, Honolulu (2007)
50. Jacobson, M.J., Richards, D., Kapur, M., Taylor, C., Hu, T., Wong, W.-Y., Newstead, A.: Collaborative Virtual Worlds and Productive Failure: Design Research With Multi-Disciplinary Pedagogical, Technical and Graphics, and Learning Research Teams. In: Proceedings of the 9th International Conference of Computer Supported Collaborative Learning (CSCL 2011), vol. III, pp. 1126–1129 (2011)
51. Jaques, P., Andrade, A., Jung, J., Bordini, R., Vicari, R.: Using pedagogical agents to support collaborative distance learning. In: Proceedings of the Conference on Computer Support for Collaborative Learning: Foundations for a CSCL Community, pp. 546–547. International Society of the Learning Sciences, Boulder (2002)
52. Ben Ammar, M., Neji, M., Alimi, A.M., Gouardères, G.: The Affective Tutoring System. Expert Systems with Applications 37, 3013–3023 (2010)

53. Holst, S.: Evaluation of Collaborative Virtual Learning Environments: The State of the Art. In: Campus 2000: Lernen in neuen Organisationsformen. Proceedings of GMW 2000. Fachtagung der Gesellschaft für Medien in der Wissenschaft. Insbruck, pp. 199–212. Waxman, Munster (2000)
54. Zurita, G., Nussbaum, M.: A conceptual framework based on Activity Theory for mobile CSCL. British Journal of Educational Technology 38, 211–235 (2007)
55. Poole, M.S., Holmes, M.E.: Decision Development in Computer-Assisted Group Decision Making. Human Communication Research 22, 90–127 (1995)
56. Kennedy-Clark, S., Thompson, K., Richards, D.: Collaborative Problem Solving Processes in a Scenario-Based Multi-User Environment. In: The 9th International Computer Supported Collaborative Learning Conference, pp. 706–710 (2011)
57. Hanna, N., Richards, D., Jacobson, M.J.: Automatic Acquisition of User Models of Interaction to Evaluate the Usability of Virtual Environments. In: Richards, D., Kang, B.H. (eds.) PKAW 2012. LNCS, vol. 7457, pp. 43–57. Springer, Heidelberg (2012)
58. Warwas, S., Fischer, K., Klusch, M., Slusallek, P.: Bochica: A Model-Driven Framework for Engineering Multiagent Systems. In: Proceedings of 4th International Conference on Agents and Artificial Intelligence (ICAART) (2012)

Improving Agent Team Performance
through Helper Agents

Marie D. Manner and Maria Gini

Department of Computer Science and Engineering, University of Minnesota
{manner,gini}@cs.umn.edu

Abstract. In this paper, we consider the problem of environmental constraints on teams and examine how the constraints impact teamwork. We simulate a realistic problem for teams in the physical world by implementing a limit on the range of communication among agents. Using BlocksWorld for Teams from Delft University of Technology, we build teams of 3-4 agents with varying communication ranges and of different agent type (regular task-performer, communication-only or reconnaissance-only) to test team performance in the constrained environment. We analyze the results and discuss implications to the team mental model. We show that adding a helper agent to the team can reduce task completion time, but not for all types of agents and environments.

1 Introduction

Imagine a dangerous, rocky terrain, strewn with unexploded bombs or traps. On one side of the field lies a civilian camp in need of food and medical supplies; on the other, a force with aide supplies to help. The aide team sends out a small deployment of robots to investigate and deactivate the bombs, possibly mapping the terrain or positioning additional hardware in the field. The agents may fail due to hardware error, such as battery drain or slow travel speeds, or software malfunction. In such a case, robots are surely more expendable than humans. They could coordinate amongst themselves, split the tasks, and return when finished, without any real human supervision. For such a team to work well, it needs to communicate in the face of hardware failures, function after failures of other team members, and recognize when parts of the goal have been completed. We use this scenario to motivate our research with teams in imperfect environments.

Teamwork is a well-known force for efficiently solving tasks. A team is different than simply a group of people – good teams have coordinated action, mutual understanding, high commitment, role differentiation, and shared goals [24]. Team members must understand the technology used, share job or task models, and hold shared concepts of how the team interacts [15]. Sharing relevant information and task knowledge, be it techniques and methods of doing or resource locations, helps each team member perform his own task faster and predict what support his team members might need and give it to them faster or even before they ask.

To build a team that can work together smoothly and effectively, we should model the structure of team information and action process in what is known as a "team mental model," which includes communication, understanding, shared goals, technological

F. Dignum et al. (Eds.): CAVE 2012, LNAI 7764, pp. 89–105, 2013.

abilities, intentions and need prediction [3,11,14]. When we develop our team in Section 4, those are the basic six components we consider. A team mental model is the particular schema used by each agent in a team, whether the agent is human or robot; as an agent experiences the world, its personal mental model will become populated with data or beliefs. The better the team mental model, the more easily agents can understand each others' actions or interests, enabling the agents to interact, cooperate, and run more smoothly as a team. Team members share ideas or information about their task, and each member adjusts his or her task based on what other team members will do, have done, or can't do. One team member's equipment breaks and it asks for help; another team member picks up the slack. One team member does the first small task in the goal, and other team members do not need to verify the task is done – they go on to other jobs to finish the team goal faster.

Now imagine that you have the perfect team. Members communicate, help each other, and accomplish the goal in front of them quickly and efficiently. What happens when you take the perfect team and stick it in an imperfect environment? Radio equipment breaks down, agent hardware or software inexplicably fails, and communication fails due to natural causes or interferences. How does our team deal with such an imperfect, and more realistic, environment? Our goal is to show that we can make teams of agents with imperfect communication abilities perform as well as (or very close to) teams with perfect communication abilities.

The main contribution of this paper is an experimental study which demonstrates that adding various agent types to a team in a constrained environment can improve team coordination up to the point of performing at the level of a team without those constraints. The context for our work is small teams engaged in an exploration task. We show how the presence of a communicator or reconnaissance agent affects team performance for different communication ranges.

We review related work in Section 2 and give an overview of the problem along with some background in Section 3. We review our experimental approach and results in Section 4, future work in Section 5, and conclusions in Section 6.

2   Related Work

The work we present builds on a large body of knowledge, which spans from mental models of team members to team structures used in human teams.

We first consider how to approach the concept of a team. Paris et al. [16] reviewed research in understanding human team performance and found no less than eight representative theories on teamwork. Such approaches examine, among other things, work-related, interdependence, capability, lifecycle evolution or maturation, and task-oriented implications of the team member interactions or relationships.

Of special relevance to our work is the study in [19] which highlights the differences between conventional and distributed teams. Distributed teams have a more flexible organization, but have a harder time in obtaining situational awareness. The lack of visual cues reduces their performance, affects their communication needs, and makes tightly coupled tasks harder to complete [7].

Knowing that we might model teams in different ways depending on things like team lifecycle or capabilities, we next address the issue of how to form a team mental model, which includes deciding which components we might include. Empirical contributions on the mental model of geographically distributed human teams are given in [5]. Work by Jonker et al. [13] considers components of a mental model and how to measure the sharedness of the model across agents. The team mental model resides in the mind, and is contrasted by any physical model. An agent has, along with its mental model, a physical model, goals, a team, a mind, an extension of the mind, and the actual system of concern. The authors argue that shared mental models apply to human-agent teams, and that agent designers can use the idea of mental models to improve teamwork.

Because we do not expressly want to leave humans out of our teams, we must consider how adding people may impact goal performance in the form of changing levels of motivation or commitment. Johnson et al. [10] investigated how human participants on a team with agents thought they worked better as a team when the agents provided explanations about their actions, even when the agents performed the same tasks regardless of human input. This belief may contribute to trusting other team members more, and this established trust helps the team work together better. When we consider human-agent teams, we should consider the happiness of the human team members, which may impact the team's task – unhappy or unmotivated humans may become indifferent to their goal, do less useful work, or sabotage the task.

Now that we have considered how to build a team and construct the mental model, we examine the practicality of human-robot communication and review some work on communicating in real-world situations. Related work shows us that human-robot interaction is feasible, and that if communication includes all facts and intentions, the team performs more efficiently. Jonker et al. [12] sought to measure the level of "sharedness" of a mental model and found that when agents communicate world and intention information, agent teams perform tasks faster. Rekleitis [17] investigated multi-agent teams with limited, line-of-sight communication, but focused on coverage of an entire area with agents. Other work considers intermittent communication or real-world problems, but uses controllers, requires networks, forms subteams, or requires close proximity [23,9]. We would like our team to explore without requiring total coverage and without using a mastermind to direct branches of the team.

Previous research tells us we can safely model teamwork, training, and even use simulations for model development, so we now look at how we can make teams operate better. Sycara and Sukthankar [20] consider the main roles agents can have on human-robot teams: agents support individuals (as personal assistants), agents support teams (as in communication or coordination), and agents act as equal team members. A huge factor is making agents and humans understand each others' intentions and responses. Additionally, human interactions depend on teammate predictability, shared understanding, redirection and adaptation abilities. Making sure that agents have all this pertinent information depends on clear communication and trust in "normal" behavior on other agents' parts.

Previous research has also examined coordination in robots, such as "combined coordination cost measure" (CCC) which increases as group productivity decreases [18]. The CCC allows the authors to measure the cost of coordination, dynamically work to decrease it, and subsequently increase productivity. Work has also examined the role of non-verbal communication between humans and robots [2] and how it might impact teams. Other relevant research on teamwork, member roles, communication, and human- agent teams (of varying distributions and complexities) includes [8,21].

We have illustrated the multiple topics inherent in our team of humanitarian robots: modelling the internal mental model, establishing the team structure, trusting other agents, considering how past performance affects an agent, accounting for problems in the environment, and accomplishing tasks despite communication or other failures.

3   Problem Description

We begin with a high level description of why human teamwork provides valuable insights, move to teamwork in agents and simulators, and then discuss how a specific example of an environmental problem impacts team performance. Consider the real-world example of a wireless communication range, in which a wireless signal can cover a smaller distance than the map size where the agents operate. We model this by implementing a limit on the distance of agent communication, and seek to help the team with imperfect communication perform as fast as a team with perfect communication. We question whether this requires updates to the mental model.

First, we discuss mental models in teams in more detail. A shared mental model[6] explains how each agent reacts to his fellows and environment with communication, action, information gathering, or some other goal-oriented activity. Team coordination and task assignment is made clear through implicit and explicit communication among team members. Teams are devoted to a particular task, which has some life span, and that task dedication brings extra communication and process overhead (from creating, organizing, and disbanding the team) along with the gain in efficiency.

While research indicates shared mental models are important to understanding how a team can communicate and operate to help members, there are few formal measurements of exactly how "shared" these shared mental models are and how helpful the model is to the task at hand. Work by Jonker et al. [12] seeks to solve this by formalizing and implementing a measure of the sharedness of the team mental model and relating this sharing to team performance. Besides the accepted mental model components of technology, task, and team interaction abilities needed by teams [15], the authors introduce new component models of the overall mental model: domain, competence/capabilities, and organization. They also include a "relevance relation" which links components to impact on team performance; the relation depends on circumstances, team task, domain, and performance criteria.

Knowledge about the task, the tools used, and how to reason and interact with teammates is a great start, but Jonker et. al. reason that additional world and agent information will assist the team goal. More knowledge about the world domain at hand, as well as about other agents' intentions, will assist developing the team mental model and give us another way to measure team effectiveness. To demonstrate the formalizations, the authors used the BlocksWorld for Teams (BW4T) application, implementing three-agent teams with varying models but the same measure of task performance. The testbed is explained in detail in Section 4.1.

Our research approaches the mental model from the angle of world problems. We want to inform the mental model structure using analysis of common team problems. Thus, our research addresses the following questions:

- How do environmental factors, like limited communication range, impact the team?
- How can we improve team performance within these constraints?
- What is the role and the impact of having a shared team mental model?

To answer these questions, we limit our study to a specific environment and set of tasks, limit the range of communication for the agents, design and implement new helper agents, and analyze the results.

4 Experimental Work

Our experiments were conducted in the BlocksWorld for Teams (BW4T) environment, version 2.0, published by Delft University of Technology. The BW4T environment can be used in the GOAL IDE, using the Prolog language, or through the Repast environment, using the Java language. This work uses the Java language.

4.1 Testbed

BlocksWorld is a classic planning domain in artificial intelligence – an agent is tasked with stacking blocks into a vertical stack, moving only one block at a time, and without moving a block on the bottom of the stack. BlocksWorld for Teams (BW4T) from Delft University of Technology [4] adds complexity to the problem by expanding the environment from a table to a map with multiple rooms, limiting visibility of where the blocks are, and allowing the user to have any number of robot or human players on a map. The map contains rooms, hallways, zero or more blocks of various colors inside a room, and a number of agents.

The agent team's goal is to deliver a sequence of blocks in the assigned order. To accomplish the goal, agents have to explore the rooms, find the blocks, and deliver them in the required order to the DropZone. Boxes that are dropped outside rooms and outside the DropZone disappear.

BW4T allows up to one agent in a room at a time, any number of agents in a hallway, and any goal sequence of blocks for the agents to find and deposit in the DropZone on the south end of the map. Agents cannot see other agents, but they can hear other agents' messages, and they can see when a room is occupied.

Fig. 1 shows nine rooms, RoomC1 ... RoomC3, RoomB1 ... RoomB3, and RoomA1 ... RoomA3, as well as the DropZone. Underneath the DropZone, the user sees the required sequence of blocks to be delivered, as well as which blocks have been delivered. In this case the sequence is blue, white, red, cyan, orange, and magenta; the blue block has been delivered (indicated by a green triangle). Agent Smith has picked up a white block in RoomC3, indicated by the agent's change in color from black to white.

An agent cannot see blocks until it moves inside of the room, as shown in the cross section of the environment in Fig. 2. If we assume the agents have memory, they can remember in their own mental model what blocks they have seen and where. This will enable them to retrieve blocks of specific colors they have seen without having to repeat the exploration phase. Obviously when multiple agents run around looking for blocks and do not share all information they have about the blocks found, memory has

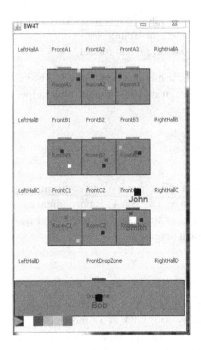

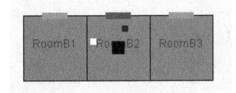

Fig. 1. BlocksWorld For Teams (BW4T)

Fig. 2. An agent (black) in a room; it can view only the objects (a white box and a blue box) in this room

a limited value. Another agent could go into a room and pick up a block, rendering the information stored in an agent's memory out of date.

Agents are able to communicate with each other through predefined questions, answers, and statements, such as "Who is in RoomB2?", "I am in RoomB2," "Someone, we need a Blue block," and "Ok." [4]. Humans can participate in the BW4T world by controlling one agent, which has the same environmental constraints as any other agent; the human-controlled agent will hear and say messages the same way.

Our agents use a control process similar to the agent decision model from [12], shown in Fig. 3. The main differences discernible at such a high level are that first, after failing to find a block color, our agents continue to search for that color, in case a different agent had been holding that block and has now deposited it in a room. The original decision cycle told an agent to stop searching for a block color after failing to find it, assume that the color was found, and update its goal sequence. Second, our agents save blocks in the room closest to the DropZone instead of any nearby room.

An agent starts without knowing where any blocks are, so it must choose a room to look in for the next color block. If it finds it, it can pick up the block and carry it to some location (either the DropZone to deposit, or a nearby room for storage). Then the agent decides again – is the task finished? Should it explore another room? Does it know where the next color is? When other agents communicate information, an agent's job is easier because it no longer needs to explore some rooms (if it just heard what

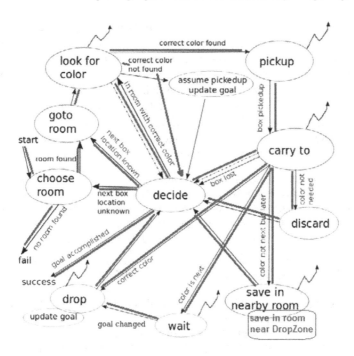

Fig. 3. Abstract decision cycle for regular agents in BW4T. [12] model is in black (thinner lines, ovals surrounding action points), with our model overlaid in red (thicker lines, rounded boxes for differing action points).

blocks are in a particular room) or because it no longer needs to get every block in the sequence (if another agent has just informed the team it will pick up the next block).

4.2 Approach

The first task was to implement a scalable team model that was robust to failures, remembered required task information, and could communicate without overburdening other agents with communication processing. The second task was to implement the limited communication range for the agent team, design and implement useful helper agents, and record the resulting task performance.

Our hypothesis was that with the addition of communication helpers, our team should be able to coordinate better and improve (decrease) the time taken to finish the task.

While developing the agents and the model, we kept the following key topics in mind: implication of interdependence of team members [16]; agent communication; beliefs, desires, intentions [6]; what factors affect task performance [20]; technology used; how to share job or task models; and how the team interacts [15]. While some items were easily known (such as the task model: get all colors in the color sequence into the DropZone), we are most interested in how the team members interact. We can choose which messages agents should say or listen to, and we need to account for repeated information and processing power required for message interpretation.

We must also choose what domain information (from the world or the agent's intentions) an agent should communicate and remember from others' messages.

To make the team as capable as possible, we built a team without leaders; the first agent to communicate an intention 'wins' that portion of the task. However, we also wanted to account for situations where agents fail, as real agents might in a physical environment due to unavoidable environmental accidents or agent hardware failure. Therefore, while agents will predict future needs in the form of which block to fetch next based on communicated intentions, the agents limit the lookahead task and at one point will revert to fetching the next block required in the sequence.

How the team interacts: Agents are responsible for
  – speaking and hearing messages from other agents;
  – remembering what they have been told (agents do not need to confirm or perform handshakes to verify information was received);
  – sending messages when they have changed the environment (i.e., picked up a block or dropped one off);
  – sending messages when they have detected something in the environment (i.e., the agent saw a block in a room);
  – making sure duplicate messages are handled (other agents may communicate the same information several times).

World domain information that agents should communicate: block colors in a room; room names; deposited blocks in the DropZone; which blocks are removed from a room.

Agent domain information that agents should communicate: intention to pick up a block; intention to go to a room; which room the agent is in; when an agent picks up a block and what color it is.

4.3   Experimental Setup

We started with a baseline of task completion times for a team of three agents. The team had perfect communication: all agents could hear all other agents regardless of location, all agents were regular-type, and all agents communicated all types of information. This baseline is given in all results graphs as a black short-dashed line with the label "Baseline – perfect."

Our goal was to develop a team of four (three regular agents, and one helper agent) with limited communication that performed as well as the team of three with perfect communication. Previous research [12] explored how communicating different types of information (none, world, intention, or all) assists agents in task completion, so all of our agents communicated or repeated both information types. World information includes facts like "There is a Blue block in RoomA1," while intention information includes goals like "I will get an Orange block from RoomB3."

We modified the BW4T environment by limiting communication range to a radius roughly the size of one, two, or three rooms. Agents can hear messages originating from within the circle of this radius centered on them.

Our experimental results surprised us. An exploratory agent helped only when the communication limitation was neither very small nor close to no communication limitations. very large.

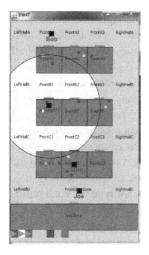 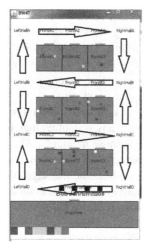 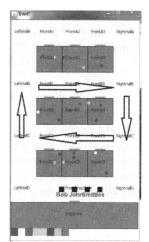

Fig. 4. Agent Smith can hear any message originating from within the circle around it. Currently, all other agents are out of range.

Fig. 5. The Figure 8 agent route. The agent repeats the route until the task is completed.

Fig. 6. The Circler agent route. The agent repeats the route until the task is completed.

We next considered facets of the environment that helper agents might take advantage of. Because the environment is small and may have widely distributed goals (blocks in far-away rooms), we first designed an agent that would walk the entire map. Next, we noted that even with a reduced radius, most agents would be able to hear communications coming from the center of the map. We designed two agents to take advantage of this – a traveling agent and a stationary agent. All three agents were designed to help spread communications from one end of the map to the other. Lastly, we created an agent for pure reconnaissance, which also repeated messages as an afterthought rather than as its primary purpose. The four additional agent types we created are:

- Figure 8: the agent follows a figure 8 pattern on the map (see Fig. 5).
- Circler: the agent makes a large circle in the middle of the map, around the B rooms (see Fig. 6).
- Scout: the agent explores all rooms, communicating information about the room contents but not attempting to deliver any blocks. The order of the visits is room C1 to C3, B3 to B1, A1 to A3, and random after that sequence is complete.
- Town-crier: the agent posts himself in one location (FrontB2) for the duration of the task.

In the first three cases wherein the agent moves, it repeats the last message heard when it reaches an intersection. This helps reduce interpretation and computation overload on other agents. For simplicity's sake, the communicator filters out "I am going to RoomX" messages. When agents start in the environment, they are so close that they are able to hear each other regardless of communication radius. We thus stop the communicator from repeating this message type, to prevent initial confusion (e.g., Agent A says it is going to RoomA1, the communicator repeats this message, and Agent A decides that since another agent has said it will go to the same room, Agent A will update its next destination and go to a different room). The town-crier repeats messages every one-half second. Each team consisted of three agents who attempted to deliver all blocks in the proper order, with one extra teammate of exactly one of the four new communicator agent types. In all cases, the regular agent types knew how many regular agent types existed in the environment, but not how many communicators; regular agents did not try to take advantage of the helper in any way other than to repeat messages often in the hope that other agents will receive those messages. The regular agent, in turn, cannot assume that other agents really received its messages, and may repeat the last message sent even if all agents were able to hear the message. We took measurements of task completion (using each block delivery as a marker) for each team type for each radius value: 10 (one room width), 20 (two rooms width) and 30 (three rooms width).

4.4   Results

As mentioned previously, each team was made of three "regular" agents (each tries to deliver blocks) and one "communicator" agent. We give a baseline (the solid black line in each results graph) for each communication distance. The baseline is built from a team of three agents who communicate with the specified radius, and a fourth teammate who wanders through hallways communicating and contributing nothing.

We tested against four different environments, to reduce the chance of biasing any particular agent type, as seen in Fig. 7. Two maps were heavily biased in block location – either the top two or bottom two rows in the map. In two maps blocks were randomly located without any empty rooms. Each agent team with different helper agents was tested in each map and the results averaged per team.

Results for team helper type for three different communication ranges on a time vs. block delivery graph are given in Figures 8, 9, and 10. Each graph contains two baselines: the average time taken by a team with perfect communication to do the task, and the average time taken by a team of three regular agents with the specified range.

Recall that our goal is to help limited communication teams perform faster; therefore, the closer a team's average block delivery times are to the perfect communication team's average, the better our team has done. In the graphs, we see a decrease in average block delivery time as increased team performance. We also consider any team that performs better than the limited range baseline team to be a success, even if it did not match the perfect team's performance.

In all cases, we expected at least a very small increase in performance for all agent communicator types. We expected communicator agents to repeat necessary and useful information (block locations) at some point during their travels (though they are also likely to repeat intentions or traveling-to messages), alerting nearby agents to room contents. Because agents always are searching for their next chosen block, the communicators will give regular agents new information as to which rooms contain which blocks, in cases where agents had not heard the original communication. Thus agents who were blindly searching will come to know which room they should go to next.

In teams of agents working with a reduced communication range of 10 units (about 1 room width), no agent helper improved results up to the perfect baseline; furthermore,

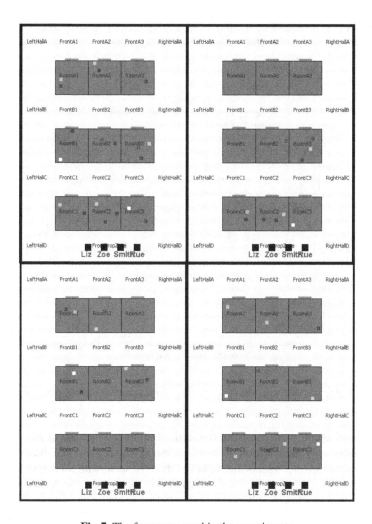

Fig. 7. The four maps used in the experiments

the added overhead actually hurt the teams. The team with the Circler agent was the only one to come close to the baseline of regular agents with a radius of 10. We did not expect agent teams with reduced communication range with helper agents to perform worse than teams with reduced communication range only, but additional agents may carry stale data throughout the environment and give fellow agents the wrong impression about the current world state. For example, a helper agent may repeat information about Room A1 and the blocks contained within, causing a regular agent to 'think' the room contains a block that is no longer in it. The regular agent may update its state information about the room every time it hears the agent, because the helper agents do not try to keep track of stale data. A helper agent with incorrect information doesn't try to verify the information; additionally, the designed helper agents do not interact with other agents to see which other agents have the most up to date information.

A way to improve and counteract this misinformation would be to keep a time stamp of information (in this environment, the most recently received message about a room's contents).

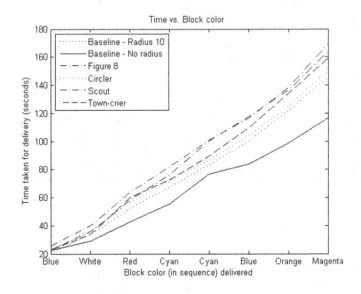

Fig. 8. Average delivery time for each block with a communication range of 10

For teams of agents working with a reduced communication range of 20 units (about 2 room widths), only the addition of the Scout agent actually assisted the team; teams with Figure 8 and Circler agents did no better than the team with no helper agent. The team with the Town-Crier agent did significantly worse, possibly because it communicates more often to team members than other helper agent types and therefore passes more stale information, or because it communicates too often and distracts team mates (adds overhead without adding value).

The useful agent, the Scout, halved the time difference in performance between the agent team without reduced communication and the team with reduced communication.

Finally, the teams of agents working with a reduced communication range of 30 units (about three room widths) were not assisted by any helper agents. An interesting note is that while neither agents with a very small communication range (of 10 units) or a larger communication range (30) units were helped, the team with the larger range was impacted more negatively than the other teams.

From these results we can draw a few conclusions: exploratory agents (with some added communication ability) were of more help than simple repeaters of information; adding helper agents can be either detrimental or beneficial; and that helper agents may be of more assistance when the team's communication range is neither very small nor very large compared to the environment. In either of those two cases, the added overhead may simply not be worth the time and expense of adding assistance.

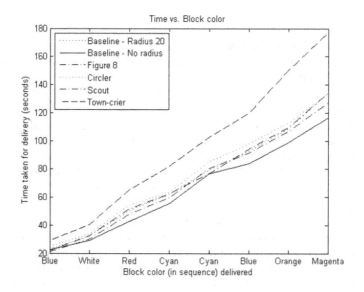

Fig. 9. Average delivery time for each block with a communication range of 20

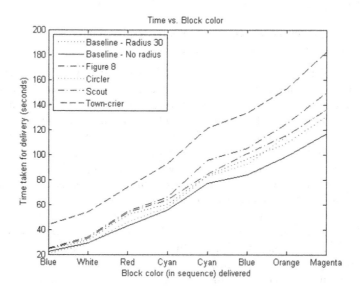

Fig. 10. Average delivery time for each block with a communication range of 30

5   Future Work

In future work, we will expand the environment size, investigate interesting performance results in which teams performed much differently than expected (better or worse), and model different sorts of communication failures.

Making the environment larger, say into a 4×3 or a 5×5 room set, will help indicate if the results found in the smaller room setup are scalable and if the same environment features can inform agent type. For example, if a 5×5 room set has hallways mixed into the rows of rooms (say between rooms A2 and A3, B3 and B4, C2 and C3, etc.), an agent similar to the Figure 8 agent will now take much longer to reach the original point. We will also investigate the simulator's potential in adding multiple-exit rooms, dead-ends, and other features that make navigation more difficult or complicated for agents.

We would like to explore and verify causes of poorer performance in teams for specific additional agent types, and we will also examine unexpectedly better performance by certain agents. For example, is our theory on what communication feature makes the Figure 8 agent decrease performance correct? We will also explore what might possibly make teams of three agents with extra agents perform better than our perfect baseline, as in the case of a Figure 8 agent team with a radius of 30. Along these lines, we will make several improvements or options on our existing communicator agents:

- repeat world information (facts) only, such as room contents, instead of agent intentions as well as facts
- repeat room contents as the communicator passes that room
- use a priority to decide which messages to repeat

We intend to explore how repeating different information types (world facts vs. agent intentions) affects the team. For example, we suspect that allowing communicator agents to repeat intention information may hinder some teams instead of improving performance. In some cases, it might save processing time and therefore speed-up agent task assessment if the communication does not repeat intentions. Additionally, implementing responses (such as "ok" to a received message) may drastically cut down on the number of messages sent and received. We will also develop at least one additional agent type – a Follower, who moves to the location from which its last message was heard. This should allow the Follower to trail other agents and serve as a sort of echo for previous communications.

We will implement message loss in the form of some k% (for example 10% or 20%) of messages getting completely dropped. This simulates environments with bad reception, like dropped cellular calls or environments with a lot of radio interference.

A more complex and interesting future direction we would like to take is a team vs. team challenge. Because the BW4T environment supports both humans and agents, as well as a server-client setup, we would like to include one to two humans with two to three agents in a race to find a sequence of blocks. This might be a programming challenge (each team is allowed to code their robotic agent) or a simple usage challenge, where the human team member must learn how best to interact with the robotic agent. Lastly, we are also interested in additional metrics, such as how much work duplication (efficiency loss) occurs because of lost communication.

These experiments suggest updates to the structure of the team mental model itself:

- Can we update the organizational model with environment features, such as expected or known flaws like communication limitations? For example, if the environment will limit range communication range, can we guess a nice ratio of communicator-type agents to regular-type agents to improve team performance? Some communicator agents might also serve double duty by exploring while they are on the way to pass messages.
- Are there cases where agents should swap roles? For example, due to a regular agent's failure, an agent switches from messenger to regular agent. We may want some minimum number of regular agents operable at all times, and convert communicator agents when a threshold is reached.
- Are there certain time periods during task execution when the number of a particular agent type should increase or decrease? For example, at the beginning of the task agents should have more communicator agents, but in the middle of the task execution, it might be more efficient to have all agents performing the task without extra communicators.
- Can we predict the most helpful agent types based on simulated environments? For example, are agents that focus on reconnaissance always more helpful than agents who repeat messages in environments where exploration is required?

Answering these questions can help us include environment features in team models, and improve completion rate of a task before we test in the real environment.

Another piece of future work is implementing and extending the concept of the Gatekeeper [1,22]. The Gatekeeper agent is responsible for collecting information about agents in the environment, deciding if some set of those agents can accomplish a task, and assigning those agents to a team to do that task.

The Gatekeeper can further be improved by using a Monitor agent to monitor the status of the team and the team members (for hardware failure or other unexpected occurrences). The Gatekeeper, having knowledge of the tasks and task requirements throughout the environment, may need to move around the environment and assign one or several teams in one or several different tasks.

The Monitor agent would be responsible for notifying the Gatekeeper agent of sudden team failures. Why have a Monitor agent at all? Say that the agents assigned to a team by the Gatekeeper have cheap, local communication abilities. If the Gatekeeper moves far enough away from the team, each team member may no longer reach the Gatekeeper with messages. This means the team either needs to be permanently equipped with more robust communication requirements (in case failures occur which require notifying the Gatekeeper), or the team needs to send a team member to the Gatekeeper to alert it of team failure (allowing the Gatekeeper to reassign task roles, etc). The first option causes more expense than necessary; after all, why equip 20 agents scattered throughout an environment with expensive, robust equipment that they might not need? The second option removes a team member for some unknown length of time from action in the environment – potentially negatively impacting the team. Assigning the Monitor agent to collect failure results and reporting them to the Gatekeeper allows us to equip fewer agents with expensive hardware as well as reducing the handshaking or other protocol overhead of discussion with the Gatekeeper agent.

Further work with agent helpers will integrate Gatekeeper and Monitor agents for heterogeneous agents and tasks within the BW4T environment. In this way, we seek to further improve agent teamwork with reduced agent capabilities and distributed decision making.

6   Conclusions

We motivated our research with an example of a humanitarian team of robots, and reviewed a range of research impacting the team. Using this example, we chose a manageable subproblem of limited communication range and implemented helper agents to adjust our team's performance. We generated results using the multi-agent system simulator BlocksWorld for Teams (BW4T), and showed that teams can be assisted by new agent types to accommodate for the environment problem. We showed that communicator agents can improve or decrease the rate of task completion when compared to a team without the extra communicator. Lastly, we proposed additional considerations for mental models, and gave future research for communication and teams with the BW4T simulator.

Acknowledgments. The authors would like to thank Birna van Riemsdijk for her much needed assistance in the BW4T setup, and her intrepid students and creators of BartJohnAgent.java, which contributed much knowledge and example environment function calls.

This material is based upon work supported in part by the National Science Foundation Graduate Research Fellowship under Grant No. NSF/IIS-1208413, NSF/IIS-1216287, and NSF/IIS-1216361. Any opinion, findings, and conclusions or recommendations expressed in this material are those of the authors(s) and do not necessarily reflect the views of the National Science Foundation.

References

1. Aldewereld, H., Dignum, V., Jonker, C., van Riemsdijk, M.: Agreeing on role adoption in open organisations. KI - Künstliche Intelligenz 26, 37–45 (2012), doi:10.1007/s13218-011-0152-5
2. Breazeal, C., Kidd, C.D., Thomaz, A.L., Hoffman, G., Berlin, M.: Effects of nonverbal communication on efficiency and robustness in human-robot teamwork. In: Proc. of IEEE/RSJ Int'l. Conf. on Intelligent Robots and Systems, pp. 708–713 (August 2005)
3. Dedre, G., Stevens, A.L. (eds.): Mental models. Lawrence Erlbaum Associates, London (1983)
4. Delft University of Technology. BW4T2 Specification (2011)
5. Alberto Espinosa, J., Kraut, R.E., Slaughter, S.A., Lerch, J.F., Herbsle, J.D., Mockus, A.: Shared mental models, familiarity and coordination: A multi-method study of distributed software teams. In: Int'l. Conf. in Information Systems, pp. 425–433 (2002)
6. Fan, X., Yen, J.: Modeling and simulating human teamwork behaviors using intelligent agents. Physics of Life Reviews, 173–201 (2004)
7. Fiore, S.M., Salas, E., Cuevas, H.M., Bowers, C.A.: Distributed coordination space: toward a theory of distributed team process and performance. Theoretical Issues in Ergonomics Science 4, 340–364 (2003)

8. Giampapa, J.A., Sycara, K.: Conversational Case-Based Planning for Agent Team Coordination. In: Aha, D.W., Watson, I. (eds.) ICCBR 2001. LNCS (LNAI), vol. 2080, pp. 189–203. Springer, Heidelberg (2001)
9. Howard, A., Parker, L.E., Sukhatme, G.S.: Experiments with a large heterogeneous mobile robot team: Exploration, mapping, deployment and detection. The International Journal of Robotics Research 25(5-6), 431–447 (2006)
10. Johnson, M., Bradshaw, J.M., Feltovich, P.J., Hoffman, R.R., Jonker, C., van Riemsdijk, B., Sierhuis, M.: Beyond cooperative robotics: The central role of interdependence in coactive design. IEEE Intelligent Systems 26(3), 81–88 (2011)
11. Johnson-Laird, P.N.: Mental models. Harvard University Press, Cambridge (1983)
12. Jonker, C.M., van de Riemsdijk, B., van de Kieft, I.C., Gini, M.: Towards measuring sharedness of team mental models by compositional means. In: Proc. 25th Int'l. Conf. on Industrial, Engineering and Other Applications of Applied Intelligent Systems (IEA/AIE), pp. 242–251 (2012)
13. Jonker, C.M., Birna van Riemsdijk, M., Vermeulen, B.: Shared mental models: A conceptual analysis. In: Workshop on Coordination, Organization, Institutions and Norms in Multi-Agent Systems at AAMAS, pp. 132–151 (2010)
14. Klimoski, R., Mohammed, S.: Team mental model: Construct or metaphor? Journal of Management 20, 403 (1994)
15. Mathieu, J.E., Heffner, T.S., Salas, E., Cannon-Bowers, J.A.: The influence of shared mental models on team process and performance. Journal of Applied Psychology 85(2), 273–283 (2000)
16. Paris, C.R., Salas, E., Cannon-Bowers, J.A.: Teamwork in multi-person systems: a review and analysis. Ergonomics 43(8), 1052–1075 (2000)
17. Rekleitis, I., Lee-Shue, V., New, A.P., Choset, H.: Limited communication, multi-robot team based coverage. In: Proc. Int'l. Conf. on Robotics and Automation, vol. 4, pp. 3462–3468 (2004)
18. Rosenfeld, A., Kaminka, G.A., Kraus, S., Shehory, O.: A study of mechanisms for improving robotic group performance. Artificial Intelligence 172(6–7), 633–655 (2008)
19. Salmon, P., Stanton, N., Houghton, R., Rafferty, L., Walker, G., Jenkins, D., Wells, L.: Developing guidelines for distributed teamwork: Review of literature and the HFI DTC's distributed teamwork studies. In: HFIDTC (2008)
20. Sycara, K., Sukthankar, G.: Literature review of teamwork models. Technical Report CMU-RI-TR-06-50, Robotics Institute, Carnegie Mellon University (November 2006)
21. Tambe, M.: Towards flexible teamwork. Journal of Artificial Intelligence Research, 83–124 (1997)
22. van Riemsdijk, M.B., Dignum, V., Jonker, C.M., Aldewereld, H.: Programming role enactment through reflection. In: 2011 IEEE/WIC/ACM International Conference on Web Intelligence and Intelligent Agent Technology (WI-IAT), vol. 2, pp. 133–140 (August 2011)
23. Wagner, A., Arkin, R.: Multi-robot communication-sensitive reconnaissance. In: Proc. Int'l Conf. on Robotics and Automation, April26-May1, vol. 5, pp. 4674–4681 (2004)
24. West, M.A., Tjosvold, D., Smith, K.G.: International Handbook of Organizational Teamwork and Cooperative Working. Wiley (2003)

Visualisation on Demand
for Agent-Based Simulation

Athanasia Louloudi and Franziska Klügl

Modelling and Simulation Research Center
Örebro University, Sweden
{athanasia.louloudi,franziska.klugl}@oru.se

Abstract. Agent-based simulation can be a useful tool when analysing complex systems such as real world scenarios. In multi-agent models when no quantitative data are available we have to search for new solutions in order to verify that the simulated model is appropriate with respect to the real one. Typical solutions approach the problem of missing data by considering contributions of human experts. In our work, we enhance the transparency of the simulation via a detailed visualisation in order to enable an immersive evaluation of the simulated model. We initially identify several conceptual and technical problems regarding the combination of a multi-agent simulation system with a game engine. We then propose a framework which implements a solution for generic processing and communication of information while maintaining consistency between the two systems. The end result automates several processes in a context independent manner and minimises the overall modeller's effort.

Keywords: Agent-based Simulation, Visualisation tools, Validation.

1 Introduction

Agent-based simulation is increasingly used as a tool for analysing complex systems, given that data collection from the real-world is expensive in terms of time, money or when the experimental conditions are harmful to humans. Models representing real-world systems are formulated and evaluated by how well they capture the behaviour of the actual system. This aspect is based on both quantitative and qualitative comparison of the model's dynamics.

Often, lack of data makes it difficult to ground and validate the model's output, thus leading the research towards the investigation of new validation methodologies. One such methodology involves human experts that evaluate the plausibility of the simulation (i.e., face validation [1]), especially when objective validation techniques are feasible. This validation technique could benefit from a detailed visualisation.

However, in multi-agent simulation visualisation is often restricted to simplistic 2D representations which cannot always capture and convey enough information regarding the model's dynamics. Hence, more complex environments, such as 3D virtual worlds, could improve the transparency and understandability of

F. Dignum et al. (Eds.): CAVE 2012, LNAI 7764, pp. 106–119, 2013.

the running simulation. Virtual Reality (VR) systems are well known for achieving a credible degree of visual truth and such characteristic is essential when performing face validation.

Our vision is to create a new validation technique which we call *Immersive Face Validation*, by developing a generic component for interfacing an agent-based simulation environment, to a VR system which is able to control visualisation in an immersive virtual environment, such as CAVE (Cave Automatic Virtual Environment) [2]. In a setup like that, a human immersed in the simulated environment, can observe the simulation's dynamics by altering his/her perspective from the often limited bird's eye view relative to the agent's point of view. This component will be used only when necessary and can be disabled when deploying or testing a new simulation run (i.e., visualisation on demand). This of course implies that the modeller should be able to set up a VR visualisation, in addition to the intended simulation, something which is not trivial. The design and construction of the 3D virtual world is a time consuming job that may hinder the actual objective of the modeller which is to develop a valid simulation.

In this paper we focus on finding an efficient way to interconnect an agent-based simulation platform, with a powerful visualisation engine that enables real-time interaction. The combination of such technologies mentioned above clearly adds new features when conveying the model's dynamics. However such a coupling involves several conceptual and technical challenges, mainly triggered by the separation of concerns between the two systems. Our contribution lies on the systematic examination of the related issues while we describe and analyse an actual solution to these problems.

In the remainder of this paper we begin by giving a better insight into the overall concept of connecting an agent-based simulation platform to virtual worlds (§ 2). In § 3 we introduce and briefly evaluate our initial work towards the realisation of the intended system. Then we present a new framework architecture in § 4 where we describe the *ConnectionComponent*. In § 5 a discussion regarding the related approaches follows, while we summarise our findings and the future outlook in § 6.

2   Combining Multiagent Simulation with 3D Virtual World

The idea of combining agent-based technology with virtual reality environments has been explored in several application areas such as virtual agents [3,4], or training and educational applications [5]. Central point of discussion in all these cases is how to efficiently combine the technologies mentioned above which have such a diverse focus. Agent-based simulation aims to represent the relevant structural and behavioural aspects of the intended system in the simplest yet valid way. Contrarily, the focus of the VR system is on the realism of the 3D object models and their animations. This implies a great amount of detail equivalent to what a human observer would expect to see in the real world. Consider for example, those two representations i.e., a large scale pedestrian simulation [6] and a virtual world crowd simulation [7], we can identify different requirements and separate concerns regarding the two systems. It is clear that the simulation system lies on high-level abstract domain-specific agent properties while the VR system uses low-level information (i.e., position and animation information) so as to represent the environment and the object-models. Therefore we choose to couple the two systems instead of integrating them in one larger platform.

Since our previous work [8], we consider that both the simulation engine and the VR visualisation system represent the same multi-agent model, however on different levels of temporal and representational granularities. Due to these granularities the interconnection of the two systems is not an easy task, as consistency has to be maintained between the two platforms. From now on we call the simulation system, *Simulator* and the VR visualisation system, *Visualisation System* respectively.

The *Simulator* has a more qualified representation with refined object structures which are to be fed to the *Visualisation System* with the 3D object models, displaying sophisticated animations. In addition, the *Simulator* is driving the dynamics while managing the actual model that is tested. The *Simulator* drives the dynamics and manages the actual model in question while the *Visualisation System* always follows the *Simulator*. Nevertheless both components represent the same system, hence both representations have to be aligned. This means that a correspondence of representations has to be guaranteed, otherwise the *Immersive Face Validation* that is based on the VR visualisation is useless as it does not display the actual simulation model. Despite the asynchronous performance, the two platforms should explicitly communicate information related to any given state of the simulated multi-agent situation. The question then becomes, which data is necessary and sufficient for the *Visualisation System* regarding the current state and behaviour of the *Simulator*.

2.1   Information Mapping

The first challenge is to define the type of information that is exchanged between the two systems, so that the *Visualisation System* can efficiently create a realistic scene. Regardless of the simulation model, there exists some common information we need to know about the agents and their activities, their state, their positioning in the environment and any possible communication with other agents. Similarly information concerning the environment should be also communicated. We need to translate this information, so as to meet the requirements of the *Visualisation System*.

Mapping Agents to Object Models. Starting from a given multi-agent simulation model, every agent or passive entity in the *Simulator* has to be associated with a detailed 3D character in the *Visualisation System*. A lot of information about the object model describe the simulated entity (e.g., shape, size and scale). During the execution of the behaviour, all measurements / information should correspond to each other so as to avoid discrepancies between the two systems. For instance, if in the *Simulator* an agent is avoiding an obstacle that is represented by a 2D shape, the bounding box of the 3D object model should be of equivalent size in order to maintain the effects of the collision avoidance behaviour.

Mapping Agent Behaviour to Animations. Displaying an agent's behaviour in a credible way is more than connecting an action to an animation. There are several issues related to the way a character in the *Visualisation System* can adapt it's behaviour / animation to changes in runtime. If the agent's internal state changes during the simulation, the animations and geometries have to follow. For example, assume that we want to visualise the pregnancy period of a female agent. Morphing operators can be used in order to enable changes in the shape and movement of the object model. On the other hand, not all activities can be visualised. For instance the *Simulator* may hold inappropriate information for visualisation or information that is not visible at all (e.g., level of hunger or fatigue). Finally, every time an animation or a set of animations is triggered, the *Visualisation System* should display a smooth transition.

Environmental Dynamics. A multi-agent simulation may also contain dynamics which are triggered by special environmental entities with global effects. These can be for instance, climate dynamics or an evacuation signal. Such dynamics cannot be assigned to a single agent. They are part of the model, influencing the agents' behaviour and therefore they should be included in the VR visualisation as the displayed behaviour reacts on that (e.g., smoke in a case of fire or change of weather conditions).

Interaction Between the Agents. Apart from the individual dynamics of the characters, their interactions have to be visualised as well. Visualisation must be coordinated and similarly animations cannot be independently displayed when we have interacting agents while group-level information should be also considered.

Then, on the simulation side, all aspects of an agent that might affect the other agents' behaviour are accessible to the modeller, whereas in the virtual world only what is within the observer's field of view is supposed to be visualised. In this case, concepts connected to level of detail (LOD) [9] are used to promote a more efficient rendering.

2.2 Temporal Granularities and Consistency

In this section we are presenting synchronisation; the second challenge, that is mere technical and is related to the temporal granularities of the two systems.

Synchronisation. The synchronisation issue is a central prerequisite for maintaining consistency between the aligned representations. It is important to assure, that regardless the way the systems perform, at a given time t (simulation or virtual time), both platforms will display or simulate matching situations. The *Simulator* and *Visualisation System* operate in different time scales. The *Visualisation System* works in real-time whereas the *Simulator's* time depends on the type of simulation and it can be discrete (time-based) or event-based. In every simulation the update is usually the fastest possible and varies according to the simulation models and also depends on the number of agents. Thus, in many applications, simulated time is intentionally different from real time (i.e., faster or slower than real-time).

We assume asynchronous operation modes between the two systems, hence it is possible for a delay to occur in the updates. Especially in the case that the *Simulator* is slower than real-time and not capable to provide the *Visualisation System* with data on time. The *Visualisation System* has to maintain the required realism and therefore it becomes necessary to compensate this lack of information as well as predict the flow of simulation when real simulation data are not provided.

2.3   VR System Configuration

In order for the *Visualisation System* to render the scene, further configuration is necessary in addition to the simulated situation. Each scenario / scene, may have special properties such as specific cameras and lighting, which have to be treated accordingly. The positioning of the cameras is important because they control the observer's perspective and in our case may affect the process of face validation.

3   Proof of Concept

In the previous section we have identified some of the challenges involved, when connecting multi-agent simulation to VR visualisation. Before we move further into the framework design and implementation we materialised a proof of concept system which we briefly describe in this section. In order to verify and potentially overcome some of the technical and conceptual issues, we focused on making a simple connection between the two systems. Therefore initially we created a prototype that combines SeSAm[1]; a general modelling and simulation platform with the Horde3D[2] GameEngine [10]. The high-level behaviour of the agent is programmed using activity graphs. This structure facilitates the connection to combination of animations as the behaviour program is already structured. SeSAm has the overall control of the model's behaviour for the transfer of information to the game engine. This is based on socket communication which uses a string-based buffered protocol which contains information regarding each relevant entity's position, orientation and activity on every update. Tags are already connected to animations. In addition, information about states or other events (e.g.,generation or removal of agents from the overall scene), is also captured by the simulation platform.

We developed a process in SeSAm that generates a complete description of the visualisation scene out of the simulated situation in XML format. In the generated XML file tokens replace object models, which implies that pointers to the object models have to be inserted manually.

---

[1] SeSAm: http://www.simsesam.de
[2] Horde3D GameEngine: http://hcm-lab.de/projects/GameEngine

We performed several experiments in different application scenarios, such as a 2D evacuation scenario and a 3D boids example, through which we identified several drawbacks. Some of those include that strings cannot maintain any semantic information and that the parser had to be modified according to the given model. Furthermore, we had to manually set the path of to the 3D object models and animations while more complex animations required specific implementation of their behaviour in the game engine. To overcome these issues, we had to revise this initial setup as well as develop novel ideas for a framework architecture that can handle the problems stated above.

4 Framework Design

In this section we present the proposed framework intending to bridge the multi-agent simulation platform with the a VR visualisation system. In order to efficiently connect the two systems, we consider the creation of a middle layer (*ConnectionComponent*) that essentially isolates the logic of the *Simulator* from the specificity of the *Visualisation System*. The framework includes two main processes; the *runtime process* (see Fig. 1) and the *setup process*. The runtime process describes the information flow and the functionality of the *ConnectionComponent* during the simulation, whereas the setup process is responsible for the configuration of the VR visualisation by setting up requests for rendering events.

4.1 Runtime Process and the ConnectionComponent

During the simulation run, agents execute activities which need to be visualised in the virtual environment using combinations of animations or other operators. In each time step, explicit information about the current situation is aggregated and sent to the *ConnectionComponent* for further processing and then it is stored in a buffer. The rendering engine, retrieves information from the buffer while forms and executes in the game engine the corresponding instantiations.

Then we need to describe two essential functionalities in the *ConnectionComponent*. Initially, all incoming simulation data is translated to specific visualisation data, which then form the (event-based) rendering instructions. This data translation involves both mapping of simulation entities to 3D object models and association of their activities to animations. The *ConnectionComponent* is then responsible for maintaining consistency between the two systems. This is handled mainly via a buffered connection to the *Visualisation System*. A representation of the simulation data is stored in memory until the game engine requests a rendering event.

SimulationStatePacket. The *ConnectionComponent* is based on an abstract meta model that serves as a data structure for buffering the incoming data as depicted in Fig. 2. During the simulation run, `SimulationState` holds information regarding time, the environment and the entities in it, as well as the human in the CAVE (`SimulationAvatar`).

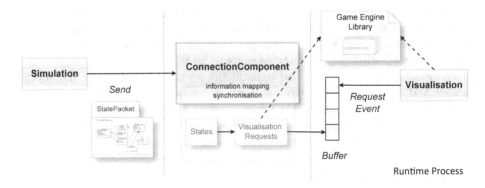

Fig. 1. Graphical illustration of the framework's components and their relations. Information flows from the Simulation which is transformed to a StatePacket and reaches the ConnectionComponent. The ConnectionComponent transforms the states into visualisation requests and stores them into the buffer. Finally the Visualisation processes the requests from the buffer.

With entities, we refer to both agents and passive entities in the simulation world (e.g., agents, resources or obstacles). All entities in the `ObjectList` are `PhysicalObjects`, which means that they have a unique name and translational information. To facilitate mapping to the visualisation data and eventually the generation of the initial visualisation scene (scene graph), we make a distinction behind agents and passive entities in this meta-model, depending on whether an entity possesses a *state* or not. In this context, *state* is associated to any activity or internal state of the agent which triggers animations in the *Visualisation System*. For instance, the activity "walk" can be connected to the particular animation of a human agent but similarly a door that is passive entity should "open" when an agent opens it. In practice this means that the door holds some internal states "open / closed" and it is classified as `Agent` in the `PhysicalObject` list. This is because we need to display animations, despite that in the *Simulator*, door might be represented as a passive resource. In case the environment has an activity, changes are triggered in the virtual scene too (e.g., daytime vs night-time, weather conditions or signal activation etc.).

Database System. In order to provide a better description of the transferred information, we created a relational model as depicted in Fig. 3. This relational model provides a declarative method which specifies all the incoming simulation information as well as their mappings to visualisation data. In turn, the visualisation data contain the object models, animations and other operators as well as describe how activities of the simulated agents correspond to combinations of animations.

Even though Fig. 2 appears similar to Fig. 3, there exist important differences especially in the way that activities are translated into *actions*, in the *Visualisation System*. Actions are different from activities in the simulation system. In the ideal case, we have 1-1 correspondence of information (e.g., activity:walk =

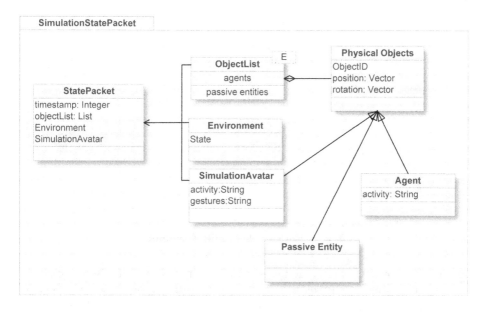

Fig. 2. UML diagram of the simulation data structure

action: walk → <walk.anim>), however this is not always the case. An agent eventually needs more than a single animation for a given activity. For example, the activity "sit" corresponds to multiple actions in the *Visualisation System* such as "walk" then "turm" and finally "sit". In addition, an action may also have a referent. This referent can be any 3D object model in the virtual world where we have to define the interaction of the referent (e.g. how an agent can pick up different objects). Finally, a simulation activity may trigger, not only animations but other visual effects such as morphing operators, sound, lighting condition etc. When augmenting all this information in the database, we still have to instantiate the *visualisation requests* which later on form the basic elements of visualisation events.

From States to Visualisation Requests. The *visualisation request* is a collection of specific information which is used by the *Visualisation System* in order to render events. The modeller has to include pointers to the object models, animations and their attributes. For example, a *GoToPosition* request should contain all the related information for the "walk" and "run" actions of an agent (e.g., speed, space, animation type etc.).

Any *visualisation request* is temporally associated with a simulated situation at time t_{Sim}. Due to the asynchronous nature of operation between the two systems, all *visualisation requests* are stored into a buffer represented by a queue. The *Visualisation System* (which is temporally independent from the *Simulator*) retrieves and processes the first available request in the queue, therefore the implementation of the buffer is based on a first-in first-out (FIFO) queue. However

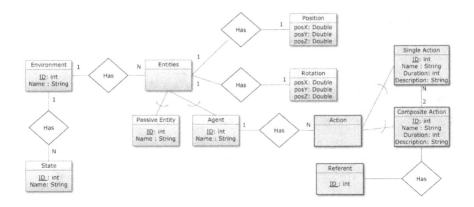

Fig. 3. Entity Relationship Diagram

not all *visualisation requests* are necessarily rendered. The *Visualisation System* imposes constrains on the selection of the *visualisation requests* so as to render only the relevant information. Only the visible events as well as events matching specific criteria are rendered (e.g., when the central agent is placed in a room, isolated, there is no need to render what is happening in another room of the same building etc.).

The *visualisation requests* depend on the availability of the specific 3D object model with the relevant animations or geometry capable of supporting the visual expression of the intended dynamics. Therefore a library of models is used to formulate events, however it depends on the simulation model whether the library is sufficiently rich. In the later case, the modeller might has to build or somehow acquire 3D object models including their appropriate animations before using them in the relevant context.

We summarise the process of the *ConnectionComponent* in the following algorithm:

Algorithm 1. Information Mapping from States to Visualisation Requests

---

1. Input: new $statePacket(t_{sim})$
2. parse $statePacket(t)$
3. calculate $deltas(statePacket(t_{sim}), statePacket(t_{sim} - 1))$
4.   **if** $deltas = \{\}$ **then**
         return
     else
         create *visRequest* from *deltas*
         augment *visRequest* with information from visualisation-map-DB
         store *visRequest* to buffer for rendering at t_{sim}
     end if

4.2 Setup Process

The *ConnectionComponent* automates several processes, thus minimises the modeller's effort in only defining the relevant 3D object models and animations. More specifically, once the simulation model is complete, the modeller can enable the VR visualisation tool by using the given interface and 3D object models. He/she should also define the translation from activities to actions as discussed previously, to provide a link to the relevant set of animations and other operators, as well as to parametrise the final visualisation result (e.g., setup of animation duration, speed, stage, timeoffset and weight).

Finally, since there is a threaded connection between the two systems, the overall initial state is provided automatically to the *Visualisation System*. This initial state contains information regarding the exact number of entities, their spatial distribution and their assigned object models, besides the information about the size of the world. Cameras and lights are configured automatically following some generic heuristics regarding the size of the virtual environment.

5 Related Work

3D multi-agent models are popular since the first movies of the animated evolving creatures of Karl Sims [11]. Later developments in microscopic pedestrian simulation produced an increasing need to provide detailed spatial representations in physically simulated 3D worlds, as a method to increase transparency and visibility on generic multi-agent simulation platforms such as Repast[3] or MASON[4] which embedded Java3D into their simulation platforms. Our approach here is different, in that we aim at hiding the increased complexity from the modeller.

In the context of representation, the breve[5] platform was recently extended with the simple programming language "steve" which is comparable to the language used in NetLogo for supporting inexperienced programmers when using the 3D simulation platform. However, besides not really being agent-based, a clear separation between visualisation and model representation seems to be difficult. There is a number of other agent-based simulation platforms specialised for 3D modelling yet breve seems to be the most well known among the free open source platforms. MASSIVE[6] visualisation and agent simulation platform is clearly the leading commercial simulator, famous for the highly impressive capabilities presented in a number of blockbusters.

Regarding the combination of virtual worlds and simulation, we meet several prominent approaches in crowd simulation [7,12]. Hereby it is important to mention that our main consideration is to provide a solution that does not relate to any specific application domain, but rather maintains a generic character. Several agent architectures have been used together with graphic or game engines as

---

[3] Repast: http://repast.sourceforge.net/
[4] MASON: http://cs.gmu.edu/eclab/projects/mason/
[5] Breve: www.spiderland.org/
[6] MASSIVE: www.massivesoftware.com

means for combining the reasoning capabilities with 3D representation and visualisation and rich environments [13,14]. In our case however, the game engine is responsible only for visualising only the dynamics of the simulated situation.

Middleware solutions such as Pogamut [15], Gamebot [16] or CIGA [17] address several inherent conceptual and technical challenges. From a technical point of view, our proposed framework has similarities with the one of Oijen et al. [17], which considers coupling of the two systems and not their embodiment. Nevertheless their vision is to use BDI agents in 3D game engines, for building intelligent behaviour. Here exactly lies the main difference to our approach. We consider this combined system as a helpful tool to evaluate the model's dynamics. Similarly, Vizzari et al. [18] present a framework for visualising crowd simulations, based on interacting situation agents. However, they do not handle the synchronisation issue but rather reduce the simulation's speed so as to visualise properly the simulation's dynamics while maintaining consistency.

Consistency is quite important for our work. Therefore, a relation can also be found with the area of distributed interactive systems, such as multiplayer network games, where consistency needs to be maintained in order to present the same situation to different users. Several techniques have been developed for avoiding or dealing with inconsistencies coming from latency and jitter [19,20]. In our case, we find the major problems to be the different resolutions as well as the synchronisation between the two heterogeneous representations of the same system. Nevertheless we should mention that the interpolation of agent's behaviour has similarities with the consistency problem of distributed interactive systems. Clearly we will have a closer look into techniques of dead reckoning, etc.

Furthermore, the Model View Controller (MVC) paradigm [21] is related to some degree to our work. MVC design patterns have been widely used in Web applications which promote the separation of visual presentation from logic. However our methodology has a core difference. The simulation platform is already separated from the visualisation. Korhauser et al. [22], give design guidelines for multi-agent simulation visualisations, adapting general design principles and techniques (e.g., shapes / colours of the agents or the use of entity groups for giving advice) when visualising the dynamics of a simulation. Their focus is on 2D models implemented in Netlogo[7]. Similarly our research is related to interfaces for multi-agent systems. Avouris [23] classify different multi-agent system architectures for identifying specific challenging when designing interfaces to multi-agent simulations. In this work only cases limited to top-down perspective (bird's eye view) are considered in contrast to our immersive visualisation approach.

6   Discussion and Future Work

In this contribution we discussed the problem of interfacing on-demand an agent-based simulation with a virtual reality system. We proposed a generic framework that facilitates the bridging of the two systems in order to enable an immersive evaluation of the simulated model by a human expert.

---

[7] Netlogo: http://ccl.northwestern.edu/netlogo/

In the proposed framework, we setup a high level connection between the two systems, offering generic processing of information while we described the formation of events in the *Visualisation System*. The shared meta model allows the scene graph to be automatically generated from the *Simulator*, reducing significantly the modeller's effort. Most importantly the overall solution is not application specific as the modeller has the flexibility to visualise different simulation models. By using a data buffer, we decouple the information stream from the *Simulator* to the *Visualisation System* while offering a solution to the synchronisation issue.

While this framework tackles certain aspects of the information mapping issue between the simulation and the visualisation, it only deals with a part of the problem. Specifically, we do not yet consider a bidirectional connection which could allow the immersed human to be accounted for in the representation. The overall complexity rises significantly as the behaviour of the human would affect the behaviour of the simulated agents. In this bidirectional connection, both the action and their results of the interaction of the human have to be relayed back to the simulation. Then, this presupposes a translation of action to activities in the *Simulator*. We need to make a distinction between the actions performed by the populated agents in the virtual world and the actions triggered by the avatar (i.e., human in the CAVE). Therefore we need to consider how the human influences the input of the simulation when defining an action. This issue is not investigated yet and remains an important task of our future work.

An additional challenge lies on the different time scales of the two systems. Until now we have only considered the case in which the *Simulator* is faster than the *Visualisation System*. There exists also the opposite situation where the *Visualisation System* needs data faster than what the *Simulator* can provide. Realism cannot be achieved as eventual stops will hinder the underlying objective of our endeavour. The system should be able to estimate a movement based on previous values or even extrapolate behaviour. However, the relation between activities and actions, allow us to enable predictions by using interpolation or extrapolation. This predictive behaviour of the system can be expressed via algorithms which are based on dead reckoning [24]. Still the accuracy of the predictions is critical and the agents have to compensate for the eventual error.

An alternative approach could be a more intelligent *ConnectionComponent* which is able to analyse and actively align the two representations based on the actions that the human in the CAVE triggers. This alignment should come as a result of the calculation of deltas between the current and the subsequent situation. If there is enough knowledge regarding the effects of actions and there is not large time difference between the *Simulator* and the *Visualisation System*, the effects of the human interaction might be isolated and the *Simulator* might be just forced to restart from a time significantly later than the current visualisation time.

Acknowledgements. This research work is part of the "Human-in-the-Loop Modeling and Simulation" project funded by VINNOVA. We also thank Augsburg University for supporting and providing us with their Horde3D GameEngine.

References

1. Klügl, F.: A validation methodology for agentbased simulations. In: Wainwright, R.L., Haddad, H. (eds.) Proceedings of the 2008 ACM Symposium on Applied Computing, pp. 39–43. ACM (2008)
2. Lee, H., Tateyama, Y., Ogi, T.: Realistic visual environment for immersive projection display system. In: Proceedings of the 16th Int. Conference on Virtual Systems and Multimedia (VSMM 2010), pp. 128–132 (2010)
3. Mac Namee, B.: Agent based modeling in computer graphics and games. In: Meyers, R.A. (ed.) Encyclopedia of Complexity and Systems Science. Springer (2009)
4. Dignum, F., Westra, J., van Doesburg, W.A., Harbers, M.: Games and agents: Designing intelligent gameplay. International Journal of Computer Games Technology 2009(837095) (2009)
5. Silverman, B., Bharathy, G., Johns, M., Eidelson, R., Smith, T., Nye, B.: Sociocultural games for training and analysis. IEEE Transactions on Systems, Man and Cybernetics, Part A: Systems and Humans 37(6), 1113–1130 (2007)
6. Klügl, F., Rindsfüser, G.: Large-Scale Agent-Based Pedestrian Simulation. In: Petta, P., Müller, J.P., Klusch, M., Georgeff, M. (eds.) MATES 2007. LNCS (LNAI), vol. 4687, pp. 145–156. Springer, Heidelberg (2007)
7. Pelechano, N., Allbeck, J., Badler, N.I.: Virtual Crowds: Methods, Simulation, and Control. Morgan and Claypool Publishers (2008)
8. Louloudi, A., Klügl, F.: Visualizing Agent-based Simulation Dynamics in a CAVE - Issues and Architectures. In: Proceedings of the Federated Conference on Computer Science and Information Systems (FedCSIS), pp. 651–658 (2011)
9. Wißner, M., Kistler, F., André, E.: Level of Detail AI for Virtual Characters in Games and Simulation. In: Boulic, R., Chrysanthou, Y., Komura, T. (eds.) MIG 2010. LNCS, vol. 6459, pp. 206–217. Springer, Heidelberg (2010)
10. Louloudi, A., Klügl, F.: A new framework for coupling agent-based simulation and immersive visualisation. In: Proceedings of the 26th European Conference on Modelling and Simulation (ECMS) (2012)
11. Sims, K.: Evolving 3d morphology and behavior by competition. In: Brooks, R.A., Maes, P. (eds.) Artificial Life IV Proceedings, pp. 28–39 (1994)
12. Thalmann, D., Musse, S.R.: Crowd Simulation. Springer (2007)
13. Norling, E.: Capturing the quake player: using a BDI agent to model human behaviour. In: Proccedings of the 2nd Int.Conference of Autonomous Agents and Multiagent Systems (AAMAS 2003), pp. 1080–1081. ACM, New York (2003)
14. van Lent, M., Laird, J., Buckman, J., Hartford, J., Houchard, S., Steinkraus, K., Tedrake, R.: Intelligent agents in computer games. In: Proceedings of the Nat. Conference on Artificial Intelligence, Orlando, FL, pp. 929–930 (July 1999)
15. Gemrot, J., Kadlec, R., Bída, M., Burkert, O., Píbil, R., Havlíček, J., Zemčák, L., Šimlovič, J., Vansa, R., Štolba, M., Plch, T., Brom, C.: Pogamut 3 Can Assist Developers in Building AI (Not Only) for Their Videogame Agents. In: Dignum, F., Bradshaw, J., Silverman, B., van Doesburg, W. (eds.) Agents for Games and Simulations. LNCS, vol. 5920, pp. 1–15. Springer, Heidelberg (2009)
16. Adobbati, R., Marshall, A.N., Scholer, A., Tejada, S.: Gamebots: A 3d virtual world test-bed for multi-agent research. In: Proceedings of the Second International Workshop on Infrastructure for Agents, MAS, and Scalable MAS (2001)
17. Oijen, J.V., Vanhee, L., Dignum, F.: CIGA: A middleware for intelligent agents in virtual environments. In: Proceedings of the 3rd International Workshop on Agents for Education, Games and Simulations, AAMAS 2011, Taipei, Taiwan (2011)

18. Vizzari, G., Pizzi, G., da Silva, F.S.C.: A framework for execution and 3d visualization of situated cellular agent based crowd simulations. In: SAC, pp. 18–22 (2008)
19. Diot, C., Gautier, L.: A distributed architecture for multiplayer interactive applications on the internet. IEEE Network 13, 6–15 (1999)
20. Delaney, D., Ward, T., McLoone, S.: On consistency and network latency in distributed interactive applications: a survey–part i. Teleoperators and Virtual Environments 15, 218–234 (2006)
21. Doray, A.: The MVC design pattern. In: Beginning Apache Struts, pp. 37–51. Apress (2006)
22. Kornhauser, D., Wilensky, U., Rand, W.: Design guidelines for agent based model visualization. Journal of Artificial Societies and Social Simulation 12(2) (2009)
23. Avouris, N.M.: User interface design for DAI applications. In: Avouris, N.M., Gasser, L. (eds.) Distributed Artificial Intelligence: Theory and Practice, pp. 141–162. Kluwer Academic Publisher (1992)
24. Beauregard, S.: Omnidirectional pedestrian navigation for first responders. In: Proceedings of the 4th Workshop on Positioning, Navigation and Communication (WPNC 2007), pp. 33–36 (2007)

A Cognitive Module in a Decision-Making Architecture for Agents in Urban Simulations

Quentin Reynaud[1, 2], Etienne de Sevin[2], Jean-Yves Donnart[1], and Vincent Corruble[2]

[1] Thales Training & Simulation, 1 Rue du Général de Gaulle 95520 Osny
{quentin.reynaud,jean-yves.donnart}@thalesgroup.com
[2] LIP 6, Université Pierre et Marie Curie, 4 place Jussieu 75005 Paris
{quentin.reynaud,vincent.corruble,etienne.de-sevin}@lip6.fr

Abstract. This paper addresses the issue of hybridization between reactive and cognitive approaches within a single decision-making architecture for virtual agent in an urban simulation. We use a reactive module in order to manage reactive behaviors and agent autonomy, and a cognitive module for anticipation, learning and complex behaviors management. The purpose of the cognitive module is to increase the agent's behavior credibility. The agent's reactive and proactive behaviors are sent to a decision module which is able to integrate, decompose, combine and select an action.

Keywords: Cognitive module, agent architecture, decision making.

1   Introduction

Virtual agents simulation is a very active area of research, and finds more and more applications. In this paper we focus on urban simulation, which has a wide range of applications: video games (particularly serious games), urban planning, transportation systems, security...

This work is being carried out within the context of TerraDynamica[1], a collaborative project aiming at building an artificial intelligence framework for the simulation of human-like agents in virtual urban environments. Because of the wide range of applications targeted in this project, we need a flexible agent architecture, fit for several domains. Depending on their objectives, urban simulation designers have to take into account several issues:

- Scalability: a great number of agents might be required in the simulation [1]
- Real-time: agent's response time could be critical [2]
- Rich environments: large cities are complex systems, because of their dynamicity and wide range of interactions [3]

This motivated our initial orientation towards reactive agents because of their low cost in terms of computational resources. It is also easier to simulate a great number

---

[1] http://www.capdigital.com/projet-terra-dynamica

F. Dignum et al. (Eds.): CAVE 2012, LNAI 7764, pp. 120–133, 2013.

of agents, in real-time and in a rich environment. In fact, nowadays in urban simulation, significant effort is put on the topics of 3D representation and path-planning, including pedestrian motion [4–6] and road traffic [7]. This work falls usually within the "human crowd simulation" trend [8, 9].

Nevertheless, reactive agents are not sufficient in order to exhibit credible and complex behaviors [10], which is a central goal of our work. Therefore, we add a cognitive dimension allowing an agent to adopt more complex behaviors, and to anticipate its future using its knowledge. In this paper, our basic assumption is that to be credible a simulation must "suspend the disbelief" of observers [11, 12]. According to Sengers [13], the observer's ability to make sense of the agent's behavior is fundamental to immerse him in the virtual environment. It is therefore important to reproduce believable and consistent behaviors, like rational behaviors [14] (maximizing performance taking stimuli and knowledge into account), including behaviors resulting from complex reasoning.

The main contribution of this paper is to describe the interest of a cognitive module plugged in a generic agent architecture. That is why we will not provide much details about our decision module and our reactive module. Further papers will present these modules more precisely.

Firstly, we present the state of the art in agent decision-making architectures, then a generic reactive architecture. Next, we give more details about the cognitive module we want to plug in this generic architecture and explain its impact on the decisional process, especially on the behaviors' integration phase. Before concluding this paper we rapidly discuss the architecture's complexity and its consequences on the scalability issue.

2   State of the Art

Two main approaches coexist concerning decision-making architectures: the reactive approach and the cognitive one [15, 16]. A reactive agent acts in response to external (and sometimes internal) stimuli. An internal representation can be used but the agent handles no reasoning. A cognitive agent functions by reasoning on a symbolic representation of itself and its environment. More recently, the concept of hybrid architecture has emerged. Its principle is to use both of the two latter approaches in an attempt to combine their advantages. In this section we base our classification on a recent paper by Duch [17]. But this classification is not as clear-cut as it could be, and others remain possible. In particular, the gaming field does not fit well in this classification. It is a dynamic domain which proposes many decision-making architectures using techniques such as finite state machines, behavior trees, or hierarchical reactive planning, in order to permit credible behaviors while limiting complexity, design and runtime cost ([18, 19]).

Initially, reactive architectures were developed to model simple behaviors for robots. Later, emerged the "animat" approach, which took inspiration from ethological models [20, 21]. Reactive architectures are strongly related to the bottom-up trend, which advocates the thesis that intelligence can spring from cooperation between simple modules. A good example of this trend is Brooks' subsumption architecture [22]. In this hierarchical architecture, several modules (each in charge of a specific behavior) judge the suitability of their own activation. To avoid conflicts, the modules are strictly prioritized: a high level module inhibits all lower level modules.

Maes proposed a system where each behavior decides on its own activation using an activation level [23]. These levels change dynamically and receive bonuses or penalties which are favoring multi-goals, opportunistic behaviors, while avoiding conflicts. DAMN [24] is also an important work based on a voting mechanism. A DAMN agent has one module for each possible behavior (follow a road, avoid obstacles, maintain internal variable...). Each module grades each feasible action, relevant to its interest. The top-rated action is the most relevant to all behaviors: it is selected.

Based on Rosenblatt and Payton's work [25], Tyrrell proposed another way to handle action selection [26]. The central idea is to decompose behaviors into sub-behaviors until "elementary actions level" are reached. At each step, all relevant stimuli are taken into account. An agent does not take any decision before the final elementary action level is computed. The decision-making process is delayed in order to allow the agent to make compromises (actions which are useful for more than one behavior/goal). That model is called "free-flow hierarchy".

The other decision-making modelling approach is the cognitive trend. Two key cognitive architectures are SOAR [27, 28] and ACT-R [29]. They are based on production rules and follow a top-down paradigm. Behaviors are the result of planning functions that use different types of memory.

The BDI approach [30, 31] is currently widely used. A BDI agent is made up of three parts. It contains desires that can be conflicting or can be irrelevant in the current situation. It has beliefs about itself and its environment and uses them to choose intentions, which are helping the agent to accomplish its desires.

Hybrid architectures try to combine the strengths of reactive and cognitive approaches. For example, the InteRRaP architecture [32] separates the decisional process into three steps. The first one is a reactive step: an InteRRaP agent has a set of behaviors, which can respond to its current objective. If none of them matches, the decisional process goes to step two: planning. The agent tries to organize several behaviors in time to reach its goals. If it does not work, the last step is reached: cooperation. The agent tries to contact the others and asks them for help.

The ICARUS architecture [33] was inspired by SOAR and uses four modules. "*Argus*" selectively perceives the environment. "*Daedalus*" plans agent's behaviors (means-end analysis from GPS [34]). "*Meander*" deals with reactive behaviors and executes plans from "*Daedalus*". "*Labyrinth*" stores the agent's knowledge.

The PECS architecture [35] uses four modules too, but they are not organized into a hierarchy. A physical module deals with homeostatic variables, an emotional module is in charge of the agent's emotional state, a social module manages the cooperation between agents and a cognitive module takes care of the knowledge. They are in permanent conflict in order to take control of the agent. The PECS architecture determines which module is the most relevant to deal with the current situation. Afterwards, that module has to drive the agent. PECS is a winner-takes-all architecture: never more than one module can drive the agent at a single time.

However, in relation with our work, we pay special attention to Maes' bonus/penalty system which is a simple and efficient way to take the global situation into account. We are also particularly interested in the DAMN voting mechanism which is a fair manner to take many expert modules into account (although each module is disconnected from all others). Each hybrid architecture presented has its own way to organize reactive and cognitive modules. An InteRRaP agent uses his "cognitive" module only if the reactive one does not find any solution: the cognitive module can therefore be bypassed. We find this harmful to the agent's behavior depth. In fact, an InteRRaP agent acts always in the same way every time it finds a reactive way to fulfill its goals. ICARUS agent's reactive behaviors can be considered as "reflex". We prefer the PECS modules organization, but PECS is a winner-takes-all architecture. No compromise and no cooperation is possible, a single module takes full control of the agent.

3   Generic Reactive Architecture

In the following section, we present a generic reactive architecture, inspired by some recent work [36–38]. We stay at a pragmatic level; we do not try to obtain a psychologically realistic model. We want to imitate human cognitive abilities, not human cognition itself (which is a far more complex work). In addition, we want an architecture which can be applied to a great range of applications. A generic reactive architecture based on the perception-action loop was chosen. A high-level reactive module is in charge of behavior proposals, and a decision module arbitrates and select actions (see figure 1). The high-level module manipulates the agent's internal state and updates it in response to the external or internal stimuli. This module should insure agent's autonomy (for example, de Sevin [37] used a motivational module which handles homeostatic variables).

The reactive module sends behavior proposals to the decision module. In the following, we consider that they are equivalent to the agent's desires (a behavior proposal corresponds to a desire the agent wants to fulfill). Let $B_A^t = \{B1, B2, ..., Bn\}$ be a behavior proposal for the agent A at time t, where each Bi is a behavior. We define the size of a behavior proposal by the number of behaviors available at the same time. A behavior corresponds to an objective that can be fulfilled by several different sequences of elementary actions (actions that cannot be decomposed).

In the rest of the paper, we use this running example to make explanations more comprehensible:

*Let Paul be an agent. **Drinking** is a behavior. To drink, Paul can "**go to the kitchen, take a glass, fill it,** and **drink out of the glass**" or "**go to the machine, buy a soda at the machine,** and **drink out of the can**", etc.*

*Paul is in the kitchen, holding a full glass in his hand. The behavior **drink** can be decomposed in the sub-behavior **drink out of the glass**, which is an elementary action.*

The behaviors are not equally important. In order to represent this importance and communicate it to the decision module, the proposed behaviors are prioritized. This priority is a numeric value between 0 and 1: 1 is vital and 0 indicates indifference. The reactive module proposes only behaviors judged as useful. That is why we do not take negative priorities into account. Let P_B^t be this priority for a behavior B at time t.

We also define the dissatisfaction level of an agent A at time t: $D_A^t = \sum_{i=1}^{n} \left(\frac{P_{Bi}^t}{n} \right)$. We assume that an agent without any desire is satisfied.

*Paul wakes up at the morning (t = 0). $B_{Paul}^0 = \{B_1, B_2, B_3\}$, with B_1: **go to WC** ($P_{B1}^0 = 0.6$); B_2: **eat** ($P_{B2}^0 = 0.35$); and B_3: **stay in bed** ($P_{B3}^0 = 0.3$). His current dissatisfaction level is $D_{Paul}^0 = \frac{P_{B1}^0 + P_{B2}^0 + P_{B3}^0}{3} \cong 0.42$*

The decision module takes several behavior proposals as input, and gives only one elementary action as output. The actual sequence of actions selected by an agent is called its effective behavior. In order to do so, the decision module has to decompose input behaviors into sub-behaviors until elementary action levels are reached. This decomposition depends on the agent's knowledge: the more knowledge the agent has, the wider the decomposition can be. Behavior priorities have to be correctly spread during the decomposition. In particular, the decomposition should take the agent's individuality (preferences, personality, etc.) into account: it can prefer Indian or French food, water or soda, etc.

Once all action priorities are computed, the decision module selects the action with the highest priority: it is the preferred action. The agent starts doing that action.

In this paper we remain at a generic level: we do not present in detail the reactive module or the decision module, because the main contribution of this paper is the addition of a cognitive module. The generic reactive architecture where the cognitive module is plugged is not central and any other architecture fulfilling the constraints that we discussed in this section can be used.

4   Cognitive Module

We need to add a cognitive dimension to this generic reactive architecture in order to observe more diverse and advanced behaviors. For that purpose, an additional cognitive module is plugged at the same level as the reactive module. It works the same way externally: it sends behavior proposals to the decision module, which is able to decompose reactive and proactive behaviors and choose the preferred action in the same manner (see figure 1).

In the following sections we present the functionality of our cognitive module. We chose to use this module to give the agent anticipatory [39], learning and planning skills in order to increase the depth and relevance of the agent's behavior [40, 41].

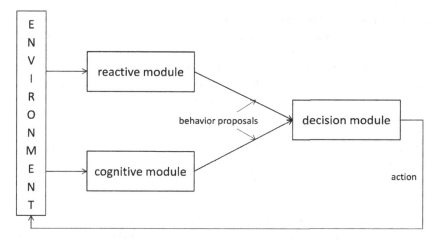

Fig. 1. Schema of the global architecture

4.1   Anticipatory Planning

As mentioned before, our basic architecture is generic: it is composed of a high-level reactive module and of a decision module. From the perspective of the cognitive module, these two other modules are seen as black boxes. The cognitive module knows their inputs and outputs but nothing else. In fact, the cognitive module can access perceptions (same inputs as reactive module), behavior proposals (reactive module's output and decision module's input) and preferred actions (decision module's outputs). Our reasoning module ignores why the agent has desires, or why it prefers doing an action rather than another. However, the cognitive module can use a model of itself, in order to anticipate its inner state. In a similar way, the cognitive module can use a model of the environment, in order to anticipate future events. To go further, the cognitive module would also require a model of agent-environment interactions.

We first consider that all these anticipatory models are provided by the simulation designer, but they can also be built though learning (see section 4.2). Each one of these models can be associated confidence index (CI), expressing the confidence that the agent has in its anticipation skill. The cognitive module uses such models to carry out an "anticipation plan", that is a projection into its future. The cognitive module tries to anticipate the outputs of the decision module, based on the anticipation of its own future desires.

The "anticipatory planning" process runs asynchronously with the action selection process.

First Step: The End of the Current Action. The cognitive module tries to anticipate the time when the agent ends its current task. To do so, the cognitive module needs knowledge of the action parameters (time before the action finishes) and travel time (time before the next action starts). For the moment, we assume that the cognitive module knows the duration of every action (fixed time) and that it can obtain a good estimation of travel times.

Second Step: Future Desires and Dissatisfaction Level. The cognitive module tries to estimate the agent's future state (at the end of its current action). It predicts the agent's future internal state and the state of the environment using the models provided as input by the simulation designer. It also needs to simulate the effects of the current action. Using this prediction, the cognitive module tries to infer the agent's future desires (B_A^t*) and dissatisfaction level (D_A^t*). In fact, it predicts the reactive module's behaviors proposal at this future time ($B_A^t* = \{B_1*, B_2*, ..., B_n*\}$).

Third Step: The Search for Anticipatory Useful Behaviors. The cognitive module starts a reasoning process whose purpose is to find (if it exists) a plan giving a lower future dissatisfaction level (i.e. better future satisfaction).

A huge dissatisfaction can be caused by a predictable event: Paul is walking home, when rain starts suddenly to fall, his dissatisfaction increase. If Paul had been aware of that sooner, a better plan for him could have been to take an umbrella before leaving his workplace. In order to have knowledge about the meteorological conditions, Paul can look at the newspapers, or infer them watching at the cloudy sky.

A better plan is in practice the selection of a myopically sub-optimal action because of a possible future reason (taking the umbrella is better than leaving the umbrella because it may rain). We note that if the agent currently knows about the rain, its optimal action is to take the umbrella. It does not need a cognitive module to notice that. These behaviors (called "anticipatory useful behaviors") can in the end be useless, or even harmful as in our example.

Paul goes back and takes his umbrella, but eventually rain does not come.

Fourth Step: The Sending of Anticipatory Useful Behaviors. If anticipatory useful behaviors are detected, the cognitive module has to determine their priority. It is calculated using the anticipated gain of satisfaction (ΔD) and the confidence index (CI) of the different anticipatory models used. We notice that CI usually decrease in time: the more distant in time, the less confident the predictions are.

These anticipatory useful behaviors are saved in the cognitive module and sent to the decision module when they are deemed useful. In our current example the behavior **"go back and take the umbrella"** is immediately useful, but it is not always the case, especially if the agent anticipates his distant future. These proactive behaviors are at the same level as the reactive behaviors. The decision module can ignore them if something else is more important (*Paul is in a hurry. He does not really care about the rain*). The decision module keeps complete control over the agent's effective behavior.

Fifth Step: The Next Preferred Action. The cognitive module has a prediction of the agent's future desires. This prediction comes from step two (if no anticipatory useful behaviors were found), or from step three (if anticipatory useful behaviors were found). Actually, in order to know if a plan is better than the current one, the cognitive module has to process again steps one and two with the new plan and compare the results. Then, in any case, the cognitive module tries to predict the agent's future decision, i.e. its future preferred action. In order to do so it has two main possible solutions. It can directly use the decision module as a simulator of itself, give it its own behaviors proposal prediction as input, and get its output back. Or it can use a model of the decision module to do the same thing (that option is not detailed in this paper). At the end of this step the cognitive module should have an estimate candidate for the future preferred action (called C_A^t*).

The process can iterate by going to step one again. We define the depth of that process as the number of iterations. We notice that if the effective choices of an agent are not the choices predicted by the cognitive module, this module has to update its predictions. The unpredictability of the future is represented by the decrease of the CI in time. An agent has no advantage in anticipating too many actions in the future, because his anticipatory useful behaviors' priority would get close to zero.

4.2   Anticipatory Learning

Using the anticipatory planning process, the agent should exhibit more consistent behaviors. It should be able to think about the future and adapt its behavior accordingly. This mechanism also provides additional tools to the simulation designer. Indeed, he has the opportunity to associate to an agent different types of anticipatory models, more or less correct, in order to exhibit several kinds of behaviors, more or less consistent. In particular, it would be possible to observe inconsistent behaviors because of false anticipatory models (*Paul thought it would rain today, so he decided to take his umbrella; but the weather ended up being totally fine*). For a simulation designer, it is a great opportunity to introduce variety in the agent's behavior (in addition to personality and personal preferences).

An anticipatory learning process is rapidly presented here. It consists in giving to the agent the ability to learn (or complement) their anticipatory models themselves, using techniques inspired from machine learning. If the anticipatory planning gives the agent the ability to take into account future events, the anticipatory learning gives to an agent the ability to take into account the surprise generated by the actual observed events so as to refine its predictions (see [42] for a similar process).

This ability simplifies the simulation designer's work (he does not have to give to each agent any anticipatory model). Two models are concerned: the reactive module model and the environment model. The learning process uses the behavior proposals to improve the reactive module model and external stimuli to improve the environment model. For example, using this learning process, an agent will be able to infer the evolution of its own motivations without any basic knowledge. In the following section, the main example (Paul's hunger) is chosen because it is simple to understand, and not because it would be the most relevant (indeed, it mostly boils down to learn something which has been given as input).

The anticipatory learning process is composed of three generalization levels:

- The first level of anticipatory learning is to collect facts about an agent without interacting with its behavior (*Paul eats at 8a.m, then at 13p.m, then at 20 p.m*).
- The second level is to search for patterns among these facts. These patterns can be detected using the number of occurrences in a period of time (*Paul is hungry three times a day*), an hour of appearance (*Paul eats at 20p.m.*), a location, etc.
- The third level is to infer generic knowledge from the second level. The cognitive module has to abstract the patterns from their surrounding context (*each day, Paul wants to eat at 13p.m.*, or *Paul wants to eat three times per day*). In fact, the anticipatory learning process accesses the agent's desire priorities. It can also infer numeric rules by watching the progression of the desires (*every hour without food intake, Paul's hunger increases by 0.1*).

Given that CI depends on the number of consistent observations (facts according to a prediction), high quality predictions should be automatically stored and low quality predictions should be automatically eliminated. This learning process allows an agent to get its own anticipatory models, which can be more or less correct, and which are used by the anticipatory planning (4.1) and impact the agent's behavior.

4.3   Complex Behaviors Management

In parallel to its anticipation role, the cognitive module can also be in charge of complex behaviors. Indeed, in order to improve credibility, we want agents to be able to exhibit complex behaviors, e.g. a "mission" in a military tactical sense. A complex behavior is also the specification of many high-level objectives and sub-objectives (i.e. high-level behaviors and sub-behaviors) with failure and success conditions. These conditions can have levels, indicating the force of failure or success. The articulation between (sub-) behaviors can be dynamic and adapted to the effective sequence of events. In order to be integrated in the agent's decisional process, complex behaviors and sub-behaviors have to be prioritized like other behaviors. In the scope of that paper, we assume that these missions are given by the simulation designer. The capacity to manage complex behaviors relies on the previously seen anticipation capacity (within the capacity to anticipate, an agent improves its management of complex tasks), but in an unpredictable future (the success of the mission is not certain). It is another tool for the simulation designer, in order to describe the simulation scenario.

*Paul is not the common citizen he seems to be. In fact he is a dangerous terrorist. During the afternoon, his mission **plant a bomb** is activated. It consists in **taking the bomb**, which is hidden under his desk, then **choosing a crowded location**, **planting the bomb without being seen**, **escaping**, and **hiding**. At any time, if he has the impression that he is being followed or spotted, his mission is aborted and he has to **hide**. Whatever the result of the mission, after a while, he **calls his accomplice** and **meets him**.*

That kind of mission cannot be simply decomposed into independent sub-behaviors. Additional information is required: failure and success conditions, goal updates, etc. In order to achieve these kind of complex behaviors, the agent has to be able to follow many heterogeneous sub-behaviors (in parallel or sequentially), during a long time frame. Instead of making the decision module more complex, in order to make it able to manage complex behaviors; we choose to locate this capability into the cognitive module. That choice has a double advantage. We keep the behavior description language as simple as possible and we are able to manage a hierarchical behavior system such as a hierarchical task network [43], which reduces the complexity.

In the particular case of complex behaviors, because of the long time frame considered and of the impossibility to predict the future (Paul has no way to know if he will be detected or not), it is easier to think about sub-tasks instead of whole mission. The key point is to isolate behaviors that are immediately useful from behaviors that are not. In our example, Paul does not need to think about his meeting with his accomplice until the last moment. Furthermore, he cannot know the time and the location of the meeting in advance. In contrast, while Paul is looking for a good location for the bomb, he could be looking for a hideout.

An important role for the cognitive module is to arbitrate between behaviors that must be sent to the decision module and those that must stay inactive. The complexity of the mission is also hidden to the decision module, and stays in the cognitive module.

*Back to our example: During the first part of the mission, the decision module receives two behaviors from the cognitive module: **find a location for the bomb** and **find a hideout**. The first one comes directly from the description of the mission, but the second one is not present in the mission. The cognitive module infers its "anticipatory usefulness".*

Priority of cognitive behaviors proposals are here derived from the mission and submission priority.

5   Impact on the Decision Module

The decision module takes behavior proposals as inputs and gives an elementary action as output. In between, it has four steps to take care of: the integration of heterogeneous behaviors, the decomposition into elementary actions, the combination into new behaviors, and the selection of the preferred action. We rapidly discussed the three last points in section 3, so the interesting point left is the integration.

One could think that the behavior's proposal formalism shared by the two high-level modules is not sufficient to compare directly their behavior's priorities in the decision module. Indeed, the high-level modules could not be sharing a common set of values. The "0" and "1" priorities are known, but the scale between them is not specified. One could also want to ensure that no module is going to take precedence over the other. In order to do so, one could want to normalize the behavior's proposal priorities, by applying to each module a coefficient that equalizes (on average) the behavior proposals' priorities. In the same vein, one could want to verify that the standard deviation is equivalent. If not, a high-level module that always proposes two behaviors, one with very high priority and the other with very low priority, has the same average priority than a module that always proposes middle-prioritized behaviors; but the first module always drives the agent's behavior. That way, we are certain that the high-level modules share a common set of values, and that the priorities they send are comparable.

That is not the choice we made. There are two main reasons for that. Firstly, simulation designers could want, in a specific situation or for a given application, to model agents that are mostly driven by the same high-level module. In the same way that there are people who are provident and others who are inadvertent, there could be agents who listen more to their cognitive or reactive module. This is a way to personalize agents, but can also be a way to adapt them to the application needs. Secondly, we do not think that it makes sense to try to find a common set of values between these modules. The heterogeneous behaviors' priorities do not have the same meaning. Our pragmatic reason is that there is no objective comparison between a plan we made and a reactive desire we suddenly feel. The only possible comparison is subjective, determined by the personality or the current situation.

Consequently, we only give a weight to each high-level module that depends on the personality of the agent. That weight increases or decreases all the priorities sent by the high-level module. The current situation, for its part, is taken into account during the decomposition process (see section 3). The next step is to perform learning about these weights (detect harmful behaviors and adjust the related weight).

In our architecture, we made the choice to combine reactive and cognitive behaviors. That places us in the hybrid approach. As we have seen in the related work section, many hybrid architectures are possible.

- The action selection process can be decomposed into several steps as in the InteR-RaP architecture
- The reactive and cognitive modules can be organized in a hierarchical manner, as in the ICARUS architecture
- They can be at the same level, as in the PECS architecture.

We selected this last form of organization because it allows us to introduce a "voting mechanism" as in the DAMN architecture (here there are weighed priorities instead of grades), in order to take all high-level modules into account. In addition, by placing the cognitive module at the same level as the reactive one, its behavior proposals are at the same level too. The decision module is able to find compromise actions between reactive and cognitive behaviors. That way, we are able to overcome limits from other hybrid architectures. Reactive and cognitive behaviors can be created in parallel and no module can be bypassed (as opposed to the InteRRaP architecture); the arbitration between reactive and cognitive behaviors is outside the reactive module, not any module is a priori preferred (as opposed to ICARUS); and our architecture is not working in a winner-takes-all manner (as opposed to PECS).

6   Discussion and Conclusion

Despite its benefits, the previously presented cognitive module increases the complexity of our architecture. It is necessary to find ways for our architecture to therefore deal with the urban simulation's scalability objective. Our central idea here is to create several dynamical types of agents, according to their importance (defined by the simulation designer) or their location (visibility from an observer). The cognitive module can be inactivate (or simplified) for some types of agent. This method, related to a level of detail artificial intelligence approach [44], allows us to allocate in priority the computing resources to the most important agents. The main objective is to save computing resources without losing agent's behavior credibility.

In this paper, we propose a decisional architecture for virtual agents in urban simulation. We have huge constraints: we want to be able to simulate a great number of agents (scaling up) in a real-time fashion, into a large and complex environment. In addition, our architecture must fit various application domains (video games, urbanism, transports, security, etc); we also try to model credible agents. In order to do so, we proposed an architecture based on the collaboration between a reactive high-level module (in charge of reactive behaviors and of the autonomy of the agent) and a cognitive module (which allows the agent to have anticipation and learning skills and manages complex behaviors). These modules propose behaviors to a decision module in charge of the arbitration between them and the action selection. That brings us to a new kind of hybrid approach, without hierarchy between reactive and cognitive behaviors and allowing compromise behaviors.

The model we described is currently being integrated into the TerraDynamica platform. The next step for us is to test and validate this model. We have many perspectives in mind. In the short term, we want to improve our decisional process in order to take agendas into account. These agendas impact also the anticipatory planning. In the longer term, we want to generalize the interface between high-level module and decision module. This gives us the possibility to design an agent with various high-level modules. Of course, they have to respect our formalism, but theoretically, any type of module (and any combination between them) could be accepted. In particular, affective and cooperative modules would be interesting, as the agent's effective emergent behavior would gain in depth. Finally, we plan to add in the cognitive module a mechanism able to memorize plans that the agent constructs. The interest of the plan has to be verified in order to avoid the storing of uninteresting one. A mechanism for comparing current and stored goals, and for adapting stored plans to the current situation is also needed.

References

1. Ceranowicz, A., Torpey, M.: Adapting to urban warfare. The Journal of Defense Modeling and Simulation: Applications, Methodology, Technology 2, 3–15 (2005)
2. Jepson, W., Liggett, R., Friedman, S.: An environment for real-time urban simulation. In: Proceedings of the 1995 Symposium on Interactive 3D Graphics (SI3D 1995), p. 165. ACM Press, New York (1995)
3. Waddell, P., Ulfarsson, G.: Introduction to urban simulation: design and development of operational models. In: Handbook in Transport, vol. 5, pp. 203–236 (2004)
4. Werner, T., Helbing, D.: The social Force Pedestrian Model Applied to Real Life Scenarios, pp. 17–26 (2003)

5. Shao, W., Terzopoulos, D.: Autonomous pedestrians. In: Proceedings of the 2005 ACM SIGGRAPH/Eurographics Symposium on Computer Animation, SCA 2005, p. 19. ACM Press, New York (2005)
6. Ronald, N., Sterling, L., Kirley, M.: An agent-based approach to modelling pedestrian behaviour. International Journal of Simulation (2007)
7. Bloomberg, L., Dale, J.: Comparison of VISSIM and CORSIM Traffic Simulation Models on a Congested Network. Transportation Research Record Journal 98104, 52–60 (2000)
8. Treuille, A., Cooper, S., Popović, Z.: Continuum crowds. ACM Transactions on Graphics 25, 1160 (2006)
9. Maïm, J., Yersin, B., Thalmann, D.: Real-time crowds. In: SIGGRAPH Asia 2008, pp. 1–16. ACM Press, New York (2008)
10. Ochs, M., Sabouret, N., Corruble, V.: Simulation of the Dynamics of Nonplayer Characters' Emotions and Social Relations in Games. IEEE Transactions on Computational Intelligence and AI in Games 1, 281–297 (2009)
11. Coleridge, S.: Biographia Literaria: Or, Biographical Sketches of My Literary Life and Opinions (1872)
12. Bates, J.: The role of emotion in believable agents. Communications of the ACM 37, 122–125 (1994)
13. Sengers, P.: Designing comprehensible agents. In: Proceedings of the 16th International Joint Conference on Artificial Intelligence, vol. 2, pp. 1227–1232. Morgan Kaufmann Publishers Inc., San Francisco (1999)
14. Russell, S.J., Norvig, P.: Artificial intelligence: a modern approach. Prentice hall (2010)
15. Bryson, J.: Hierarchy and sequence vs. full parallelism in action selection. In: From animals to animats (2000)
16. Langley, P., Laird, J.E., Rogers, S.: Cognitive architectures: Research issues and challenges. Cognitive Systems Research 10, 141–160 (2009)
17. Duch, W., Oentaryo, R.J., Pasquier, M.: Cognitive Architectures: Where do we go from here? In: Proceeding of the 2008 Conference on Artificial General Intelligence 2008: Proceedings of the First AGI Conference, pp. 122–136. IOS Press (2008)
18. Orkin, J.: Three states and a plan: the AI of FEAR. In: Game Developers Conference (2006)
19. Isla, D.: Handling complexity in the Halo 2 AI. In: Game Developers Conference (2005)
20. Meyer, J.A.: Artificial Life and the Animat Approach to Artificial Intelligence. In: Boden (ed.) Artificial Intelligence, pp. 325–354 (1996)
21. Guillot, A.: The animat contribution to cognitive systems research. Cognitive Systems Research 2, 157–165 (2001)
22. Brooks, R.A.: A Robust Layered Control System For a Mobile Robot. Massachusetts Institute of Technology, Cambridge (1985)
23. Maes, P.: Situated agents can have goals. Robotics and Autonomous Systems 6, 49–70 (1990)
24. Rosenblatt, J.: DAMN: A Distributed Architecture For Mobile Navigation - Thesis Summary. Journal of Experimental and Theoretical Artificial Intelligence, 339–360 (1995)
25. Rosenblatt, J.K., Payton, D.W.: A fine-grained alternative to the subsumption architecture for mobile robot control. In: International Joint Conference on Neural Networks, vol. 2, pp. 317–323. IEEE (1989)
26. Tyrrell, T.: The use of hierarchies for action selection. Adaptive Behavior 1, 387 (1993)
27. Laird, J.E., Newell, A., Rosenbloom, P.S.: SOAR: an architecture for general intelligence. Artif. Intell. 33, 1–64 (1987)

28. Laird, J.E.: Extending the Soar Cognitive Architecture. In: Proceeding of the 2008 Conference on Artificial General Intelligence 2008: Proceedings of the First AGI Conference, pp. 224–235. IOS Press, Amsterdam (2008)
29. Anderson, J.R., Bothell, D., Byrne, M.D., Douglass, S., Lebiere, C., Qin, Y.: An integrated theory of the mind. Psychological Review 111, 1036–1060 (2004)
30. Rao, A.S., Georgeff, M.P.: BDI Agents: From Theory to Practice. In: Proceedings of the First International Conference on Multi-Agent Systems (ICMAS 1995), pp. 312–319 (1995)
31. Georgeff, M., Pell, B., Pollack, M., Tambe, M., Wooldridge, M.: The belief-desire-intention model of agency. Intelligent Agents V: Agents Theories, Architectures, and Languages, 1–10 (1999)
32. Müller, J.P., Pischel, M.: The Agent Architecture InteRRaP: Concept and Application (1993)
33. Langley, P., Choi, D.: A unified cognitive architecture for physical agents. In: Proceedings of the 21st National Conference on Artificial Intelligence, vol. 2, pp. 1469–1474. AAAI Press (2006)
34. Newell, A., Simon, H.A., rand corp Santa Monica Calif.: GPS, a program that simulates human thought. Defense Technical Information Center (1961)
35. Schmidt, B.: Human factors in complex systems: The modelling of human behaviour. In: Simulation in Wider Europe, 19th European Conferance on Modelling and Simulation, pp. 5–14 (2005)
36. Robert, G., Guillot, A.: MHiCS, a modular and hierarchical classifier systems architecture for bots. In: 4th International Conference on Intelligent Games and Simulation (GAME-ON 2003), pp. 140–144 (2003)
37. de Sevin, E.: An action selection architecture for autonomous virtual humans in persistent worlds (2006)
38. Dujardin, T., Routier, J.-C.: Behavior Design of Game Character's Agent. In: 2010 IEEE/WIC/ACM International Conference on Web Intelligence and Intelligent Agent Technology, pp. 423–430. IEEE (2010)
39. Robert, R.: Anticipatory Systems (1985)
40. Meyer, C., Ganascia, J.G., Zucker, J.D.: Learning strategies in games by anticipation. In: International Joint Conference on Artificial Intelligence, pp. 698–707. Lawrence Erlbaum Associates Ltd. (1997)
41. Butz, M., Sigaud, O., Gérard, P.: Anticipatory Behavior in Adaptive Learning Systems. Springer, Heidelberg (2003)
42. Burke, R.: Great expectations: Prediction in entertainment applications. Life-Like Characters Tools, Affective Functions, and Applications (2004)
43. Erol, K., Hendler, J., Nau, D.S.: UMCP: A sound and complete procedure for hierarchical task-network planning. In: Proc. 2nd Intl. Conf. on AI Planning Systems, pp. 249–254 (1994)
44. Navarro, L., Flacher, F., Corruble, V.: Dynamic level of detail for large scale agent-based urban simulations. In: The 10th International Conference on Autonomous Agents and Multiagent Systems, vol. 2, pp. 701–708. International Foundation for Autonomous Agents and Multiagent Systems (2011)

Improving Situation Awareness in Intelligent Virtual Agents

Surangika Ranathunga and Stephen Cranefield

Department of Information Science, University of Otago,
PO Box 56, Dunedin 9054, New Zealand
{surangika,scranefield}@infoscience.otago.ac.nz

Abstract. Virtual worlds are inherently complex, dynamic and unpredictable in nature. The interface they provide to external agent systems consists of low-level events and primitive data. This introduces an information representation gap between virtual worlds and declarative BDI-based agent systems. As a result, BDI-based intelligent virtual agents (IVAs) are not capable of identifying the complex abstract situations unfolding in their surrounding environment. In this paper, we describe a two-step process that enables an IVA to identify the complex situations they encounter. First, complex event recognition mechanisms are applied on the low-level sensor data received by an IVA. Complex events identified in the first step are compared against a domain-specific situation model to identify active situations. The situation model helps the agent to be aware of the start and end of situations, and also to be aware of any active situation at any given time.

1 Introduction

Due to their success in many application areas, BDI-based agent systems have been a natural selection for implementing Intelligent Virtual Agents (IVAs). However, attempts to interface BDI agents with virtual worlds have faced many practical difficulties due to the inherent differences between these two types of system [9,6]. BDI systems are declarative and have been criticised for their over-reliance on the notion of individual events and for not having enough capabilities to cope with complex abstract situations taking place in the environment [16,4]. Virtual worlds are complex, dynamic and unpredictable in nature, and a BDI agent deployed in a virtual world mainly receives low-level event and primitive state information as sensor data. Virtual worlds also have much faster execution cycles than BDI-based agent systems. Due to these incompatibilities, a BDI-based intelligent agent deployed in a virtual world is overwhelmed with large amounts of low-level sensor data that are being received in a speed that exceeds processing capabilities of the agent system. Information on interesting situations unfolding around an IVA is hidden beneath the heap of low-level sensory data, making them directly unavailable for the deliberation process of the agent.

Researchers argue that how a person characterises a situation can help in determining the decision process chosen to solve a problem, and also can help

F. Dignum et al. (Eds.): CAVE 2012, LNAI 7764, pp. 134–148, 2013.

in increasing his or her performance [8]. This applies to artificial agents as well. Researchers have already identified the need for such an abstract concept to improve the reasoning process of intelligent agents, where the recognition by an agent as being in a particular situation may affect its complete reasoning process [16]. As for an IVA, with a perceived situation, it can establish focused attention, predict possible reactions of other participants in the environment, intelligently allocate limited resources and provide explanations of the decisions taken [18].

For a BDI-based IVA to realise the benefits of having high-level domain-specific situational knowledge, information representation gap between the two systems should be minimised. In order to accomplish this, intermediate processing mechanisms are needed to identify situations embedded in the received virtual world sensor data.

According to the definition by Endsley [8], situation awareness is "perception of the elements in the environment within a volume of time and space, the comprehension of their meaning, and the projection of their status in the near future". This paper focuses on situation recognition, which is a sub-component of situation comprehension. We describe a two-step process that enables an IVA to identify the dynamic situations taking place in its environment.

In the first step, low-level sensor data received from a virtual world is processed to identify complex events taking place in the virtual environment. For this step, we use a framework that we developed in previous research that is capable of handling large amounts of sensor data received from a virtual world [13]. This previous version of the framework focused on identifying *events* taking place in virtual environments, with a specific focus on Second Life[1].

In the second step, these identified complex events are compared with a domain-specific situation model, which shows the connection between different events and how events trigger transitions between situations. Complex events that mark the start and end of situations are communicated to the agent to be used as beliefs in its deliberation process. This extended framework is also aware of the currently active situations, and whenever the IVA is notified of the current state of the world, it is also notified about the currently active situations that the agent might be interested in. This way, the persistence of the situations is maintained, and the IVA can make use of this situational knowledge as beliefs in its decision making process.

Based on the related literature in the area of situation awareness, we categorise situations identified in a virtual environment into three abstraction levels: situations based on the attributes of individual entities (objects and avatars), situations arising from the relations between different entities, and compound situations that arise from correlations of situations in the previous two levels.

We briefly discuss how the concept of situations is integrated with the BDI paradigm. We demonstrate our system using Jason [3] BDI agents deployed in a Second Life virtual environment.

---

[1] http://secondlife.com/

The rest of the paper is organised as follows. Section 2 discusses previous research related to situation modelling in BDI agents, and approaches for situation recognition by intelligent agents. Section 3 presents a categorisation of situations occurring in a virtual environment, based on their abstraction level. Section 4 and 5 discuss our two-step process of situation recognition. Section 6 presents our approach for modelling situations in BDI agents. Section 7 presents an example of how our approach is used in situation recognition by Jason BDI agents deployed in Second Life. Section 8 concludes the paper.

2   Related Work

2.1   Modelling Situations in BDI Agents

Researchers have identified different approaches for integrating the concept of situations with the BDI paradigm. Thangarajah et al. [16] capture situations as entities that are conceptually different from an agent's beliefs and at a coarser granularity. Consequently, what is associated with a situation is a 'meta program/plan (MP)', which does not directly produce behaviour, but changes other aspects of an agent such as attitude, focus, understanding, and priorities.

In the work of Buford et al. [4], situations are treated as normal beliefs. In their model, situations are a result of event correlation and situation recognition processes. Therefore situations facilitate the implementation of complex plan triggering conditions.

So and Sonenberg [14] integrate situation awareness with the standard BDI architecture using an epistemic reasoning module. This module aggregates perceptual inputs into beliefs. A situation is based on an aggregated set of beliefs. It in turn generates multiple goals for the agent to achieve. In their more recent work [15], the authors present situation awareness as a meta-level control mechanism that can be used to manage intention reconsideration in BDI agents.

2.2   Situation Recognition by Intelligent Agents

Implementation of situation recognition by BDI agents has been mainly based on simplistic approaches. Thangarajah et al. [16] make use of a temporal database to identify situations that span across a period of time. This is based on the assumption that situations are generally based on appearances of objects over time. So and Sonenberg [14] use rule-based knowledge and forward chain reasoning to capture the knowledge about dynamic situations unfolding in an agent's environment. In this approach, observed data from an agent's environment are processed to become beliefs that reflect the status of the environment. However, due to the complexity of virtual environments, both these approaches may not be scalable enough to identify complex abstract situations taking place there.

Buford et al. [4] have presented a theoretical framework that makes use of event correlation for situation recognition by BDI agents. This is similar to our use of complex event recognition in the situation recognition process. They suggest the use of case-based reasoning (CBR) mechanisms to create a library of standard situation templates. Low-level events received from an operational environment are subject to event correlation mechanisms to identify high-level 'synthetic events'. Based on the identified synthetic events, matching situation templates are retrieved from the situation library. These templates are instantiated and/or adapted according to current event information. If a situation template is adapted, this new template is also added to the situation library. In this theoretical framework, the new components for situation recognition are directly embedded in the BDI platform.

We do not see much research addressing the specific problems related to situation recognition by IVAs. Zhang et al. [18] present a pattern-driven approach to recognise situations in a virtual battle field. In order to recognise situations by an intelligent pilot bot Ehlert et al. [7] provide two mechanisms— state heuristic rules based on a state-transition diagram and a probabilistic approach; however, only simple situations have been considered.

It should be emphasised here that situation recognition by an IVA is essentially not the same as IVA perception, which has received a considerable amount of attention (e.g. [11,2]). According to the definition of situation awareness by Endsley [8], perception involves detecting the relevant elements in the environment, along with their status, attributes, and dynamics. Situation comprehension involves the integration of information related to these different elements and the determination of their significance with respect to one's goals. Situation recognition is a sub-component of situation comprehension, which involves the problem of matching relational structures identified in sensor data with stored structures or templates representing situations.

3 Situations at Different Abstraction Levels

According to Buford et al. [4], a situation is "an aggregated state of entities and inter-entity relations of the world, which are observable at a specific time period". Based on this definition, we denote a situation s as :

$s = \langle sType, AttVals, t_s, t_e \rangle.$

Here, $sType$ is the situation type. Each situation type is associated with a set of attributes $attNames(sType)$ at a suitable abstraction level. This set contains attributes that all situations of that type possess. For a given situation instance, $AttVals$ provide the variable bindings for each attribute in $attNames(sType)$. In a situation, the last two elements t_s and t_e are the start and end timestamps of the situation, respectively.

A situation instance is uniquely identified by a type in the form shown above, i.e., two situation instances belonging to the same situation type can be said to be equivalent if they started and ended at the same time, and had identical attribute values.

Situations taking place in a virtual environment can be categorised in many ways. Due to the low-level primitive nature of the sensor data received from a virtual world, situations in many abstraction levels can be identified. In the field of situation recognition, researchers have already identified the importance of presenting situations at different abstraction levels [5,10]. Based on the categorisation of Buford et al. [4], with respect to virtual environments, we broadly categorise situations into three abstraction levels. Situations identified in lower levels are useful in defining and identifying situations at higher levels, making the situation identification process hierarchical and easier to handle.

3.1 Situations Based on the Attributes of Entities

Situations based on entity attributes are the lowest level of situations that an IVA can identify in a virtual environment. We term these 'primitive situations'. Attributes that formulate a primitive situation are the entity property values or some derived value based on them (e.g. a non-zero velocity value is used to derive the abstract entity property 'moving'). Therefore, if an entity maintains the same value/s for one or more of its properties, this may lead to an interesting situation. For example, an entity maintaining a non-zero velocity for a period of time can lead to a situation of interest for the IVA.

3.2 Situations Based on Entity Relations

Situations based on relations between entities and/or any domain related concepts such as location information can be considered as the next level of situation abstraction. At this abstraction level, attributes of a situation consist of entities and other domain related concepts. For example, an enemy tank *in* one's territory may lead to an interesting situation that should be dealt with.

With respect to situations, many researchers have proposed different relation categorisations (e.g. [10]). Depending on the requirements of a selected application domain, the types of relations that may result in interesting situations should be identified. When looking at related research, use of relations as a solution to bridge the representational gap between agent systems and virtual worlds can also be seen. For example, Gemrot et al. [9] use class relationships between entities in generating generalised events for abstract object classes. Vosinakis and Panayiotopoulos [17] presented the concept of a 'geometric memory' in virtual worlds that defined spatial relationships such as near, on, front of, behind, above and below. However, in both these approaches, relational information has not been used to define abstract situations.

3.3 Compound Situations

The idea of compound situations has been proposed by Jakobson et al. [10], and Dahlbom [5]. Compound situations are identified based on the relations between other situations. Developing the example in the previous section, an observation of an enemy tank inside one's territory *and* the observation of a squadron of enemy aircraft flying towards that territory mark an interesting situation for an IVA.

4 Identifying Complex Events Taking Place in Virtual Environments

4.1 Events

Events play a very important role in IVA situation identification. In many virtual worlds such as Second Life and an extended version of Unreal Tournament [1], IVAs receive sensory data from the virtual environment mainly in the form of event notifications. Several frameworks that integrate agent systems and virtual worlds have also assumed that sensor readings are received as events (e.g. [6]).

In the context of virtual environments, these received event notifications are the observed changes in the virtual environment state. According to the dynamic virtual environment formalism presented in our previous research [13], these events are identified as primitive events. An event notification received from a virtual world can be a result of an entity property change, or an event that affects the virtual environment as a whole, such as the posting of a message in public chat channels. Thus, they may result in the occurrence of different situations. The observed state space can be constructed based on the received event notifications. This state space can again be used to infer any other primitive events of interest, such as the appearance and disappearance of entities.

It should be noted that situations and events have a fundamental difference with respect to how they are perceived and how they are being acted upon by an agent. Situations are considered to be persistent. An agent's practical reasoning strategy may vary across different situations, because the knowledge of the current situation/s provides a useful mechanism for selecting plans for execution. This means that, for the same observation in the environment, the agent may react differently based on its understanding of the currently active situations. Moreover, if the agent is aware of the situation model, identification of being in a particular situation helps in anticipating the future situations that it may encounter, and the agent can pro-actively be ready for those future situations or take actions to stop them from occurring. As for events, an agent is mainly interested in identifying an instantaneous notification of an event, and reacting to this occurrence.

Events can also be considered as triggering changes in a more abstract state space, defining the transitions between different situations. Therefore events are also useful in notifying an IVA of any situation transitions of interest, by monitoring an incoming state sequence for the existence or absence of any situations. In fact, according to Dahlbom [5], when there is a large number of objects and relations, and when the situation sequence is quickly developing, explicit use of all state predicates to detect situations may not be optimal. Therefore describing situations using events provides an alternative for this problem.

4.2 Complex Event Identification Framework

We make use of a framework that was developed in previous research [13] for the identification of complex events taking place in a virtual environment. This framework has three precessing steps to identify complex events from the sensory data received from a virtual world.

Construction of a Discrete State Representation of the Environment
In this framework, the first step of identifying situations in a virtual environment is the construction of a discrete state representation of the environment. As per the virtual environment state definition given in our previous research [13], the discrete state space of the virtual environment as perceived by an IVA contains the state of the observable entities in the environment, and any messages publicly exchanged or privately received by the IVA.

If the virtual environment provides periodic state updates to an IVA, this can be directly used as the discrete state representation. If the received event notifications contain the state of all the entities in that environment, then these event notifications also can be directly used as the states of the virtual environment. However, if these event notifications contain attribute values only of the entity corresponding to that event, an explicit inference mechanism has to be employed to generate the state of the environment in the time instant represented by the received event notification.

Our framework implements data amalgamation and inference mechanisms to generate complete state information corresponding to the time instant represented by the received state update or the event notification. The data structure corresponding to a state (which we call a 'snapshot') consists of a set of individual entity states, and optionally may contain any events (received from the virtual world or events inferred by the framework), and a set of messages exchanged in the public chat channels at the given time instant. The state of an individual entity contains the observed or derived values of the properties of that entity at the given instant of time.

Identifying Relations between Entities
This step focuses on identifying the various dynamic (e.g. spatial, structural) relationships between the entities included in a snapshot. Static (e.g. functional) relationships between entities can also be used in relation identification. Identification of relations between entities in a snapshot makes it possible to derive new information at a higher abstraction level than the low-level data received from the virtual world. This information is useful in the subsequent complex event recognition step, as well as in defining interesting situations, as explained in Section 3 .

The importance of identifying relational information was identified in the previous version of our framework. However, it was applied in a very limited context. There we introduced the concept of "contextual information", which can be identified in conjunction with some externally supplied static information such as location data, or position information of static objects such as buildings. Moreover, contextual information was treated as information related to individual entities. Treating relational information as belonging to individual entities can introduce ambiguity to relation representation. For example, consider a relation that encodes the information that two avatars are close to each other. Then we are faced with a question of how to include this relationship; does it belong to only one entity (and if so, to which entity), or does it belong to both of the entities. Therefore in this extended version of the framework, we differentiate between entity-specific relations and state-specific relations.

Given a data structure corresponding to a constructed state instance, the framework identifies these relationships using a rule-based script. These relations are added to the original state instance, forming an abstract state space. However, if the number of relations that should be identified increases, this approach may not be efficient. In future work we expect to investigate some efficient mechanisms for relation identification.

In order to identify spatial relations in a virtual environment, Vosinakis and Panayiotopoulos [17] present a perception module that applies a set of rules on the identified objects in a virtual environment and generates beliefs for IVAs. These beliefs are essentially relations between different entities. Zhang and Hill [18] propose a tree-structured representation for identifying spatial and organisational relationships in a virtual military domain.

Complex Event Detection

In simple terms, complex event detection involves identifying pre-defined patterns in the incoming low-level sensor data stream. As per our requirements, this involves monitoring the individual entity property values and or entity relationships and identifying any changes that can possibly result in interesting situations.

Identifying complex events taking place in virtual environments is hard for reasons such as the large amounts of unreliable low-level sensory data received by an IVA and the high frequencies of data receipt. If events based on longer durations of temporal relationships have to be identified, it is necessary that an efficient complex event recognition mechanism is employed to ensure real-time situation recognition by IVAs. Otherwise the cost involved with complex event recognition outweighs its benefits. Some techniques used in pattern recognition are graph matching, probabilistic techniques, temporal constraint based techniques, rule-based techniques and state transition techniques [5]. All these recognition mechanisms have their advantages and disadvantages, and the suitable mechanism for a given application domain should be selected based on the requirements.

In the framework that was presented in our previous work [13], patterns related to complex events are instantiated using an open source complex event processing engine called Esper[2]. In Esper, event pattern matching is implemented using state machines, and it has a very expressive language that supports many of the complex event processing operators. Event identification in Esper has very low latency when handling high-frequency data streams coming from a virtual world. Even the most complex event pattern we defined in our previous research did not take more than 1 millisecond to be recognised by Esper [13]. However, since the underlying pattern matching mechanism of Esper is based on state

---

[2] http://esper.codehaus.org/tutorials/tutorial/tutorial.html

machines, Esper cannot address the uncertainty aspect of situation recognition. Moreover, it is hard to implement partially matching temporal patterns in Esper. This opens up new avenues for future research to identify efficient mechanisms that address both uncertainty and partial matching of patterns.

5   Situation Identification

Construction of a situation model is a main prerequisite for real time situation recognition in complex dynamic systems [4]. A situation model represents the situations taking place in an operational environment, and their relationships. Observation data received from monitoring the application environment are matched against the situation model to identify the unfolding situations.

In our framework, we use a finite state machine to specify the situation model. Situations that are to be identified in a virtual environment serve as the states of the model, and the identified complex events serve as the triggering conditions of the state transitions. Transition from and to situations mark the start and end of situations, and this information is passed to the agent as events. The situation model is also useful in identifying active situations in the environment. Whenever the framework sends a state update to the IVA, the active situations are also included in this state update, thus notifying the agent about the persistence of the situations. At the agent side, these can be converted into beliefs to be used in the decision making process.

The idea of maintaining currently active situations is similar to the concept of active situations maintained in the agent model proposed by Thangarajah et al. [16]. They also model separate entry and exit conditions for a situation, which are similar to our situation transition events of a situation. However, these entry and exit conditions refer only to the appearance of objects, while our events may be results of more complex event patterns.

The use of finite state machines is a simplistic approach to implement a situation model. Complex reasoning related to situation identification needs the use of complex mechanisms such as Case-Based-Reasoning as described in Section 2.2. Such an approach facilitates partial matching and adaptation of the defined situations to the sensor data received. Another limitation of this simple approach is the inability to support hierarchical situations (situations belonging to different levels of abstractions, but based on the same entity states) that may co-exist in an environment. This limits the full realisation of the benefits of categorising situations into different abstraction levels.

6   Modelling Situations in BDI-Based IVAs

We model situations as belief constructs in the BDI paradigm. The agent is notified about the entry and exit to situations by means of events that become beliefs for the agent. The agent is also notified of the active situations when it is notified about the state of the environment. If the agent programmer is familiar with the situations and their relationships for a given domain, he can implement agents that make use of the knowledge of active situations in their deliberation process. This enables the agents to base their plan selection on complex conditions of the environment. Therefore we believe that there is no need to treat situations as conceptual entities different to beliefs as suggested by Thangarajah et al. [16].

Our approach for modelling situations in BDI agents is similar to the approach used by Buford et al. [4]. In their proposed theoretical framework, event correlation and situation recognition processes are integrated in the BDI platform, and the abstract situation templates are part of the agent internals. Internal events generated in the agent's reasoning process and events identified in the external environment are correlated in the situation recognition process. However, we think that an agent's internal events generated by belief and/or goal additions and/or deletions are conceptually at a different abstraction level than the events taking place in an agent's external environment, and should be treated separately. Moreover, keeping the situation recognition mechanism outside the BDI agent system brings the advantage of not having to change the internal logic of the existing BDI agent systems to integrate the concept of situations. However one drawback of keeping the situation model outside the agent's internal processing mechanism is that the agent is not aware of the complete situation model to be used in its proactive reasoning.

We do not wish to provide a comprehensive discussion of modelling situations in BDI agents, as this is out of the scope of this paper.

7   Example

Our framework developed in previous research [13] includes an interface that can connect any multi-agent system with Second Life, and it has been already demonstrated with the Jason agent development platform. Therefore in this example, we use the same setting and demonstrate how Jason agents can make use of the identified situations to react better to the dynamism in their virtual environment. Jason is an open source Java-based multi-agent systems development platform that incorporates an interpreter for the BDI-based agent programming language AgentSpeak.

The types of situations that should be identified in a virtual environment depend on the type of simulation being used. Therefore situation identification can best be explained in the context of a specific simulation. In this example, we use the SecondFootball[3] virtual soccer simulation to demonstrate how the situation identification process works.

SecondFootball is a simulation in Second Life that facilitates playing virtual football. It provides most of the functionality and features of a real-life football game. A SecondFootball match includes the concurrent actions of multiple players and a soccer ball that move around the field. Because of the team environment in this simulation, it contains a multitude of interesting situations that are of use to an IVA deployed as a player in this simulation.

---

[3] http://www.secondfootball.com/

In this example, we consider a Jason agent deployed in a SecondFootball simulation, and for simplicity, assume that it is interested in three separate situations: when the opponents have got the possession of the ball (*op*), when his team has got the possession of the ball (*tp*), and when no team has got possession of the ball (*np*). The simulation is implemented with three players: two controlled by humans, and one controlled by a Jason agent.

Here, the first situation type (*op*) can be represented as,

$\langle opposition\_has\_ball, \{player\}, t_s, t_e \rangle$

The second situation type (*tp*) can be expressed as:

$\langle own\_team\_has\_ball, \{player\}, t_s, t_e \rangle$

and the third situation type (*np*) can be expressed as:

$\langle no\_team\_has\_ball, \{\}, t_s, t_e \rangle$.

Below we show the pattern *got_lost_possession* that is implemented in Esper for identifying the time instant that a player gets the possession of the ball directly from another player. An event listener component associated with the Esper engine generates two events *lost_possesion* and *got_possesion*, corresponding to the first player losing the possession of the ball and the second player gaining the possession of the ball, respectively.

```
SELECT * FROM
PATTERN
 [EVERY
  a =  EntitySnapshot(Entity.Name = 'ball',
       EU.GetContextVal(ContextDic, "possession") !=
       "No possession"))
  ->
  b =  EntitySnapshot(Entity.Name = 'ball',
       EU.GetContextVal(ContextDic, "possession") =
       EU.GetContextVal(a.ContextDic, "possession"))
  ->
  c = EntitySnapshot(Entity.Name = 'ball',
       EU.GetContextVal(ContextDic, "possession") !=
        EU.GetContextVal(a.ContextDic, "possession"),
       EU.GetContextVal(ContextDic, "possession") !=
       "No possession"))
  ->
  d = EntitySnapshot(Entity.Name = 'ball',
       EU.GetContextVal(ContextDic, "possession") =
       EU.GetContextVal(c.ContextDic, "possession"))
WHERE timer:within(2.5 sec)]
```

Here, *a*, *b*, *c* and *d* are aliases for four data item inputs to the Esper engine, which are of the type 'EntitySnapshot'. The EntitySnapshot data structure refers to the state of an entity, which also includes any abstracted relational information. The pattern searches for a sequence of four data items that are coming one after other (identified by the sequence operator '$->$'). The *a*, *b* data items

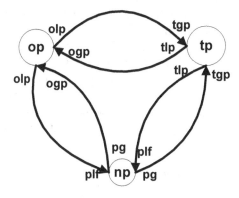

Fig. 1. Situation model for the soccer scenario

correspond to entity states where the first player had the possession of the ball, and c and d data items correspond to entity states where the second player had the possession of the ball. In theory only two data items (one corresponding to the state in which the first player had the possession, and the other corresponding to the state in which the second player had the possession) should suffice to define this pattern. However, due to the unreliability of the data stream coming from Second Life, this resulted in low accuracy, and as a remedy we use four data items. This pattern makes use of the spatial relationship between the ball and the player that identifies the player who has the possession of the ball. The GetContextVal method in the class EU[4] is used to extract the name of the player in possession of the ball from the relational information. This relation is treated as a relation belonging to the ball. Using a timer avoids the necessity of keeping the data items related to the ball in memory for unnecessarily long periods. The wild card option in the select clause specifies that all the attributes of all data items should be selected.

The situation model corresponding to the three states op, np and tp is shown in Figure 1. In this model, situation transitions are labelled with two events to mean that both events must hold for the transition to take place. In this model, *ogp* and *tgp* are events that are identified based on the *got_possession* event above, and refer to *opposition_got_possession*, and *own_team_got_possession*, respectively. *olp* and *tlp* events are identified based on the *lost_possession* event above, and refer to *opposition_lost_possession*, and *own_team_lost_possession*, respectively. These events are identified by the mapping functionality that associates the events generated by Esper patterns with model transition events. In this process, it uses the static relational information that specifies the team each player belong to. *plf* and *pg* events correspond to *possession_lost_ball_free* and *possession_gained*, respectively.

---

[4] EU stands for the utility class EsperUtility that includes additional complex logic needed for Esper pattern processing.

A transition into a situation always generates a *start_situation* belief addition event in Jason, with the actual situation information as parameters. A transition into a situation also generates an *in_situation* percept to be sent to Jason, which states that the given situation is active. This transition also updates the active situations maintained in the framework, and the *in_situation* percept is sent to the agent every time a new state update is being sent.

For example, the Jason plan below is executed when the *opposition_got_possession* situation is started, and the agent reacts to it by running to the field area 'penaltyB', to stop a possible goal scoring by the opposition at goal B.

```
+start_situation(opposition_has_ball(Player_name))
<-
action("run", "penaltyB").
```

The main difference between simple event-based reasoning and situation-based reasoning comes through the introduction of active situations. For the same event received from the environment, the agent can take different actions based on any active situation that the agent is aware of.

For example, consider the following Jason plan, which is initiated by an event stating that the agent is being called by a fellow team member to move to where he is[5]. Given that it is faced with a situation where the opposition has the possession of the ball, the agent decides not to go to where his team mate is, and simply adds a mental note to itself to remember about the team member's call.

```
+teammate_called(Player_name):
 in_situation(opposition_has_ball(Player_name))
<-
+remember(teammate_called, Player_name);
```

8   Conclusion

This paper addressed the specific problem of situation recognition by IVAs. We presented a two-step process to identify situations at different abstraction levels. The first step makes use of a framework that was developed in previous research [13] to identify complex events taking place in the virtual environment. As the second step, this framework was extended to include a domain-specific situation model, and situation transitions are identified with the help of the complex events identified. With the situation model, it is possible to maintain information about active situations, and inform the agent about them whenever a new state update is sent. Thus the framework maintains the persistent nature of situations, and the agents are made aware of this persistence. The solutions

---

[5] We are currently working on how participant utterances can be used by IVAs in the situation recognition process.

we proposed not only help in creating IVAs that are more aware of the dynamic situations they are faced with, but they also help in bridging the representational gap between agent systems and virtual worlds, with respect to dynamic information comprehension. Performance tests of the system up to the complex event recognition step (inclusive) show that the framework takes approximately 45 milliseconds in identifying a complex event in a sensor data item received from Second Life [12]. We have tested the system with up to six concurrent moving avatars in the environment, and the results did not show any significant drop in performance. Also, there was no noticeable performance degradation by the introduction of the situation recognition component.

The framework uses a simple script-based mechanism for identifying relations present in an incoming sensor data stream, which has to be replaced by a more efficient mechanism (e.g. a rule engine) in the future. Moreover in future work, there is a need to investigate different complex event recognition approaches that can cater for the uncertainty of virtual environments, and to use evolving or learning approaches to pattern recognition. Situation recognition phase can also be improved to support sophisticated situation recognition with parameter matching (s.a. case-based-reasoning).

References

1. Adobbati, R., Marshall, A.N., Scholer, A., Tejada, S., Kaminka, G., Schaffer, S., Sollitto, C.: Gamebots: A 3D virtual world test-bed for multi-agent research. In: Proceedings of the Second International Workshop on Infrastructure for Agents, MAS, and Scalable MAS (2001)
2. Bordeux, C., Boulic, R., Thalmann, D.: An efficient and flexible perception pipeline for autonomous agents. Computer Graphics Forum 18(3), 23–30 (1999)
3. Bordini, R.H., Hubner, J.F., Wooldridge, M.: Programming multi-agent systems in AgentSpeak using Jason. John Wiley & Sons Ltd., England (2007)
4. Buford, J., Jakobson, G., Lewis, L.: Multi-agent situation management for supporting large-scale disaster relief operations. Intelligent Control and Systems 11(4), 284–295 (2006)
5. Dahlbom, A.: Petri nets for Situation Recognition. PhD thesis, University of Sköve, Örebro University (2011)
6. Dignum, F., Westra, J., van Doesburg, W.A., Harbers, M.: Games and agents: Designing intelligent gameplay. International Journal of Computer Games Technology, 2009, 18 pages (2009)
7. Ehlert, P.A.M., Mouthaan, Q.M., Rothkrantz, L.: A rule-based and a probabilistic system for situation recognition in a flight simulator. In: Mehdi, Q.H., Gough, N., Natkin, S. (eds.) Proceedings of 4th International Conference on Intelligent Games and Simulation (GAME-ON 2003), Eurosis, pp. 201–207 (2003)
8. Endsley, M.R.: Toward a theory of situation awareness in dynamic systems. Human Factors: The Journal of the Human Factors and Ergonomics Society 37(1), 32–64 (1995)
9. Gemrot, J., Brom, C., Plch, T.: A Periphery of Pogamut: From Bots to Agents and Back Again. In: Dignum, F. (ed.) Agents for Games and Simulations II. LNCS, vol. 6525, pp. 19–37. Springer, Heidelberg (2011)

10. Jakobson, G., Buford, J., Lewis, L.: Situation management: Basic concepts and approaches. In: Popovich, V.V., Schrenk, M., Korolenko, K.V. (eds.) Information Fusion and Geographic Information Systems. Lecture Notes in Geoinformation and Cartography, pp. 18–33. Springer (2007)

11. Peters, C., Castellano, G., Rehm, M., André, E., Raouzaiou, A., Rapantzikos, K., Karpouzis, K., Volpe, G., Camurri, A., Vasalou, A.: Fundamentals of agent perception and attention modelling. In: Cowie, R., Pelachaud, C., Petta, P. (eds.) Emotion-Oriented Systems, Cognitive Technologies, pp. 293–319. Springer, Heidelberg (2011)

12. Ranathunga, S., Cranefield, S., Purvis, M.: Extracting Data from Second Life. In: Discussion Paper 2011/07, Department of Information Science, University of Otago (2011), http://otago.ourarchive.ac.nz/handle/10523/1802

13. Ranathunga, S., Cranefield, S., Purvis, M.: Identifying events taking place in Second Life virtual environments. Applied Artificial Intelligence 26, 137–181 (2012)

14. So, R., Sonenberg, L.: Situation awareness in intelligent agents: Foundations for a theory of proactive agent behavior. In: Proceedings of the IEEE/WIC/ACM International Conference on Intelligent Agent Technology, pp. 86–92. IEEE Computer Society (2004)

15. So, R., Sonenberg, L.: Situation awareness as a form of meta-level control. In: Proceedings of the First International Workshop on Metareasoning in Agent-Based Systems at the Sixth International Joint Conference on Autonomous Agents and Multiagent Systems, Honolulu, Hawaii (2007)

16. Thangarajah, J., Padgham, L., Sardina, S.: Modelling situations in intelligent agents. In: Proceedings of the Fifth International Joint Conference on Autonomous Agents and Multiagent Systems, pp. 1049–1051. ACM (2006)

17. Vosinakis, S., Panayiotopoulos, T.: Programmable Agent Perception in Intelligent Virtual Environments. In: Rist, T., Aylett, R.S., Ballin, D., Rickel, J. (eds.) IVA 2003. LNCS (LNAI), vol. 2792, pp. 202–206. Springer, Heidelberg (2003)

18. Zhang, W., Hill Jr., R.W.: A template-based and pattern-driven approach to situation awareness and assessment in virtual humans. In: Proceedings of the Fourth International Conference on Autonomous Agents, pp. 116–123. ACM (2000)

Generating Corpora of Activities of Daily Living and towards Measuring the Corpora's Complexity

Rudolf Kadlec, Michal Čermák, Zdeněk Behan, and Cyril Brom

Faculty of Mathematics and Physics
Charles University in Prague
Czech Republic
rudolf.kadlec@gmail.com, mikajel@yahoo.com,
rain@matfyz.cz, brom@ksvi.mff.cuni.cz
http://amis.ms.mff.cuni.cz

Abstract. Episodic memory modeling enjoys increasing interest in virtual agents, autonomous companions or computer games research communities. To evaluate memory models, it is often necessary to "fill" them with appropriate data - streams of activities corresponding to what would happen to a real human during a particular time period. However, such activity corpora, freely available, are, to our best knowledge, lacking. This paper has two goals. First, it shows two already implemented complementary approaches to generating activity corpora. While the first one uses HTN planning to create a corpus with relatively abstract activities, the second one utilizes a 3D simulation to generate a stream of more fine-grained actions. The key question is evaluation of the resulting corpora in terms of their resemblance to streams of activities of real humans. Thus, the second goal of this paper is to compare the generated corpora to several known datasets of human activity, based on their entropy, compressibility and statistics of transitions between actions. This can be conceived as a first step towards creating general complexity measures of streams of human actions and we see it as the main contribution of this paper.

Keywords: Virtual agents, Behavior complexity measurement, HTN planning, AND-OR trees, Compressibility, Entropy.

1 Introduction

Episodic memory [30] modeling, that is, modeling a memory for personal history of an entity, enjoys increasing interest in agents and robotic research communities. Possible applications of autonomous entities with episodic memory range from videogames in large role playing games to artificial companions (reviewed in [7]).

Every day in human life brings a number of events that can be possibly remembered. When equipping an autonomous entity with episodic memory abilities, a

F. Dignum et al. (Eds.): CAVE 2012, LNAI 7764, pp. 149–166, 2013.
© Springer-Verlag Berlin Heidelberg 2013

researcher must be able to generate streams of such events to evaluate the memory model; otherwise, the model would exist in a vacuum. Two open questions are how to generate these *event streams* so that they are similar to event streams of real humans, and how to objectify the similarity. In this paper, we address these questions. We extend previous approaches to generation of event streams and present new complexity measures of these streams.

There are many types of events. Their list includes, but is not limited to, conversational events, physiological events, thought events, perceptual events concerning surrounding entities, and events about starts and ends of activities an agent is engaged in directly. Here, we specifically focus at streams of events of the last kind. Technically, these streams can be conceived as lists of activities that the agent is performing and that change the environmental state.

Such activities are of various complexities: moving a finger is a more fine-grained action than visiting grandparents in Rome. Our goal is to generate event streams with atomic level roughly corresponding to activities such as "sleep," "wake up," "brush teeth," "eat," etc. For example we are not interested in modeling every step in walking, nevertheless our approach enables adding this level of detail if needed. At the same time, our goal is to generate streams for months-long periods (think of a persistent world of a MMORPG). Thus, we also need to group these actions recursively into clusters of increasingly more abstract activities such as "eat," "dinner in restaurant" and "enjoying an evening," a hierarchical approach.

In this paper, we use two complementary methods for generating corporas of activities of daily living (henceforth ADL corpora or ADL stream). While one generates a preliminary ADL stream and then executes it in a 3D environment producing a final stream, the other employs only the first step. The 3D simulation used by the former approach can add an interesting detail to the stream, e.g. interruption of actions, but the cost is increased computational time. Consequently the former approach is suitable for generating shorter streams, e.g. for a month long period, and the latter is suitable for half year long periods. Both mechanisms output a hierarchically represented ADL corpora. These two techniques capitalize on already known approaches to action selection and corpora generation and do not present significant contribution *per se*.

The main contribution is defining new measures of behavior complexity and applying them on our corpora and also on behavior data obtained from real settings. We will demonstrate that the outputs of our two methods are similar to real world data according to these measures. From the methodological perspective, this work can be also conceived as evaluation of these measures *per se*. We discuss in the paper the possibilities of general application of the measures, their limitations and next steps. We see these measures as a first step towards a set of more expressive measures capturing also other aspects of the behavior. Relation of these measures to humans' judgment of the behavior also remains as a future work.

The rest of the paper continues as follows. In the next section we describe requirements that we have on our programs for generating the corporas. In Section 3 we detail our two programs and show how the requirements are implemented. In Section 4 we define several measures, apply them on the generated streams and compare the results with real datasets. We close the paper with Discussion and Future Work.

2 Requirements

The goal is to generate a parameterizable corpus of ADL. Most notable requirements on the programs are:

1. Capture daily human activity regularities.
2. Create different behavior variants through nondeterminism.
3. Use hierarchical behavior representation.
4. Provide non-trivial number of alternative behavior decompositions.
5. Include objects as resources of some behaviors.
6. Assert plausible frequency of different behaviors.
7. Provide open-source implementation of the programs.

Both our programs address these requirements.

3 Corpora Generation

In this section we detail our two programs. The former uses HTN planner for generating ADL and the latter uses hierarchical reactive planner and also includes 3D simulation in the production loop. For example, concerning movement, the output of both programs is one action $MOVE(FROM, TO)$; however, the latter simulates walking the agent along the respective navigation graph step by step, which may result in altering the final destination.

We first describe the HTN approach and then the hierarchical reactive planning approach.

3.1 Planning Approach

Our planning algorithm is based on a randomized version of the HTN planner SHOP2 [23] developed by [5]. Besides simple randomization of possible alternative goal decompositions introduced in [5] we extended the planning algorithm with probabilities of alternative decompositions used to fulfill different goals. Previous version [5] used only uniform distribution in selection of alternatives. We decided to use HTN because our previous work [21] comparing several PDDL planners shows that they suffered serious performance degradation issues when applied to a domain of our size. The source code of the modified SHOP2 planner explained here and a code of our domain is available online[1] under GNU GPL license.

---

[1] Homepage of our planning program is at http://code.google.com/p/epis-planner/ [16.9.2011].

Technical Details. The SHOP2 planner does not operate directly with time and generally outputs a satisfactory plan. Thus to meet Req. 1 we create a hierarchy of tasks starting with one root task *DAY* that is decomposed to tasks corresponding to various parts of the day: *MORNING, BEFORE-NOON, NOON, AFTER-NOON, EVENING and NIGHT*. These tasks are not part of the real stream of an agent's actions. They serve as a tool that helps to simulate different parts of the day and ensure time flow continuity. Each task representing a real activity of an agent is then associated with some time interval, which ensures that tasks are performed in corresponding time.

Req. 2 on nondeterminism was already addressed by the previous work [5] that we are building upon. In [5] all alternative task decompositions have the same probability of being chosen, that is the probability of choosing decomposition T of parent Pa is: $P(T|Pa) = \frac{1}{|children(Pa)|}$, where $children(Pa)$ denotes a set of all applicable decompositions. We extended this simple schema and introduced *weight of the decomposition* $W_T \in (0, \infty)$. Now the probability of selecting decomposition T is given by:

$$P(T|Pa) = \frac{W_T}{\sum_{t \in children(Pa)} W_t}$$

This way we can introduce some rare events like illness etc.

Req. 3 and 5 are naturally addressed by the SHOP planner. Hierarchical decomposition is an innate property of the HTN formalism and objects can be easily incorporated into the plan as parameters of actions in a STRIPS like notation.

High number of alternatives (Req. 4) for each goal is fulfilled by the domain, e.g. in our domain goal *satisfy hunger* has three different decompositions that have further variants. At the end there are 15 different ways the goal can be accomplished. Similarly, Req. 6 is addressed by the domain. More detailed description of the domain is available on the program's web page.

Example Code. Here is an example of definition of our domain.

Listing 1.1. Example of method definition

```
(:method :weight 2 (ASatisfyHunger)
    eat-outside
    ((hungry)
     (affordance ?place to-eat)
     (affordance ?place menu ?food))
    ((GetTo ?place)
     (!order ?food) (!eat ?food)
     (!drink))
)
```

Listing 1.2. Example of operator definition

```
(:operator (!eat ?food)
    () ((hungry)) ()
)
```

Listing 1.1 shows an HTN method *ASatisfyHunger* defining one possible decomposition of satisfying hunger. Each definition of a method is equivalent to an OR-node in the AND-OR tree formalism. Each child in the decomposition is equivalent to an AND-node. In this case, we describe a way how to satisfy a hunger by finding a place where we can eat, traveling there, picking a random item from a menu and eating it. Operators are elements that can have a direct influence on a state of the world. The operator *!eat* defined in Listing 1.2 removes the fact *hungry* from the current world state. Listing 1.3 shows an example of output of our program: a stream of actions corresponding to a visit of the pub *PUB1*. Some of the actions are parameterized with objects or places needed for their proper execution.

Our domain consists of 56 operators, 8 top level methods, 19 methods in total plus another 16 auxiliary methods used to capture different parts of the day and finally 81 atoms representing places and objects in the world.

Listing 1.3. Example of generated stream of actions

```
GET-TO-TRAMSTOP STATION_WORK
WAIT-FOR-TRAM TRAM22
BOARD-TRAM TRAM22
RIDETRAM TRAM22 STATION_WORK STATION_PUB1
EXIT-TRAM TRAM22
GET-TO STATION_PUB1 PUB1
ENTER PUB1
DANCE
ORDER-BEER
DRINK
CHAT
LEAVE PUB1
GET-TO PUB1 STATION_PUB1
WAIT-FOR-TRAM TRAM14
BOARD-TRAM TRAM14
```

3.2 3D Simulation Approach

Our second program using hierarchical reactive planning produces a flat preliminary stream of ADL, which is then executed in a 3D virtual environment in an accelerated way. This helps with dealing with visibility of objects, action failures etc. An agent's decision making is based on a concept of AND-OR trees, see [8]. The scheduling algorithm chooses a top-level goal that will be executed by the agent and execution of this goal is then driven by the AND-OR tree representing possible behavior to accomplish the top-level goal. The chosen tree is then executed in the virtual environment. During the actual simulation the agent also collects objects required to perform those actions. The final output is a hierarchical ADL.

Technical Details. Requirements 1 and 2 on regularity and nondeterminism are addressed by a scheduling mechanism used to create the agent's schedule for each day. The schedule defines which goals can be executed at a particular simulation time.

To define the schedule we will introduce following terms:

1. G is a set of all top-level goals that can be performed by the agent. G_0 is this set plus no_goal element, that is $G_0 = G \cup \{no\_goal\}$.
2. Transition λ is a triplet (g_1, g_2, T) where $g_1 \in G_0, g_2 \in G$ and T is a time interval when this transition can be applied.
3. Schedule S is a set of transitions λ and a function p assigning each transition a probability of being applied $p(\lambda)$. A valid schedule must fulfill: $\forall t \forall g_1 \in G_0$: $\sum_{\lambda \in S, \lambda = (g_1, g_2, T), t \in T} p(\lambda) = 1$, where t denotes simulation time.

During the simulation the agent performs top-level goals from the schedule. When the execution of a top-level goal is finished, all transitions applicable to the current simulation time and the previous top-level goal are found and one of them is chosen according to their probabilities. In some cases (e.g. start of simulation, no applicable transition is found) the agent may not follow any goal. In this case the next goal will be chosen from the transitions that are applicable to the current simulation time where $g_1 = no\_goal$. For any time such transition has to be defined in a valid schedule.

Scheduling top-level goals is done with granularity of 1 hour, meaning the boundaries of a time interval in a transition will always be whole hours. Beside hours, day of week can be defined for each time interval, e.g. *[08:00, 11:00] on Monday.* It is also possible to define general intervals valid for any day of a week or change the granularity of 1 hour.

In contrast with the HTN approach where the generated plan was immediately outputted as an activity stream here the schedule serves only as an "advice" for the simulated agent, some goals in the schedule can be for example interrupted during the simulation by external forces. This also adds to the nondeterminism of the simulation.

Req. 3 is met by using the AND-OR tree formalism. For each atomic action executed in the environment we have a trace of possibly several higher level goals, e.g. $Work \rightarrow Commute \rightarrow Walk$.

High number of alternative decompositions for higher level goals (Req. 4) is given by design of the domain. For our simulation we have created a schedule representing top-level goals of a single worker living in a city. He is following a general plan based on a working week; he sleeps each night, goes to work on week days, enjoys free time during evenings and weekends. Our agent can follow 27 different top-level goals. These range from basic goals like sleeping to more complex ones like going to work, drinking in a pub or doing physical activities.

Complex goals are defined by more complex AND-OR trees. Therefore every execution of the top-level goal can generate a different stream of atomic actions.

Currently the most complex goal defined in our program is the top-level goal *to work*. Courses of executions of this goal can differ in details like going to work by foot or taking the public transportation, or in more important points like working in the office building or working from home. Altogether our *to work* goal can be completed by 160 unique sequences of atomic actions.

Of course not all available top-level goals offer such variability and there are several goals, like sleeping, that offer no variability at all. Altogether more than half of our 27 different top-level goals offer at least 10 different ways how the goal can be achieved.

As in the HTN approach, objects or places are needed as preconditions for performing some actions (Req. 5). For example, in order to buy some groceries, the agent needs to localize a place with type *supermarket* and needs to acquire an object of type *money*.

Defining different frequencies for different behaviors (Req. 6) is enabled due to the scheduling mechanism described above. Frequency can range from several executions a day to less than one execution in a week.

Virtual Environment. Actual simulation is run in Pogamut platform [11] on Unreal Tournament 2004² engine. A specific map of a small town that contains all the objects and places necessary to follow an agent's plan is used. Different buildings in the map represent his home, work, shops, restaurants, etc. It is possible to watch an agent as he moves in the virtual world. The actual atomic actions, except for walking and running, are not literally executed by the agent; he simply runs to the adequate place on a map and sends a message about execution of an atomic action without performing the low level animation (Fig. 1).

Fig. 1. Screenshot of a simulation showing an agent in a virtual kitchen

---

² Epic Games, 2004,
   http://en.wikipedia.org/wiki/Unreal_Tournament_2004 [19.9.2011].

4 Behavior Statistics and Complexity

Requirements 1, 2 and 4 from Section 2 call for generating streams of actions that will be similar to activity of humans. Note we are not discussing here believability of animations, gestures or facial expressions of agents, which are studied in the field of virtual agents often, but believability of long streams of actions as defined in Introduction. It is unclear how to measure this quality, to our knowledge the field is lacking some widely accepted measure of complexity and believability of agent's behavior. Some initial steps in this direction have already been done. Arrabales et al. [2] provide scale for a measurement of single agent's complexity but it depends on subjective human assessment of the agent's behavior and its decision making algorithm. Alternative to this approach is [19] that proposes objective measures like *size of a procedural knowledge* but these measures are not always related to believability of the observed behavior.

We have to ask what properties of an activity stream can contribute to its believability. Is a sequence of actions *raise hammer, hammer in nail* and so on repeatedly believable? In some contexts it could be but not for a long time. We would say that this behavior is too predictable and lacks deviations that are inherent to behavior of any creature, be it a human or an animal. To reveal these highly predictable behaviors we take two sources of inspiration from the information theory. We can model the activity stream as a Markov source and we can measure its entropy. Similar technique that tries to measure the amount of predictability of the sequence is compression ratio. Finally properties of the transition matrix can be also inspected.

Eventually to compare results obtained from our artificial domains to reality we use the same measures on several dataset obtained in real settings. Following sections detail the measures and datasets used and results of our analysis.

4.1 Measures Used

Behavior Entropy. Entropy rate can be used as a measure of unpredictability of an agent's actions. Because the agent's behavior often includes dependencies between executed sub-behaviors we can model it as a Markov source. Under Markov assumption we can measure entropy of the source and use it as one descriptor of the behavior. Assuming the action source is 0, 1st and 2nd order Markov source the calculation of respective entropy rates H^0, H^1 and H^2 is given by the following equations:

$$H^0(S) = -\sum_i p_i log_b p_i$$

$$H^1(S) = -\sum_i p_i \sum_j p_{i,j} log_b p_{i,j}$$

$$H^2(S) = -\sum_i p_i \sum_j p_{i,j} \sum_k p_{i,j,k} log_b p_{i,j,k}$$

where p_i, $p_{i,j}$, $p_{i,j,k}$, respectively, denotes probability of action A_i, sequences of actions A_iA_j and $A_iA_jA_k$, respectively, and b is a number of actions present in the stream. We can define entropies of higher orders analogically.

To get a grasp of the quantity measured by entropies of different orders see Tab. 1. Sequence $AAAA$ that can correspond to sequence *go to work, go to work* ... is entirely predictable thus all entropy rates are 0. On the other hand sequence $ABAB$ is unpredictable if we consider it as an unordered set of symbols, both A and B are equally likely, that is $H^0 = 1$. However if we view it as a first order Markov sequence it becomes perfectly regular, A is always followed by B and vice versa. Knowledge of one last symbol is sufficient to predict the next one, thus $H^1 = 0$. The example of sequence $AABB$ takes this one step further. We have to take into account two last symbols to reveal regularity of the sequence.

Table 1. Example of entropy rates for several example sequences

Sequence	H^0	H^1	H^2
AAAA	0	0	0
ABAB	1	0	0
AABB	1	1	0

Notice that we use *log* with base b instead of 2. This is because different domains can use different number of atomic actions. Using log_b normalizes the entropy to the interval $\langle 0, 1 \rangle$ and thus makes it possible, in theory, to compare the values across different domains. The log_b normalization maintains the property that a completely deterministic sequence will have entropy 0, whereas a sequence with uniformly distributed probabilities of all actions will have entropy 1. In practice, we think it is meaningful to compare domains with a similar number of actions, but we do not claim that comparison between domains with 2 actions and 100 actions will make sense.

Compressibility. Compression ratio of a sequence can be used as another measure of its complexity. Examples of using compression algorithms to measure sequence complexity can be found in genetic optimization [12] or in ethology [25].

Compressibility is connected to a more general framework of the minimum description length (MDL) [22] principle. The idealized version of the MDL searches for the shortest program written in a Touring complete programming language that can generate a given sequence. The length of the program can then be taken as a measure of complexity of the sequence. Unfortunately this definition is rather impractical since Touring complete languages are too expressive and MDL defined in this way is uncomputable. However when choosing simpler languages than the Touring complete ones we can compute shorter descriptions of the data and that is what compression algorithms do. Thus we can use compression algorithm of our choice and apply it to the sequence of atomic actions produced by the agent.

Markov Process Perspective. Besides measuring unpredictability of the sequence we can also inspect distribution of frequency of the actions and properties of the transition matrix like distribution of *in degrees* of the actions.

4.2 Analysis Methodology

Datasets. We selected several sources of human activity data to compare their complexity with our activity streams generated by the programs. The datasets come from various sources, PLCouple1 [14], Huyhan [13], Kadlec [17] originate in ubiquitous computing, Restaurant game [24] is an online computer game, Behan-HTN and Cermak-3D datasets are our own generated datasets, Behan-HTN dataset was generated by the HTN planning (Sec. 3.1), Cermak-3D dataset by the 3D simulation (Sec. 3.2).

Even though some of those datasets contain additional sensory information (e.g. accelerometer data or GPS locations in ubiquitous computing datasets) for purposes of behavior complexity measure we are using only the activity annotation. We also merge subsequent executions of a same action into one. We now detail settings where the datasets were collected.

PLCouple1 dataset [14][3] was recorded in a smart home setting inhabited by two people, the dataset even includes video recordings. 100 hours of the activity of one inhabitant was then manually annotated.

Huyhn dataset [13][4] was recorded mostly in home and office setting, a participant was equipped with three 3D accelerometers whose readings were later used for activity recognition.

Kadlec dataset [17] comes from a project that tries to create an automatic diary from data collected by a smart phone. The dataset was collected during a training phase of the system where the user had to hierarchically annotate his activity. The dataset denoted *LL-Kadlec* is the set with the whole action hierarchy (e.g. one action could be $Work \rightarrow Commute \rightarrow Walk$) and *LLA-Kadlec* contains only the atomic actions (action from the previous example will be reduced to $Walk$ only).

Restaurant game dataset [24] consists of behavior logs recorded in an online 3D game, where players played a waitress or a customer. The original aim of the work is to create a library of behaviors from these logs that can be used by autonomous agents playing the game. We use only the customer's actions and denote this dataset as *CUSTOMER*.

Besides these datasets selected for our analysis there are also other similar datasets, e.g. [31,28,18]. We could not use them, because [31] provides 245 annotated activities only and [18] lacks the activity annotation. The dataset [28][5] is large enough, but it was released only a few weeks ago. Tab. 2 compares properties of datasets used in our analysis.

---

[3] http://architecture.mit.edu/house_n/data/PlaceLab/
PlaceLab.htm [5.7.2011].
[4] http://www.ess.tu-darmstadt.de/datasets/tud-ubicomp08 [26.8.2011].
[5] http://www.opportunity-project.eu/challengeDownload [4.10.2011].

As a baseline we also included two artificial datasets. One denoted as *det* consists of completely deterministic sequences (4 types of sequences that are repetitions of patterns AB, AABB, ABCABC and AABAAC), this simulates unnaturally long repetitive sequences of actions, e.g. mechanical *hammering in nails* over a very long period. The second denoted as *rAB* consists of random uniformly sampled sequences of 2 up to 5 symbols, this can be interpreted as the other extreme of the spectrum, activity driven by flipping coins.

Table 2. Overview of the activity datasets. Letters in the Type column means: R — data from real environments, manual annotation of human actions; V — human activity in a virtual environment; S — computer simulated agents in virtual environment. Size denotes number of actions in the dataset. *We use only a limited subset of the Restaurant Game dataset.

Dataset	Type	Size	Act. types
PLCouple1 [14]	R	900	44
Huyhn [13]	R	462	34
LL-Kadlec [17]	R	5185	369
LLA-Kadlec [17]	R	5185	40
CUSTOMER [24]	V	3472*	13
Behan-HTN	S	∞	55
Cermak-3D	S	∞	62

4.3   Dataset Analysis

For analysis we used the R statistical software [26], graphs were created using the ggplot2 [32] package.

Entropy. We measured entropy of all datasets using equations given in Section 4.1. Fig. 2 shows entropies of all the datasets. As can be seen the entropy of randomly uniformly sampled sequences is close to 1, all the other sequences including *det* has lower entropy, which is decreasing with increasing order of entropy. As we can see the *LLA-Kadlec* has higher entropy than the *LL-Kadlec*. This is because the latter dataset contains the whole hierarchy of actions, that is the atomic actions' context decreases the uncertainty. Our *Behan-HTN* has lower H^1 and H^2 entropies than others, suggesting a room for improvement.

Compressibility. When we use compressibility ratio as a measure, the length of the sequence plays a role since longer sequences with some regularity tend to have better compression ratio than the shorter ones. Therefore we took the length of the shortest sequence (462 actions long Huyhan dataset) and splitted the other datasets into multiple sequences of this length. For each sequence we measured its compression ratio with several compression algorithms, namely:

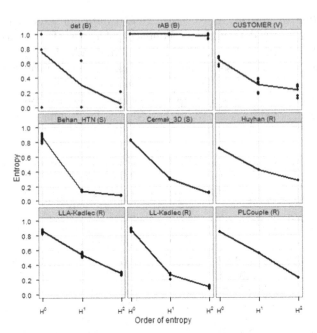

Fig. 2. Dependence of entropy on the number of past steps used for conditioning. Lines show means of the distributions. Letters V, S, R are explained in Tab. 2, B denotes baseline dataset.

GZIP[6], Snappy[7], LZMA[8], LZF[9], QuickLZ[10] and bzip2[11]. Every action in a particular sequence was coded as a single letter (e.g. *Eat, Drink, Eat* was coded as *A, B, A*). Information about duration or objects involved was removed in this phase. Eventually we combined the measured compression ratios with entropies H^0, H^1, H^2 and also H^3 and performed a principal component analysis [16] (PCA) on these observations.

Fig. 3 shows the projection of the observations. To better understand the projection Tab. 3 shows directions of the first two principal components, PC1 and PC2. PC1 depends strongly on the compression ratios, the best compressible sequences are on the left on Fig. 3, sequences with worse compression ratios are on the right, whereas PC2 depends more on the entropy rates, high entropy sequences are on the bottom, lower entropy sequences are at the top. PC1 accounts for 0.62% of variance, PC1 and PC2 together account for 0.86% of variance of the data. We can note that all compression algorithms contribute about the same to PC1, this is because of strong correlation of compression ratios (all pairwise correlations are > 0.94).

---

[6] http://www.gzip.org/ [17.9.2010].

[7] http://code.google.com/p/snappy/ [17.9.2010].

[8] http://www.7-zip.org/ [17.9.2010].

[9] https://github.com/ning/compress/ [17.9.2010].

[10] http://www.quicklz.com [17.9.2010].

[11] http://bzip.org/ [17.9.2010].

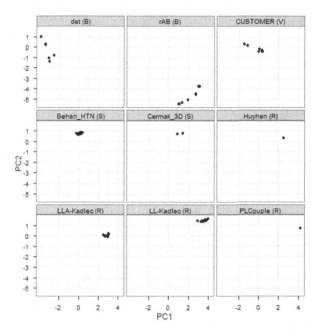

Fig. 3. PCA of behavioral datasets. Each point represents one sequence of the given type.

Table 3. Vectors of the first two principal components

	H^0	H^1	H^2	H^3	BZIP2	GZIP	LZF	LZMA	QuickLZ	Snappy
PC1	0.10	0.29	0.20	0.04	0.35	0.37	0.39	0.39	0.39	0.39
PC2	-0.43	0.37	0.50	0.57	-0.24	-0.18	-0.00	-0.09	-0.02	0.02

We can see that the datasets obtained in real settings (*PLCouple, LL-Kadlec, LLA-Kadlec, Huyhan*) all fall to similar cluster of sequences that are hard to compress but they have much lower entropy than random sequences. Datasets obtained by programs (*Behan-HTN, Cermak-3D*) are a bit easier to compress and Behan-HTN also has a bit lower entropy; there is room for improvement but still they are close to the real datasets. We also see that not only *rAB*, but also *det*, which scored similarly to natural datasets according to H^0, H^1 and H^2 alone, are substantially different.

Markov Process Perspective. PCA brought some insight into structure of the datasets but we can further inspect the datasets from other perspectives. One natural is distribution of actions' frequencies. Fig. 4 shows that all the natural datasets and both our datasets, but not the baselines, follow similar exponential like distribution, having many rare actions and a few common actions.

Small variation of the previous approach is analysis of number of the action classes preceding a given class, that is *in degree* of a given action class in a transition graph corresponding to a first order Markov process learned from the

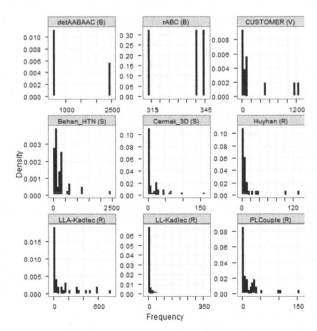

Fig. 4. Histograms of action frequencies. X axis is number of repetitions of the given action, Y axis shows density - proportion of actions with given frequency in the whole dataset.

dataset. Fig. 5 shows distributions of in degrees. We see that both our datasets and all real datasets with the exception of *CUSTOMER* dataset again follow similar exponential like distribution. *CUSTOMER* dataset has a lot of actions with many predecessors and fewer actions with only a few predecessors. This can be caused by the fact that players of the Restaurant game where this dataset originates from had to explore an environment of the game and all its possibilities to learn how the environment works. Thus they may try several combinations of actions that they would not do in real life; additional analysis would be needed.

5   Discussion and Future Work

We presented our two programs for generation of activities of daily living. Domain specifications, i.e. inputs of the programs, present an agent's life style. For every domain, we are able to generate different variants of activity streams, i.e. different courses of a particular life period; the approaches are partly nondeterministic. The generation of month long periods takes minutes of computation time. We will use the corpora for evaluating our new episodic memory model for virtual agents, which we develop in parallel.

To evaluate resemblance of the generated activity streams to streams of activities of real humans, we defined several measures of complexity of the sequences, namely conditioned entropy, compressibility and properties of transitions between actions. We compared our corpora to several other sources of activity

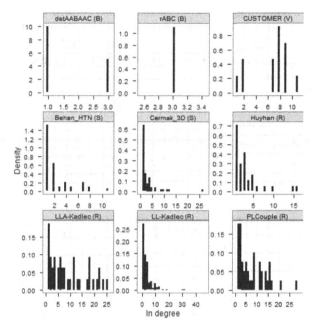

Fig. 5. Histograms of in degrees

obtained in real settings, demonstrating that our corpora resemble the real-world ones unlike two mechanistic baselines. Our corpora are still a bit more predictable than the real-world datasets since they could be compressed better and one of them has a bit lower entropy, suggesting room for improvements.

The measures *per se* are useful, because they cluster together datasets that a user would expect to share some commonalities yet reveal differences between datasets with different features.

One next step is refining the measures to show finer differences between the datasets as was the example of *CUSTOMER* dataset and its in-degree distribution. This can enhance the projections of datasets through PCA.

New measures can come from addressing limitations of the current approach: 1) we are not encoding use of objects explicitly, even though corpora are generated with objects; 2) there is no mechanism dealing with similarity of actions; 3) we are not taking into account duration of actions. In our opinion, a probabilistic graphical model [20] could address most of these issues. For purposes of episodic memory modeling we would also like to encode percepts of the agent since they can be also stored in the memory. This would make it possible to distinguish "empty" worlds from those populated with many changing objects and agents.

Another next step is improving the approaches to corpora generation. As shown above, we still "not there yet" in terms of resemblance to real datasets.

Our approach to ADL generation can be also used in the context of plan recognition, e.g. [6], or traffic simulation, e.g. [3]. Our measures could also be incorporated into development cycle of virtual agents and used along with the well established practice of unit testing. Besides unit tests whose result is fail/-

success, we can record an agent's actions and compare them with previous runs of the same agent. Unexpected shifts in the measures possibly plotted using PCA can signal unwanted changes in the agent's behavior and hence probably also in its functionality. The measures could also be tested in different simulations of human behavior (e.g. [1]), or in completely different domains like maritime simulations [15].

The work that remains to be done is to find whether there is a correlation between some of our measures and human's rating of sequences on a scale from artificial to natural. E.g. it seems reasonable to require some incompressibility of the streams we do not know if this is really the important aspect of being "natural". The same question of connectedness to human rating applies also to the other measures.

On a more general level one possible direction of a future work could be to characterize mathematically a minimal model needed to generate believable streams of actions, i.e. to find a model that is able to *fool* all measures comparing its actions to real datasets. We could see such model as an analogy to scale-free networks describing topology of World Wide Web [4], Brownian motion or recently criticized [10] Lévy flight concept [29]. Formulation of such model grounded in real data could also have implications for design of programming languages oriented on specification of virtual agents behavior like POSH [9] or AgentSpeak [27].

We do not claim that we have solved the problem of behavior complexity measure but we think that our approach combining entropy and compressibility can be used as a first step in exploratory analysis of a behavior expressed by an unknown agent. His behavior can be plotted against other known datasets and we can quickly get first impression of its complexity.

Acknowledgment. This work was partially supported by the student research grant GAUK 0449/2010 A-INF/MFF, by the SVV project number 265 314 and by the grants GACR 201/09/H057 and P103/10/1287.

References

1. Allbeck, J., Badler, N.: Simulating human activities for synthetic inputs to sensor systems. Distributed Video Sensor Networks, 193–205 (2011)
2. Arrabales, R., Ledezma, A., Sanchis, A.: ConsScale: A pragmatic scale for measuring the level of consciousness in artificial agents. Journal of Consciousness Studies 17(3-4), 131–164 (2010), http://www.ingentaconnect.com/content/imp/jcs/2010/00000017/F0020003/art00008
3. Balmer, M., Meister, K., Rieser, M., Nagel, K., Axhausen, K.: Agent-based simulation of travel demand: Structure and computational performance of MATSim-T. In: 2nd TRB Conference on Innovations in Travel Modeling, Portland (2008)
4. Barabási, A., Albert, R.: Emergence of scaling in random networks. Science 286(5439), 509 (1999)
5. Blaylock, N., Allen, J.: Generating Artificial Corpora for Plan Recognition. In: Ardissono, L., Brna, P., Mitrović, A. (eds.) UM 2005. LNCS (LNAI), vol. 3538, pp. 179–188. Springer, Heidelberg (2005)

6. Blaylock, N., Allen, J.: Fast hierarchical goal schema recognition. In: Proceedings of the National Conference on Artificial Intelligence, vol. 21(1), p. 796. AAAI Press/MIT Press, Menlo Park/Cambridge (1999)

7. Brom, C., Lukavský, J.: Towards virtual characters with a full episodic memory ii: The episodic memory strikes back. In: Proc. Empathic Agents, AAMAS workshop, pp. 1–9 (2009)

8. Brom, C., Pešková, K., Lukavský, J.: What Does Your Actor Remember? Towards Characters with a Full Episodic Memory. In: Cavazza, M., Donikian, S. (eds.) ICVS-VirtStory 2007. LNCS, vol. 4871, pp. 89–101. Springer, Heidelberg (2007)

9. Bryson, J., Stein, L.: Modularity and design in reactive intelligence. In: International Joint Conference on Artificial Intelligence, vol. 17(1), pp. 1115–1120 (2001)

10. Edwards, A., Phillips, R., Watkins, N., Freeman, M., Murphy, E., Afanasyev, V., Buldyrev, S., da Luz, M., Raposo, E., Stanley, H., et al.: Revisiting Lévy flight search patterns of wandering albatrosses, bumblebees and deer. Nature 449(7165), 1044–1048 (2007)

11. Gemrot, J., Kadlec, R., Bída, M., Burkert, O., Píbil, R., Havlíček, J., Zemčák, L., Šimlovič, J., Vansa, R., Štolba, M., Plch, T., Brom, C.: Pogamut 3 Can Assist Developers in Building AI (Not Only) for Their Videogame Agents. In: Dignum, F., Bradshaw, J., Silverman, B., van Doesburg, W. (eds.) Agents for Games and Simulations. LNCS, vol. 5920, pp. 1–15. Springer, Heidelberg (2009)

12. Gomez, F.J., Togelius, J., Schmidhuber, J.: Measuring and Optimizing Behavioral Complexity for Evolutionary Reinforcement Learning. In: Alippi, C., Polycarpou, M., Panayiotou, C., Ellinas, G. (eds.) ICANN 2009, Part II. LNCS, vol. 5769, pp. 765–774. Springer, Heidelberg (2009)

13. Huynh, T., Fritz, M., Schiele, B.: Discovery of activity patterns using topic models. In: Proceedings of the 10th International Conference on Ubiquitous Computing, pp. 10–19. ACM (2008)

14. Intille, S.S., Larson, K., Tapia, E.M., Beaudin, J.S., Kaushik, P., Nawyn, J., Rockinson, R.: Using a Live-In Laboratory for Ubiquitous Computing Research. In: Fishkin, K.P., Schiele, B., Nixon, P., Quigley, A. (eds.) PERVASIVE 2006. LNCS, vol. 3968, pp. 349–365. Springer, Heidelberg (2006)

15. Jakob, M., Vanek, O., Hrstka, O., Pechoucek, M.: Agents vs. pirates: Multi-agent simulation and optimization to fight maritime piracy. In: Proceedings of AAMAS, pp. 37–44 (2012)

16. Jolliffe, I.: Principal component analysis. Springer (2002)

17. Kadlec, R., Brom, C.: Towards an automatic diary: an activity recognition from a data collected by a mobile phone. In: Workshop Proceedings Space, Time and Ambient Intelligence (IJCAI), pp. 56–60 (2011), http://dl.dropbox.com/u/17077973/proceedings/STAMI-20110/ STAMI-11-IJCAI-Proceeding.pdf

18. Kiukkonen, N., Blom, J., Dousse, O., Gatica-Perez, D., Laurila, J.: Towards rich mobile phone datasets: Lausanne data collection campaign. In: Proceedings of the ACM International Conference on Pervasive Services (ICPS) (2010)

19. Klügl, F.: Measuring complexity of multi-agent simulations–an attempt using metrics. In: Languages, Methodologies and Development Tools for Multi-Agent Systems, pp. 123–138 (2008)

20. Koller, D., Friedman, N.: Probabilistic graphical models: principles and techniques. The MIT Press (2009)

21. Kučerová, L., Brom, C., Kadlec, R.: Towards planning the history of a virtual agent. In: ICAPS Workshop on Planning in Games (2010)

22. Li, M., Vitanyi, P.: An introduction to Kolmogorov complexity and its applications. Springer-Verlag New York Inc. (2008)
23. Nau, D., Au, T., Ilghami, O., Kuter, U., Murdock, J., Wu, D., Yaman, F.: SHOP2: An HTN planning system. Journal of Artificial Intelligence Research 20(1), 379–404 (2003)
24. Orkin, J., Roy, D.: The restaurant game: Learning social behavior and language from thousands of players online. Journal of Game Development 3(1), 39–60 (2007)
25. Panteleeva, S., Danzanov, Z., Reznikova, Z.: Estimate of complexity of behavioral patterns in ants: analysis of hunting behavior in myrmica rubra (hymenoptera, formicidae) as an example. Entomological Review 91(2), 221–230 (2011)
26. R Development Core Team: R: A Language and Environment for Statistical Computing. R Foundation for Statistical Computing, Vienna, Austria (2010), http://www.R-project.org/
27. Rao, A.: AgentSpeak(L): BDI agents speak out in a logical computable language. In: Perram, J., Van de Velde, W. (eds.) MAAMAW 1996. LNCS, vol. 1038, pp. 42–55. Springer, Heidelberg (1996)
28. Roggen, D., Calatroni, A., Rossi, M., Holleczek, T., Forster, K., Troster, G., Lukowicz, P., Bannach, D., Pirkl, G., Ferscha, A., et al.: Collecting complex activity datasets in highly rich networked sensor environments. In: Seventh International Conference on Networked Sensing Systems (INSS), pp. 233–240. IEEE (2010)
29. Shlesinger, M., Zaslavsky, G., Frisch, U.: Lévy flights and related topics in physics. Springer (1995)
30. Tulving, E.: Precis of elements of episodic memory. Behavioral and Brain Sciences 7(2), 223–268 (1984)
31. Van Kasteren, T., Noulas, A., Englebienne, G., Kröse, B.: Accurate activity recognition in a home setting. In: Proceedings of the 10th International Conference on Ubiquitous Computing, pp. 1–9. ACM (2008)
32. Wickham, H.: ggplot2: elegant graphics for data analysis. Springer, New York (2009), http://had.co.nz/ggplot2/book

Does High-Level Behavior Specification Tool Make Production of Virtual Agent Behaviors Better?

Jakub Gemrot, Zdeněk Hlávka, and Cyril Brom

Charles University in Prague, Faculty of Mathematics and Physics, Czech Republic

Abstract. Part of Academia's motivation for improving agent-based languages and architectures is the hope that some of its solutions might be, one day, adopted by the videogame industry for specification of agents' behavior. However, the games industry already employs its own techniques for that purpose. Thus we need rigorous empirical data to provide an insight to the expected utility of academic solutions and pinpoint their most promising features. Game programmers often face situations when they have to understand and modify the work of current or former colleagues, or to extend their own work from months or even years ago. Thus, one way an academia's solution could provide value would be that it outperforms the industry's typical approach under these circumstances – offering better code readability and maintainability. Here we present results of an empirical study modeling this problem. We adopt Java programming as the industry approach (modeling scripting) and choose the POSH reactive planner as an academic approach. We engaged 22 computer science students attending a university course on virtual agents on two programming assignments, in which they had to produce specific high-level behaviors of 3D virtual agents solving different game-like tasks. First, students had to produce the behavior of a particular task from scratch. Second, these behaviors were used in an assignment where students had to extend the behavior coded by someone else. Finally, three months later, 8 of these students were told to extend their own behavior they coded in the first assignment. The quantitative results indicate that Java is as good as POSH in terms of subjective programmers' preference and that there is no objective difference between qualities of created behaviors. The qualitative results suggest several useful but also troublesome features of POSH, some of which are shared by other languages, suggesting possible improvements.

Keywords: Virtual agents, Agent development techniques, Empirical studies.

1 Introduction

Reactive planning is currently the dominant paradigm for controlling virtual agents in 3D videogames and simulations. Prominent reactive planning techniques used in the industry are derivations of finite state machines (FSMs) [1] and behavior trees [2]. Technically, these are implemented in a scripting language, such as general-purpose Lua [3] or special-purpose UnrealScript [4], or they are hard-coded in a game's native language, typically C++ [5]. Advantages and drawbacks of different industry approaches have been commented on widely [6, 7, 8]. The general agreement in the academia is that scripting languages do not provide enough expressivity for creating

F. Dignum et al. (Eds.): CAVE 2012, LNAI 7764, pp. 167–183, 2013.

complex human-like agents, or it is cumbersome to use them for this task, and that there should be a better way for creating virtual agents behaviors.

At the same time, academia is producing action selection (AS) systems that seek to improve cognitive performance of agents. These include the decision making modules of cognitive architectures, e.g. Soar and ACT-R [9, 10], stand-alone BDI-based languages, e.g. GOAL [11], and reactive planners such as POSH [12]. It has been demonstrated that some of these systems, e.g. Soar [9], POSH [13], GOAL [11] and Jazzyk [14], can be used for controlling virtual agents acting in game-like environments. However, cognitive performance of an agent is not the only concern of the game industry. Ease of use, code readability and re-usability (of parts of code) play an important role in eagerness of adoption of new systems. In fact, these features may be more important than the agent's cognitive performance as the industry will be unlikely to adopt systems that are hard to use or produce code incomprehensible to anybody except the author.

Academic approaches often use custom behavioral languages to disguise underlying low-level code (in Lua, C++ etc.) forcing the programmer to think in high-level behavioral constructs, such as mental states, goals, action competences or triggers. These constructs are also defined explicitly as language primitives to be organized by programmers into behavioral plans that are interpreted by an AS system. Still, these AS systems are tied with the disguised low-level code for the purpose of communication with the environment, including information gathering and processing, and action executions and monitoring the course of the execution. The high-level languages typically lack synchronization or generic *while* statements to deal with application protocols gracefully, therefore AS systems must also define interfaces between these two levels. This two-layer architecture is thought to have several positive outcomes: 1) the low-level agent "periphery" should be reusable by different high-level plans, 2) well structured low-level code should improve comprehensibility, 3) correctly-separated high-level constructs should be easier to understand and extend, 4) a high-level plan is thought to be easily grasped by non-programmers, such as game designers, as it is more intuitive. Essentially, the high-level plan is to the low-level code what SQL is to Cobol.

Technically, one does not need an academic AS system featuring a high-level behavioral language to create complex behaviors. An option exists to hard-code everything inside the low-level code as we witness in many computer games. Which approach is better?

Two particular scenarios are encountered in game companies often and it is worth investigating this question in the context of these situations. First, when an AI developer leaves a company, somebody needs to continue his or her work. It is desirable that a developer's code is as comprehensible as possible (even without documentations and code commenting), so that it is easy to extend. Second, if a company creates a sequel to its game, it might be desirable that some existing code for the agents' behaviors is reused. Thus, it should be easy to augment or refactor existing behaviors.

The goal of this paper is to present results of a quasi-experimental, comparative study with both quantitative and qualitative measures modeling the above mentioned situations of AI developers, a method adopted from psychology and social sciences. The study's goal was to investigate whether an academic approach that combines both the lower and the higher level behavior description outperforms an industry approach employing only the lower level in the situations in question and at the same time, gain insight into the utilization of high-level constructs. We adopt Java as the industry approach and POSH reactive planner [12] as the academic approach. Java is at least as good as C++ for programming complex agent's behavior, but it is not a typical game industry language. We use it for two reasons. First, all our subjects, [22] university computer science students, know Java acceptably well, which models a situation in a company where programmers known their programming language. Second, POSH's lower level uses Java. We use POSH because it has been already demonstrated for controlling virtual agents [13]. It also benefits from a graphical tool developed for visualizing an agent's behavior plan using high-level constructs only [17]. POSH can be thought of as typical of a broad class of academic solutions such as a BDI-based systems, that include planning and primitive layers.

All our subjects attended a course on programming virtual agents for games where they learned POSH. Their situation corresponded to situation of game programmers considering using an academic system after experimenting with it for about three person-days. Our subjects were divided into two groups. Both groups worked on the same tasks from a first-person shooter domain using Unreal Tournament 2004 environment (UT04), but the first used Java only and the second used POSH to model higher level control. Our hypotheses were:

1. POSH outperforms Java in terms of subjectively-perceived usability and objective quality of the resulting agents.
2. POSH outperforms Java when the task is to catch up upon the work of someone else.
3. POSH outperforms Java when the task is to extend one's own code (three months later).

If these had been confirmed, there would have been an empirical argument for maturity of at least one particular academic solution. In fact, no hypothesis was supported by the data. This means that it is important to isolate the most beneficial and problematic features of POSH to suggest possible improvements. Features shared with different academic systems are the most important.

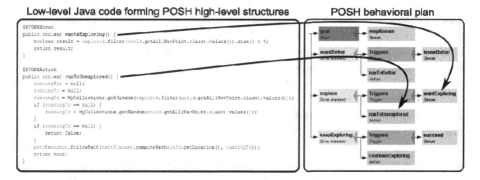

Fig. 1. Relation between high-level POSH plan and low-level Java code presenting separation of high-level behavioral code from the low-level code of sensors and actions

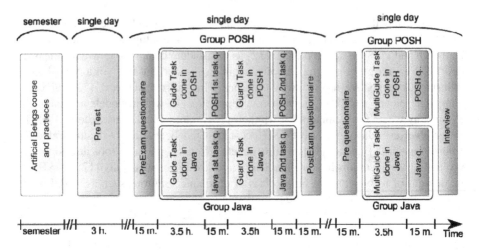

Fig. 2. The course of the experiment

The rest of the paper is organized as follows. Section 2 presents related work. Section 3 introduces POSH [12] explaining its roots, architecture and Behavior Oriented Design [15] methodology for the design of virtual agent behaviors. Section 4 describes the experiment setup and following section 5 presents its results. Section 6 discusses results and presents ideas for general improvements to AS systems, which concludes the paper.

2   Related Work

Empirical studies of academic AS systems are scarce. In our previous comparative study [28], we demonstrated that POSH, enhanced with a GUI, is at least as good as Java, but in that study, subjects programmed the high-level code only and for relatively simple tasks, which is a study's limitation. Doubts about using only the high-level constructs for programming complex agents behavior stem from the work of Píbil et al. [16], who reports on experiences from the creation of a team of agents solving a MAS game-like scenario inside a grid world using vanilla Jason [22] implementation, that is, using the Jason's high-level constructs only without modifying the low-level Java code. They report on hard Jason's corners and the inevitable implementation of complex behavior primitives in underlying Java language.

Hindriks et al. [19] conducted a qualitative analysis of the code of 60 first year computer science students developing (in teams) three Capture The Flag agents for UT04 using GOAL agent programming language. That work aimed at "providing insight into more practical aspects of agent development" and "better understanding problems that programmers face when using (an agent programming) language" and identified a number of structural code patterns, information useful for improvements to the language. However, that study was not comparative and did not report the programmers' feedback.

The fact that an AS system's usability is also closely linked to the quality of developers' tools and their ability to visualize complex behaviors in an intuitive way was recognized by Heckel et al. [20] in their work on BehaviorShop. A usability study of BehaviorShop demonstrated a well-thought GUI for editing high-level behavioral plans is easily graspable by non-programmers. However, their study was not comparative and they did not allow subjects to work with low-level code, which is arguably required for larger behavior modifications as argued by [15, 16].

The industry's interest in simple and intuitive tools is exemplified in Desai's work on ScriptEase [24]. ScriptEase is a graphical authoring tool of the BioWare's Never-Winter Nights game allowing non-programmers to create new game modules. She shows that her simplification of the GUI is welcomed by both programmers and designers.

3 POSH

POSH action selection was originally developed in the late 1990s in response to criticism of what was then an extremely popular agent design approach (at least in academia): Subsumption Architecture (SA) [23]. SA was used to produce considerable advances in real-time intelligent agents, particularly robotics. It consists primarily of two components: a highly modular architecture where every action is coded with the perception it needs to operate; and a complex, highly distributed form of action selection to arbitrate between the actions that would be produced by the various modules. Although well-known and heavily cited, the SA was seldom really used outside of its developers. Bryson hypothesized that the emphasis on modular intelligence was actually the core contribution of SA, but that the complexity of action selection, while successfully enforcing a reactive approach, confused most programmers who were not used to thinking about concurrent systems.

POSH was developed to simplify the construction of action selection for modular AI. A programmer used to thinking about conventional sequential programs is asked to first consider a worst-case scenario for their agent, then to break each step of the plan to resolve that scenario into a part of a reactive plan. Succeeding at a goal is the agent's highest priority, the thing the agent does if it can. The programmer must therefore describe for the agent how to perceive that its goal can be met. Then for each step leading up to the goal the same process is followed: a perceptual condition is defined allowing the agent to recognize if it can take the action leading most directly to its goal [12]. The actions are each small chunks of code that control the agent briefly, so-called behavior primitives (see Fig. 1).

After a period of experimenting with the system, Bryson embedded POSH in a more formal development methodology called Behavior Oriented Design (BOD) 18. BOD emphasizes the above development process, and also the use of behavior modules written in ordinary object-oriented languages (low-level code) to encode the majority of the agent's intelligence, including its memory. These modules provide the high-level behavior and sensory primitives; methods calls are the interface between a high-level POSH plan and the low-level code of the behavior modules (see Fig. 1). BOD includes a set of heuristics for recognizing when intelligence should be refactored either from a plan to a behavior module or to decompose a complex module using a plan.

Recently, a graphical editor for POSH plans has been developed. Its new version was used in the present study (Fig. 1).

4   Method

4.1   Experiment Design

The study compared the usability of an academic AS system, POSH, enhanced with a graphical tool for the creation of high- level behavioral plan, and an unenhanced classical programming language, Java. The context of the comparison was two particular situations mentioned in Sec. 1 common in the game company. The study was divided into three tasks. Each task was to create a behavior for an agent that had to fulfill a game-like goal. Subjects using Java had a complete freedom in the way of coding the behavior. Subjects using POSH were constrained by the requirement to separate low-level Java code into behavior and sensory primitives, specific constructs, which were then used inside high-level POSH behavioral plan (see Fig. 1).

The study was set in an AI course for computer science students in Faculty of Mathematics and Physics, Charles University in Prague. Subjects were given a pretest (3 hours) after the course to ensure that they had acquired elementary skills for solving sub-problems from the final exam. Only subjects that had passed the pretest were admitted to the final exam.

The final exam was organized to obtain comparative data on Java and POSH usability and provide data for the first game company scenario (see Sec. 1). The final exam consisted of two tasks, the Guide Task (3.5 hours) and the Guard Task (3.5 hours), see Sec. 4.3. Subjects were split into two groups, the Java group and the POSH group. In the first task, subjects were to create the whole Guide behavior from scratch. In the second task, each subject received a code from a randomly selected colleague from the same group and was asked to extend it into Guard behavior. There was a 30 minutes long break between the first and the second task. Finally, three months later, some subjects participated in the final task, in which every subject was given his code from the first task and was asked to extend it into MultiGuide behavior (3.5 hours). The follow-up provided data for the second game company scenario.

Subjects were given 4 questionnaires in total during the final exam (15 minutes each) and 2 questionnaires during the follow-up. Subjects solving the follow-up also underwent a structured interview that was meant to provide more accurate qualitative data as the number of subjects was rather small for quantitative data analysis. The course of the experiment is summarized in Fig. 2. Subjects were always informed how long the task will take in advance, but the structure and the exact content were revealed only during the study. The assignments were given immediately prior to each task.

The whole package featuring Pogamut platform used, task texts given and questionnaires used can be downloaded from [29].

4.2   Participants

For the initial study, we recruited 22 students out of 33 attendants of the AI course. The study was the course's final exam and students were given their final grade based on performance of their agents in the Guide task. Students had the option of withdrawing from the study if they preferred a different kind of final exam.

We excluded 2 students from the analysis due to data incompleteness. In total, we analyzed data from 20 students. Students were randomly divided into two groups. The random assignment was stratified by year of study in order to guarantee that both groups contained similar number of students in each year of study.

For the follow-up task, we succeeded in recruiting 8 subjects (5 from the Java group and 3 from the POSH group) from the original 22. They participated for reward 30 USD. The number of follow-up participants was too small for statistical analysis, but provided qualitative data.

4.3   Materials

The Course. The students attended an introductory course on the control of virtual characters. The course is intended for students without previous AI or 3D graphics knowledge but with previous programming experience. Only students from the second or a higher year of study could attend. The course comprises of 12 theoretical lectures (90 minutes each) and 6 practical lessons at computers (90 minutes each). The theoretical classes are detailed in [21]. In practical lessons, the students are taught how to work with virtual agent's library (2 lessons) and develop behavior of virtual agents using both Java (2 lessons) and POSH (2 lessons).

Pretest. The general aim of the Pretest was to rule out subjects that were not sufficiently prepared for the final exam. Unprepared subjects would bias the data as they would likely fail during the final exam which would influence their answers in questionnaires.

The Pretest task was to create an agent capable of exploring the environment of UT04 game and collect items of a specific type. The agent had no adversaries in this task. Implementation language was assigned to subjects at random.

Three programmers skilled in VR technology solved the pretest task in advance to calibrate the difficulty of the test. The time allotment (2 hours) was at least three times longer than average time needed by these programmers to finish the task. Subjects had 3 attempts to pass the Pretest. Most passed on their first attempt.

Experimental Task

Guide. The Guide Task was to create an agent capable of finding a lost Civilian agent and leading it home. At the beginning, Civilian agent was standing still at random position broadcasting its position with a "mobile phone." The Guide agent must communicate with the Civilian agent if it wants the Civilian agent to follow its lead. The communication had a fixed and rather simplistic protocol described in the assignment.

Communication was reliable but Civilian was willing to reply to Guide over the mobile only if Guide was not too far away. Apart from finding Civilian, there were two obstacles that Guide had to overcome in order to successfully lead Civilian home. First, Civilian was willing to start following Guide only if Civilian can see Guide. Second, if Civilian lost Guide from sight, it stopped walking. Thus, the challenge was not only to find Civilian and persuade it to follow Guide home, but also to constantly observe whether Civilian is doing so. Once Civilian was home, it restarted itself in another location in the map. Guide's goal was to rescue Civilian as many times as possible within 5 minutes.

Guard. The Guard Task was an extension of the Guide Task. Again, the task of the Guard agent was to find and guide the lost Civilian agent home. However, there was also an adversary Alien agent in the environment created to hunt down both Guard and Civilian. Thus resulting Guard behavior must have correctly prioritized the following intentions: 1) finding a weapon, 2) finding and leading Civilian home, 3) responding to Alien. For instance, the Guard agent should have stopped leading Civilian when Alien was spotted and started attacking Alien.

MultiGuide (follow-up). The MultiGuide Task was also an extension of the Guide Task. This time, there were two Civilian agents in the environment and the Multi-Guide agent had to get them together first and then lead both home.

Organization. For all tasks, subjects were told to code both low-level behavior primitives as well as high-level plans. Concerning the lower level, both groups used Java. For the higher level, i.e., organizing complex motor primitives based on already processed sensory information, Java group subjects hard-coded their own if-then rules or finite state machines (simple *switch* statements), whereas POSH group subjects had to use the POSH graphical editor for specification of a high-level POSH plan. POSH group was also encouraged to use the BOD design methodology. Tasks were solved by two skilled programmers in advance and their feedback was used to adjust the tasks difficulty.

Subjects received the assignment written on the paper prior to every task and they were provided with sufficient time (30 minutes) to read it and ask questions to clarify ambiguities.

Groups were working in parallel in two different rooms. Subjects were not allowed to cooperate on the solution but they were allowed to utilize any documentation about used virtual agent's library available on the Internet.

Questionnaires. Every subject received 4 questionnaires during the initial study and participants of the follow-up received an additional 2.

Questionnaires contained both quantitative (11 level Likert items; 10 maximum, 0 minimum) and qualitative questions. Questions were designed to 1) control for influences (comprehensibility of the assignment, task difficulty, whether the course has prepared subjects well, etc.), 2) investigate how appropriate was a language for a particular task, 3) report on language preferences, 4) report on how easy/hard was to extend the received code, 5) identify hard corners of Java/POSH behavior development. Follow-up subjects also undergone a structured interview.

4.4   Data Analysis

All quantitative answers from the questionnaires were analyzed. Quantitative answers from the Guide task and Guard task post-questionnaires were compared. Answers from Java and POSH groups were also compared. We have used paired and two-sample t-tests with Welch approximation to compare the means in the two groups. Having discrete data, it would seem natural to look for methods using contingency tables (chi-square test of independence) or rank-based tests (Wilcoxon test, sign test or two-sample Kolmogorov-Smirnov test). However, using contingency tables here would suffer from low number of observations in cells while rank-based tests would suffer from lots of ties in our data. Moreover, the reasons for rejecting the null hypothesis may not be clear in some situations. Therefore, we have decided to compare the means observed in the two groups by applying paired and two-sample t-tests. Assuming that two-sided two-sample t-test is used to compare two groups of size 11 (see Sec. 5) and that the standard deviation is 2, the test detects difference 2 with probability approx. 60% and difference 3 with probability more than 90%. Notice that Central Limit Theorem guarantees that t-test may be used in this setup because the observed means are approximately normally distributed, see also [26, 27] for a more detailed justification of this approach. For other data from contingency tables, we have used χ^2 tests of independence with p-values obtained by Monte Carlo simulation in contingency tables. Additionally, agents from the Guide task were tested for quality. We executed the corresponding task scenario 10 times for each agent (Civilian's random position sequence has been fixed) and checked how many Civilians the agent saved in 5 minutes. The agent's score was computed as the average of all runs. Guard-task agents were not evaluated as most subjects solved this assignment only partially due to insufficient time and increasing fatigue (the study lasted 8 hours). Statistical tests were not run for the follow-up questionnaires and the follow-up agents were not tested due to the small number of participants.

5   Results

Results can be divided into objective performance of created agents and subjective assessment of the used tool. We will show quantitative data first and discuss qualitative data later. Only the most important data are reported due to space limitations.

5.1   Quantitative Data

Quantitative data reports on:

A. how well the subjects understood the assignment; analyzing answers to the question "Have you understood the assignment?";
B. how well the subjects were prepared for solving the task; analyzing answers to the question "Did practice lessons prepare you well for solving this kind of task?";
C. how satisfied they were with the behavior they had created; analyzing answers to the question "How do you feel about the behavior you have produced? Is it ok?";
D. the agent's objective performance, in the case of Task 1;
E. how appropriate the tool the subjects were using was for solving the task; analyzing answers to the Guide Task's question "Do you find Java to be the appropriate for the assignment?";
F. satisfaction with comprehensibility of received code, in case of Task 2.

5.1.1 Task 1 - Guide Agent

Ad A. Subjects in both groups understood the assignment very well and there were no between-group differences (mean for Java group = 9.36±0.77; mean for POSH group = 9.36±0.98).

Ad B. Subjects in both groups were equally prepared for the Task 1 (mean for Java group = 8.91±1.81; mean for POSH group = 8.5±1.9; p-value = 0.621).

Ad C. Subjects in POSH group were slightly less satisfied with their agents (mean for Java group = 7.64±0.67; mean for POSH group = 5.82±2.75; p-value = 0.056). The observed difference is not quite statistically significant, but given the low N we report the trend.

Ad D. Agents' objective performances (Table 1) did not statistically differ between the groups (p-value = 0.722).

Ad E. Satisfaction of subjects with their programming tool in the Guide Task (Fig. 3, 4) was slightly higher in Java group but the difference was not significant (mean for Java group = 8.09±1.81; mean for POSH group = 7.09±3.51; p-value = 0.414).

Table 1. Task 1 agents' performances

Perf. / Group	Weak	Moderate	Good	Total
Java	3	4	4	11
POSH	1	4	4	9
Total	4	8	8	20

5.1.2 Task 2 - Guard Agent

Ad A. Subjects in both groups understood the assignment very well and there were no between-group differences (mean for Java group = 9.46±0.99; mean for POSH group = 9.73±0.62).

Ad B. Subjects in POSH were prepared slightly better for this task (mean for Java group 6.67±3, mean for POSH group 8.8±1.3; p-value = 0.075). Again we report the trend due to the low N and weak power of the test.

Ad C. Subjects in both groups were similarly unsatisfied with their agents (mean for Java group = 3.82±2.09; mean for POSH group = 3.36±2.46; p-value = 0.646).

There was also highly significant shift of satisfaction visible when answers from both groups combined from Task 2 were compared to combined answers from the Task 1 (mean for Task 1 = 6.73±2.16; mean for Task 2 = 3.59±2.24; p-value of paired t-test < 0.001).

Ad E. Subjects' satisfaction with their tool did not differ between groups (Fig. 5, 6, mean for Java group = 6.67±2.06; mean for POSH group = 6.64±3.04; p-value = 0.979).

Ad F. We also have asked subjects whether they find the received code comprehensible. The result showed no between-group differences (mean for Java group = 5.8±3.6; mean for POSH group = 6.27±2.97; p-value = 0.747).

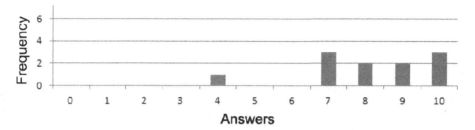

Fig. 3. Java group satisfaction with their tool (Task 1)

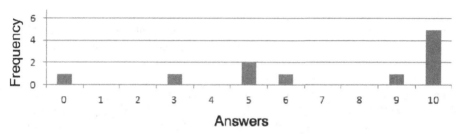

Fig. 4. POSH group satisfaction with their tool (Task 1)

5.1.3   Task 3 - MultiGuide Agent

All subjects reported that they understood the assignment perfectly (mean for both groups = 10±0). All subjects were able to extend their old code and create the Multi-Guide agent. Interviews did not bring any dramatic comments on comprehensibility of code written in Java vs. POSH. Subjects from both group reported that reading through the code took around 10 minutes for both groups. Opinions regarding Java/POSH preference are included below.

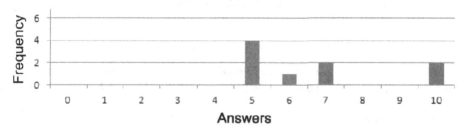

Fig. 5. Java group satisfaction with their tool (Task 2)

5.2   Qualitative Data

Quantitative results present an overall view on how subjects were satisfied with POSH or Java in the situations we modeled. These results have not revealed substantial differences between POSH and Java, suggesting that more fine-grained, qualitative approach is needed. Our qualitative data came from answers to "Explain" questions to abovementioned questions from questionnaires and from the interviews.

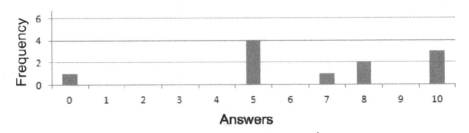

Fig. 6. POSH group satisfaction with their tool (Task 2)

Answers can be divided into two categories: conceptual, pointing out strong and weak points of behavior design using POSH, and technical, such as wrong POSH engine settings. We will discuss mainly the former category as technical points might be eliminated easily by tweaking our POSH implementation.

Recall that POSH strictly separates behavior into a high-level plan, which uses behavior modules that define low-level code of behavior and sensory primitives (see Sec. 3). A well thought out POSH plan depicts how the agent will respond to the environment without revealing any technical details of the low-level code. When summarized, the qualitative data revealed rather strong, and opposite, opinions regarding this ability of POSH and its graphical editor: this feature was praised but also hated.

Many subjects found the separate thinking about the high-level behavior plan to be positive.

"I think it is pretty easy to make the idea in POSH and then just write few simple methods."

"The plan helps you to keep track of the important stuff that your agent does and reminds you to keep the behavioral triggers simple."

"In POSH, I can clearly distinguish states."

"Behavior states written in Java are harder to debug."

"POSH enforces good behavior architecture."

However, some found that unsuitable to their style of work.

*"The lack of variables at the level of POSH plans that would visualize flow of **low-level** data from senses to actions seems limiting."* [POSH does not have variables at the high-level]

"POSH limits you when you're coding the behavior."

"You still need to write Java code." [note this is intentional in POSH/BOD approach, and cf. this with [16], who find it difficult to use vanilla Jason without underlying Java]

"Switching between POSH GUI and Java IDE was confusing me." [refers to the necessity of switching between two modes of programming; the low-level and the high-level]

The last opinion contrasts with:

"POSH is a convenient way to clearly write agent decision logic and underlying Java is powerful enough to code all details."

Some users failed to see any advantages in POSH at all or at least in having a separate graphical program and action-selection mechanism to run it.

"I can simply write POSH decision tree in Java."

We noticed that POSH subjects cannot program the required behavior exclusively inside the high-level plan. The subjects always coded also their own low-level POSH primitives or made changes to primitives of other subjects (Task 2) or their own (Task 3).

POSH was frequently criticized with technical comments. Students usually disliked writing names of actions and senses twice, first in POSH and then in Java. But there were a few comments that revealed some conceptual flaws of POSH behavioral language as well.

"POSH has fixed order of action priorities; this becomes too limiting for complex behaviors." [that points to POSH's (intentionally) simple conflict resolution mechanism]

"POSH does not provide any mechanisms for action-switching, it is hard to track that for yourself." [like in many other agent-based systems, support for transition behaviors, including *action-in* and *action-out* constructs, is limited or none, see also [25]]

"POSH does not support parallel behaviors; parallel behavior is especially hard to manage." [original POSH used on robots allowed for parallel behaviors, but this is more difficult in the present VR incarnation due to the game engine]

Qualitative data provide interesting points for further discussion. Some points can be generalized to other agent-based languages.

6   Discussion and Conclusion

This study has compared the usability of the academic AS system POSH empowered with a graphical editor to that of a common programming language Java in two situations common in a game company: a) catching up upon the work of a colleague, and b) extending one's own work from several months ago.

Unfortunately quantitative results could only be gathered on two of the three tasks we assigned. Here we showed no difference between Java and POSH groups in subjectively reported readiness for utilization of the tool in Task 1 (see Sec. 5.1.1.B). Subjects from POSH group reported they were prepared slightly better for Task 2, which could be to POSH's advantage, but the effect was rather small (see Sec. 5.1.2.B). The qualitative data seem to argue that we prepared the students well for the tasks no matter the technique; the groups were not biased. Because there are no differences in objective agents' qualities (see Sec. 5.1.1.D), the first hypothesis that POSH is better in terms of usability and efficiency of resulting behavior is not supported.

The second hypothesis also has not been supported by the quantitative data from the first condition, as subjects did not report improvements to the code's readability due to POSH's visible organization of the sensory and behavior primitives into a high-level plan (see Sec. 5.1.2.F). However, verbal comments are interesting. Whereas complete freedom of coding high-level behavior in Java was praised by some Java group subjects, it was a source of confusion for others. For POSH, negative comments were focused only on complexity of behavior primitives in low-level code, constraints of the high-level language, but never on the problems with the high-level plan comprehensibility (see Sec. 5.2 and below).

"Single routine from hell." [a Java subject referring to a single Java method that executed the whole behavior]

"The logic method was a long list of ifs that were kinda obscure and it was unclear to me which part was taking care of which part of the behavior." [a Java subject referring to overly complex if-then rules in Java, which were mixing high-level behavioral code with low-level code]

That contrasts with negative comments of POSH subjects related to the low-level code written by a different subject:

"Senses and actions were quite complex."

"Some of the primitives were unfamiliar; there was some extra stuff I did not understand."

"The naming was good, but there were about 5 senses/actions that didn't do anything."

Finally, the third hypothesis also has not been supported (see Sec. 5.1.3). Subjects from both groups did not report any problems with reading own code that they had created 3 months ago, even if they had not been interacting with the code all over the period.

This last may indicate that Task 1 and 3 were too simple to get much advantage from a programming tool, at least for the 8 programmers who had completed Task 2 and were willing to come to their code again. This is particularly true since the basic structure of POSH could be indeed replicated with Java conditional statements if the hierarchy or plan was not too complex. Had we been able to complete the full course of the study with all programmers, we may have found subjects that the POSH structure assisted.

6.1   Main Interpretation

It is useful to conceive the results from the standpoint of the metaphor separating behavioral code into the "low-level" and "high-level". When adopting this perspective, the results argue that tasks of a medium complexity (compared to common tasks of an industry programmer) already imply programming at both levels, and consequently, switching the programmer's attention between the levels. Note that POSH/BOD already recognizes that and the study of Píbil et al. [16] also supports this interpretation. However, this cast doubts on the idea that non-programmers, such as game designer, could ever use "intuitive high-level languages" *only*, except for the simplest tasks.

An interesting point is that majority of subjects seem to praise the separation of high-level behavior plan from the low-level code, which is a general finding, but they were not satisfied with concrete limitations that POSH enforces on the architecture of behavior primitives. Still, some subjects seem not to have internalized their thinking in terms of this two-level architecture at all and to have problems with switching between levels of abstraction.

What we still do not know is whether the explicit materialization of the low-level / high-level separation realized in POSH/BOD and agent-based languages in general, would eventually turn out to be more of an advantage than a burden. The fact that students think the former does not necessarily mean it really is. Some qualitative data concerning Guard task and one quantitative outcome (see Sec. 5.1.2.B) suggest that at least when one has to read the code of some else, the explicit materialization of high-level constructs is an advantage. At the same time, however, as said above, some qualitative data suggest that some students may have problems when the interface between two levels is explicit. This might be similar to object-oriented programming; one has to undergo a long journey to fully appreciate the concept, and perhaps some programmers are always happier in assembly. Future research is needed to elucidate what exactly is a POSH's and its GUI's technical limitation and what is a deeper conceptual issue.

6.2   Generalization

Many comments on Java vs. POSH can be transposed to other academic AS systems due to general approach they all share with POSH. All of them try to separate behavioral code out of low-level code. We will now summarize the study's results into the list of guidelines that should be considered when assessing AS systems for the purpose of authoring behaviors for virtual agents.

1. The study's result supported the idea that low-level code should be used for coding behavior primitives. A high-level AS system should not try to supply processing of sensory information or attempt to supply logic of low-level actions directly. An AS system should understand that behavior primitives always need to be created in low-level code forming the agent periphery and provide appropriate support for organizing it.
2. The interface of an AS system with low-level code should be simple and interface requirements should be assessed as they will indicate design patterns a programmer will need to follow. If those design patterns are complex or over-constraining, as is the case of parameter-less sensor and action methods in POSH, it may lead to time consuming implementation of agents' peripheries.
3. An AS system should be prepared for the execution of transition behaviors. Whenever an AS system decides it is time to switch from one action to another, it should also notify low-level code it is doing so, i.e., it should be part of AS interface to the low-level code.

From the methodological perspective, the lessons learnt from this study are that both quantitative and qualitative data are useful for assessing engineer performance.

Acknowledgements. This research is supported by the Czech Science Foundation under the contract P103/10/1287 (GACR), by student grant GA UK No. 0449/2010/A-INF/MFF, by student grant GA UK No. 655012/2012/A-INF/MFF and by SVV project number 263 314. Human data were collected respecting APA ethical guidelines. We kindly thank Joanna Bryson, University of Bath, UK, for her consultations regarding design of the experiment and data analysis.

References

1. Fu, D., Houlette, R.: The Ultimate Guide to FSMs in Games. In: AI Game Programming Wisdom II, pp. 283–302. Charles River Media (2004)
2. Champandard, A.J.: Behavior Trees for Next-Gen Game AI. In: Internet Presentation (June 11, 2012), http://aigamedev.com/insider/presentations/behavior-trees
3. Schuytema, P.: Game Development with Lua. Charles River Media (2005)
4. UnrealScript programming language (June 11, 2012), http://udn.epicgames.com/Two/UnrealScriptReference.html
5. Schwab, B.: AI Game Engine Programming, 2nd edn. Charles River Media (2008)
6. AiGameDev community (June 11, 2012), http://aigamedev.com/
7. Rabin, S.: AI Game Programming Wisdom series (June 11, 2012), http://www.aiwisdom.com/
8. Gamasutra webpage (June 11, 2012), http://www.gamasutra.com/
9. Magerko, B., Laird, J.E., Assanie, M., Kerfoot, A., Stokes, D.: AI Characters and Directors for Interactive Computer Games. In: Proceedings of the 2004 Innovative Applications of Artificial Intelligence Conference. AAAI Press, San Jose (2004)
10. Best, B.J., Lebiere, C.: Cognitive agents interacting in real and virtual worlds. In: Sun, R. (ed.) Cognition and Multi-Agent Interaction: From Cognitive Modelling to Social Simulation, Cambridge University Press, NY (2006)
11. Hindriks, K.V., van Riemsdijk, B., Behrens, T., Korstanje, R., Kraayenbrink, N., Pasman, W., de Rijk, L.: Unreal Goal Bots. In: Dignum, F. (ed.) Agents for Games and Simulations II. LNCS (LNAI), vol. 6525, pp. 1–18. Springer, Heidelberg (2011)
12. Bryson, J.J.: Intelligence by design: Principles of Modularity and Coordination for Engineering Complex Adaptive Agent. PhD Thesis, MIT, Department of EECS, Cambridge, MA (2001)
13. Partington, S.J., Bryson, J.J.: The Behavior Oriented Design of an Unreal Tournament Character. In: Panayiotopoulos, T., Gratch, J., Aylett, R.S., Ballin, D., Olivier, P., Rist, T. (eds.) IVA 2005. LNCS (LNAI), vol. 3661, pp. 466–477. Springer, Heidelberg (2005)
14. Köster, M., Novák, P., Mainzer, D., Fuhrmann, B.: Two Case Studies for Jazzyk BSM. In: Dignum, F., Bradshaw, J., Silverman, B., van Doesburg, W. (eds.) Agents for Games and Simulations. LNCS (LNAI), vol. 5920, pp. 33–47. Springer, Heidelberg (2009)
15. Bryson, J.J.: The Behavior-Oriented Design of Modular Agent Intelligence. In: Kowalczyk, R., Müller, J.P., Tianfield, H., Unland, R. (eds.) NODe-WS 2002. LNCS (LNAI), vol. 2592, pp. 61–76. Springer, Heidelberg (2003)

16. Píbil, R., Novák, P., Brom, C., Gemrot, J.: Notes on Pragmatic Agent-Programming with Jason. In: Dennis, L., Boissier, O., Bordini, R.H. (eds.) ProMAS 2011. LNCS, vol. 7217, pp. 58–73. Springer, Heidelberg (2012)
17. Gemrot, J., Brom, C., Kadlec, R., Bída, M., Burkert, O., Zemčák, M., Píbil, R., Plch, T.: Pogamut 3 – Virtual Humans Made Simple. In: Gray, J. (ed.) Advances in Cognitive Science, pp. 211–243. The Institution Of Engineering And Technology (2010)
18. Bryson, J.J.: Action Selection and Individuation in Agent Based Modelling. In: Proceedings of Agent 2003: Challenges of Social Simulation, Argonne National Laboratory, pp. 317–330 (2003)
19. Hindriks, K.V., van Riemsdijk, M.B., Jonker, C.M.: An Empirical Study of Patterns in Agent Programs. In: Desai, N., Liu, A., Winikoff, M. (eds.) PRIMA 2010. LNCS, vol. 7057, pp. 196–211. Springer, Heidelberg (2012)
20. Heckel, F.W.P., Youngblood, M., Hale, D.H.: Behavior Shop: An Intuitive Inter-face for Interactive Character Design. In: Proceedings of the Fifth Artificial Intelligence and Interactive Digital Entertainment Conference, AIIDE 2009, Stanford, California, USA, October 14-16. The AAAI Press (2009)
21. Brom, C.: Curricula of the course on modelling behaviour of human and animal-like agents. In: Proceedings of the Frontiers in Science Education Research Conference, Famaguta, North Cyprus, pp. 71–79 (2009)
22. Bordini, R.H., Hübner, J.F., Wooldridge, M.: Programming Multi-Agent Systems in AgentSpeak Using Jason. John Wiley & Sons, Ltd. (2007)
23. Brooks, R.A.: Intelligence Without Representation. Artificial Intelligence 47(1-3), 139–159 (1991)
24. Desai, N.: Using Describers To Simplify ScriptEase. Master Thesis. Depart-ment of Computing Science, University of Alberta, Edmonton, Alberta, Canada (2009)
25. Plch, T.: Towards Believable Intelligent Virtual Agents with StateFull Hierarchical Reactive Planning Action Selection. In: Safrankova, J., Pavlu, J. (eds.) WDS 2011, Part I - Mathematics and Computer Sciences, pp. 119–124. Matfyz Press, Prague (2011)
26. Rasch, Teuscher, Guiard: How robust are tests for two independent samples? Journal of Statistical Planning and Inference 137(8), 2706–2720
27. Heeren, T., D'Agostino, R.: Robustness of the two independent samples t-test when applied to ordinal scaled data. Stat. Med. 6(1), 79–90 (1987)
28. Gemrot, J., Brom, C., Bryson, J., Bída, M.: How to compare usability of techniques for the specification of virtual agents' behavior? An experimental pilot study with human subjects. In: Proceedings of Agents for Games and Simulations, AAMAS Workshop, Taipei, Taiwan, pp. 33–57 (2011)
29. Experiment reusable packages (June 11, 2012),
    http://pogamut.cuni.cz/pogamut-devel/doku.php?id=human-like_
    artifical_agents_2010-11_summer_semester_exam_info

Author Index